Dictionary of
MODERN ENGLISH USAGES

Dictionary of MODERN ENGLISH USAGES

Sonu Marwah

ANMOL PUBLICATIONS PVT. LTD.
NEW DELHI-110 002 (INDIA)

ANMOL PUBLICATIONS PVT. LTD.
Regd. Office: 4360/4, Ansari Road, Daryaganj,
New Delhi-110002 (India)
Tel.: 23278000, 23261597, 23286875, 23255577
Fax: 91-11-23280289
Email: anmolpub@gmail.com
Visit us at: www.anmolpublications.com

Branch Office: No. 1015, Ist Main Road, BSK IIIrd Stage
IIIrd Phase, IIIrd Block, Bangalore-560 085 (India)
Tel.: 080-41723429 • Fax: 080-26723604
Email: anmolpublicationsbangalore@gmail.com

Dictionary of Modern English Usages

First Edition, 2010

ISBN 978-81-261-4523-2

PRINTED IN INDIA

Printed at Balaji Offset, Delhi.

Contents

Preface

A Dictionary of Modern English Usage is a good reference cum textbook for English usage, pronunciation, and writing. Ranging from plurals and literary technique to the distinctions among like words (homonyms, synonyms, etc.), to foreign-term use, it became the standard for most reference books that followed. English usage is to encourage a direct, vigorous writing style, and to oppose all artificiality - firmly advising against unnecessary, convoluted sentence construction, foreign words and phrases, and archaisms. Like most practical books, its linguistics is a mixture of the prescriptive and the descriptive - thus allowing extremists to place one in the other.

There are two main approaches to the study of usage: prescriptive and descriptive. Prescriptivism involves the laying down of rules by those claiming to have special knowledge of or feeling for a language. Prescriptive advice tends to be conservative, changes being regarded with suspicion if not disdain. Descriptivism involves the objective description of the way a language works as observed in actual examples of the language. Descriptive advice -- almost an oxymoron -- about the acceptability of a word or construction is based solely on usage. Each approach has advantages and disadvantages. Descriptivism is the scientific method of linguists and lexicographers. At its best, descriptivism embraces prescriptivism, since a descriptive study should examine the prescriptive commentary that precedes it. Armed with the history of a usage and an examination of its appearance in various contexts -- spoken and written, formal and informal.

Author

Chapter 1

Introduction

DICTIONARY

A dictionary is a list of words with their definitions, a list of characters with their glyphs, or a list of words with corresponding words in other languages. In a few languages, words can appear in many different forms, but only the lemma form appears as the main word or headword in most dictionaries.

Many dictionaries also provide pronunciation information; grammatical information; word derivations, histories, or etymologies; illustrations; usage guidance; and examples in phrases or sentences. Dictionaries are most commonly found in the form of a book. Some dictionaries are also found in electronic portable handheld devices. Dictionaries are produced by lexicographers.

WORD ORDER

Today, dictionaries of most languages with alphabetic and syllabic writing systems list words in lexicographic order, usually alphabetical or some analogous phonetic system.

In many languages, words are grouped together according to their true or normal origin ("root"), and these roots are arranged alphabetically. If English dictionaries were arranged like this, the words "import", "export", "support", "report", "porter", "port", "important" and "transportation" would all be listed under "port". This method has the advantage that all words of a common origin are listed together, but the disadvantage is that you have to know how to disassemble all prefixes of a word before you look it up. Some Sanskrit dictionaries and all Arabic dictionaries work like this.

Dictionaries of languages using ideographic writing systems, may be sorted either according to one of many schemes based on the component parts of the characters (number of strokes, overall shape, or pronunciation of each letter), or according to the pronunciation of the full words when spelled phonetically. Due to the unfamiliarity of Chinese speakers with phonetic spellings, phonetic sorts are particularly unsuitable for Chinese dictionaries, while the fluency of Japanese speakers with kana makes kana spelling the most common and convenient method to sort Japanese dictionaries.

The first English alphabetical dictionary came out in 1604 and alphabetical ordering was a rarity until the 18th century. Before alphabetical listings, dictionaries were organized by topic, i.e. a list of animals all together in one topic.

VARIATIONS

Since words and their meanings develop over time, dictionary entries are organized to reflect these changes. Dictionaries may either list meanings in the historical order in which they appeared, or may list meanings in order of popularity and most common use.

Dictionaries also differ in the degree to which they are encyclopedic, providing considerable background information, illustrations, and the like, or linguistic, concentrating on etymology, nuances of meaning, and quotations demonstrating usage.

Any dictionary has been designed to fulfil one or more functions. The dictionary functions chosen by the maker(s) of the dictionary provide the basis for all lexicographic decisions, from the selection of entry words, over the choice of information types, to the choice of place for the information (e.g. in an article or in an appendix). There are two main types of function. The communication-oriented functions comprise text reception (understanding), text production, text revision, and translation. The knowledge-oriented functions deal with situations where the dictionary is used for acquiring specific knowledge about a particular matter, and for acquiring general knowledge about something. The optimal dictionary is one that contains information directly relevant for the needs of the users relating to one or more of these functions. It is important that the information is presented in a way that keeps the lexicographic information costs at a minimum.

HISTORY

The art and craft of writing dictionaries is called lexicography.One of the earliest dictionaries known, and which is still extant today in an abridged form, was written in Latin during the reign of the emperor Augustus. It is known by the title De Significant Verborum ("On the meaning of words") and was originally compiled by Verrius Flaccus. It was twice abridged in succeeding centuries, first by Sextus Pompeius Festus, and then by Paul the Deacon. Verrius Flaccus' dictionary was an abridged list of difficult or antiquated words, whose usage was illustrated by quotations from early Roman authors.

The Erya, from the early 3rd century BC, was the first Chinese language dictionary. The book organized Chinese characters by semantic groups. The intention of this dictionary was to explain the true meaning and interpretation of words in the context of older ancient texts.

The word "dictionary" comes from neoclassical Latin, diccio, meaning simply "word".

The first true English dictionary was Robert Cawdrey's Table Alphabeticall of 1604, although it only included 3,000 words and the definitions it contained were little more than synonyms. The first one to be at all comprehensive was Thomas Blount's dictionary Glossographia of 1656. This was followed by Samuel Johnson's famous and more complete dictionary of 1755.

In 1806, Noah Webster's dictionary was published by the G&C Merriam Company of Springfield, Massachusetts which still publishes Merriam-Webster dictionaries, but the term

Webster's is considered generic and can be used by any dictionary.

The most complete dictionary of the English language is the English Dictionary. The first edition was properly begun in 1860 and was completed in 1928, by which time a supplement that took an additional five years to complete was already necessary.

DICTIONARY OF ENGLISH USAGE

Every major hazard in English usage was subjected to reanalysis and, where necessary, provided with sage qualifications or 'Keep Off' signs. MEU is a collection of articles arranged under both ordinary headings (*this, thistle, thither, -th nouns, those, though*) and idiosyncratic ones (*battered ornaments, out of the frying pan, sturdy indefensible, swapping horses*). This work in particular has made the name Fowler as well known among those interested in usage and the language as Johnson and Webster, a point of reference for both those who venerate and those who regret what he has had to say. Presented as the 3rd edition, this is effectively a new book that sets Fowler himself in historical perspective.

A Dictionary of Modern English Usage is a style guide to English usage, pronunciation, and writing. Ranging from plurals and literary technique to the distinctions among like words (homonyms, synonyms, etc.), to foreign-term use, it became the standard for most style guides that followed – thus, first edition remains in print despite the existence of the second edition, and third edition. The third edition has been largely rewritten along the lines of a modern usage dictionary, making some use of corpus data.

Approach

English usage was to encourage a direct, vigorous writing style, and to oppose all artificiality – firmly advising against unnecessary, convoluted sentence construction, foreign words and phrases, and archaisms. He opposed all pedantry, and notably ridiculed artificial grammatical rules without warrant in natural English usage – such as bans on split infinitives and ending a sentence with a preposition, rules on the placement of the word *only*, and distinctions between *which* and *that*. He also condemned every cliché, and, in classifying them, coined and popularized the terms *battered ornament*, *Ward our Street*, *vogue words*, and *worn-out humour*, whilst simultaneously defending useful distinctions between words whose meanings were coalescing in practice, and guiding the user away from errors of word misuse, and illogical sentence construction. Like most *practical* guides, its linguistics is a mixture of the prescriptive and the descriptive — thus allowing extremists of both camps to place Fowler in the other.

Edition

Before writing this work, Fowler with his brother had written and revised *The King's English*.

The first edition of *Fowler's* was reprinted several times. A reprint whose copyright page mentions "1954" as the most-recent reprint year, also notes that the 1930 and 1937 reprints were "with corrections...." The second edition, *Fowler's Modern English Usage*, published in 1965, was lightly revised by Sir Ernest Gowers, who updated and contributed to the text, and removed articles deemed "no longer relevant to [current] literary fashions."

The third edition, published in 1996, revised in 2004, was edited by Robert Burchfield, whose preface says, while "Fowler's name remains on the title-page... his book has been largely rewritten." Editorially, the difference between the first and third editions is that the first edition, *A Dictionary of Modern English Usage* (1926) is a prescriptive style guide about how to write clearly and expressively, and the third edition — titled *The New Fowler's Modern English Usage* (1996) and *Fowler's Modern English Usage* (2004) — is a descriptive usage guide about how English is spoken and written in practice.

Quotations

A Dictionary of Modern English Usage is renowned for its witty passages; many of which have been widely cited:

The speaker who has discovered that *Juan* and *Quixote* are not pronounced in Spain as he used to pronounce them as a boy is not content to keep so important a piece of information to himself.

Display of superior knowledge is as great a vulgarity as display of superior wealth – greater indeed, inasmuch as knowledge should tend more definitely than wealth towards discretion and good manners.

Writers who observe the poignancy sometimes given by inversion, but fail to observe that 'sometimes' means 'when exclamation is appropriate', adopt inversion as an infallible enlivener; they aim at freshness and attain frigidity.

The English-speaking world may be divided into those who neither know nor care what a split infinitive is; those who do not know, but care very much; those who know and condemn; those who know and approve; and those who know and distinguish.

It is strange that a people with such a fondness for understatement as the British should have felt the need to keep changing the adverbs by which they hope to convince listeners of the intensity of their feelings.

Henry Fowler researched *A Dictionary of Modern English Usage* with the aid of his younger brother Francis, who died in 1918 from tuberculosis contracted during service with the BEF. The dedication begins: "I think of it as it should have been, with its prolixity's docked, its dullness's enlivened, its fads eliminated, its truths multiplied..."

Description

No book had more influence on twentieth-century writers of English *Dictionary of Modern English Usage* . It rapidly became the standard work of reference for the correct use of English in terms of choice of words, grammar, and style. Much loved for his firm opinions, passion, and dry humour, Fowler has stood the test of time and is still considered by many to be the best arbiter of good practice.

Now it is bringing back the original long-out-of-print first edition of this beloved work, enhanced with a new introduction by one of today's leading experts on the language, David Crystal. Drawing on a wealth of entertaining examples, Crystal offers an insightful reassessment Fowler's reputation and his place in the history of linguistic thought. Fowler, Crystal points out, was far more sophisticated in his analysis of language than most people realise and many of his entries display a concern for descriptive accuracy which would do any modern linguist proud. And although the book is full of his personal likes and dislikes, Fowler's prescriptivism is usually intelligent and reasoned. Crystal concludes warmly that Fowler was like "an endearingly eccentric, schoolmasterly character, driven at times to exasperation by the infelicities of his wayward pupils, but always wanting the best for them and hoping to provide the best guidance for them.... He may shake his stick at us, but we never feel we are actually going to be beaten."

In the concluding section of the book, Crystal examines nearly many entries in detail, offers a modern perspective on them, and shows how English has changed since the 1920s. This exciting and long awaited re-release of one of the classic works of English reference will delight everyone interested in language.

Dictionary makers apply two basic philosophies to the defining of words: prescriptive or descriptive. The Oxford English Dictionary (OED) is descriptive, and attempts to describe the actual use of words. Noah Webster, on the other hand, intent on forging a distinct identity for the American language, altered spellings and accentuated differences in meaning and pronunciation of numerous words. This is why American English now uses the spelling "colour" while the rest of the world uses "colour". (See American and British English differences.) While disapproved of in the UK the US spellings are universally understood; likewise the British spellings are not acceptable in America.

While descriptivists argue that prescriptivism is an unnatural attempt to dictate usage or curtail change, prescriptivists argue that to indiscriminately document "improper" or "inferior" usages sanctions those usages by default and causes language to "deteriorate". Although the debate can become very heated, only a small number of controversial words are usually affected. But the softening of usage notations, from the previous edition, for two words, ain't and regardless, out of over 450,000 Third, was enough to provoke outrage among many with prescriptivist leanings, who branded the dictionary as "permissive."

The prescriptive/descriptive issue has been given so much consideration in modern times that most dictionaries of English apply the descriptive method to definitions, while additionally informing readers of attitudes which may influence their choices on words often considered vulgar, offensive, erroneous, or easily confused. Merriam-Webster is subtle, only adding italicized notations such as, sometimes offensive or nonstand (nonstandard.) American Heritage goes further, discussing issues separately in numerous "usage notes." Encarta provides similar notes, but is more prescriptive, offering warnings and admonitions against the use of certain words considered by many to be offensive or illiterate, such as, "an offensive term for..." or "a taboo term meaning..."

Because of the broad use of dictionaries, and their acceptance by many as language authorities, their treatment of the language does affect usage to some degree, even the most descriptive dictionaries providing conservative continuity. In the long run, however, usage primarily determines the meanings of words in English, and the language is being changed and created every day. As Jorge Luis Borges says in the prologue to "El otro, el mismo": "It is often forgotten that (dictionaries) are artificial repositories, put together well after the languages they define. The roots of language are irrational and of a magical nature."

Features

- *Dictionary of Modern English Usage* is a classic, an unsurpassed resource on the correct use of English in matters of style and grammar. Now the original edition is introduced by the best-known modern expert on language usage, David Crystal, in a comprehensive edition that re-evaluates Fowler for the twenty-first century.

- The only hardback edition of this standard reference work, and the only edition to include contextualizing introduction and commentary.
- David Crystal's introduction places the Dictionary in the climate of its time, and reaches some fascinating conclusions about how the book really works, looking beyond the common notion that it is wholly prescriptive and idiosyncratic. Illustrated with numerous illuminating examples from the Dictionary.
- Notes on the entries discuss the changes in usage and attitude between Fowler and today, showing how English has changed since the 1920s by reference to modern corpus studies, grammars, dictionaries and the internet.
- Includes a chronology, bibliography, and a table of pronunciation preferences, showing how the pronunciation of words has changed during the past century.

New edition of an old and esteemed dictionary was released. The publisher courted publicity, noting the great expense and amount of work that went into its making. But the book was ill-received. It was judged "subversive" and denounced in the *New York Times*, the *Chicago Tribune*, the*Atlantic*, the *New Yorker*, *Life*, and dozens of other newspapers, magazines, and professional journals. Not every publication condemned the volume, but the various exceptions did little to change the widespread impression of a well-known reference work being cast out from the better precincts of American culture.

The dictionary was called "permissive" and details of its perfidy were aired, mocked, and distorted until the publisher was put on notice that it might be bought out to prevent further circulation of this insidious thirteen-and-a-half-pound, four-inch-thick doorstop of a book. *Webster's Third New*

International (Unabridged) wasn't just any dictionary, of course, but the most up-to-date and complete offering from America's oldest and most respected name in lexicography.

The dictionary's previous edition, *Webster's New International* Second Edition (Unabridged), was the great American dictionary with 600,000 entries and numerous competitors but no rivals. With a six-inch-wide binding, it weighed four pounds more than *Webster's Third* and possessed an almost unanswerable air of authority. If you wanted to know how to pronounce *chaise longue*, it told you, shâz long, end of discussion. It did not stoop to correct or even mention the vulgarization that sounds like "Che's lounge." When to use *less* and when to use *fewer*? It indicated what strict usage prescribed. It defined *celebrant* as "one who celebrates a public religious rite; esp. the officiating priest," not just any old party guest.

The third edition took a more empirical approach, listing variations in pronunciation and spelling until the reader looking for the one correct answer became the recipient of numerous competing answers: shâz long and Che's lounge (with *lounge* labeled a folk etymology). Shades of meaning were differentiated with scads of quotations from the heights of literature and the lows of yesterday's news section. The new unabridged dictionary was more rigorous but harder to use. And all this made some people quite irate, which *Webster's Third* defines as "feeling and showing a high degree of anger : WRATHFUL, INCENSED."

At first glance, the controversy over *Webster's Third* seems to symbolize a lurch in American culture from a late fifties' respect for standards to a sixties' rebellion against establishment values. The ensuing debate over the dictionary's methodology did owe much to the anxiety of midcentury intellectuals about the rise of a national popular culture, as attested to by the involvement of Dwight Macdonald, who became the definitive critic of *Webster's Third*. But the dictionary-bashing that began in 1961 has continued well beyond America's shift from square to hip. In 2001, *Harper's* magazine published a cover story by David

Foster Wallace that contained a fresh assault on *Webster's Third* and its editor, Philip Gove. Like many earlier critiques, it showed little understanding of the thinking that went into*Webster's Third.* It was unique, however, in its brazen misrepresentation of the book itself.

All the material from the *Webster's Second* (W2) could not be reprinted without making W3 a two-volume work, and much of the second edition's material cried out for revision, such as the supplement "Names of Noteworthy Persons,". W3, like W2, would be called unabridged, but words not used since 1755 were deleted. In all, 250,000 entries were retired to free up space for new material.

Gove, in Morton's telling, comes off as an impatient and technocratic editor. He did not shrink from drawing hard lines. A dictionary should give primacy to generic terms, he asserted, not proper names, not geographical appendixes, not biographical information, not famous sayings, nor names from the Bible and the plays of William Shakespeare. This way of cutting encyclopedic material and proper nouns is also the approach of the *English Dictionary,* but it was completely novel to American dictionaries, which tended to be one-stop, all-purpose reference works, as W2 had been.

Gove's decision quickly cleared a lot of dead wood, but deprived users of helpful material and resulted in some general peculiarity. Charles Dickens, for example, no longer warranted an entry but*dickensian* (with a lowercase d) did. Words almost always capitalized in print were shown in lower case but followed by the notation *usu. cap* (usually capitalized)—a policy Morton wrote was "universally deplored."

READ A DICTIONARY

The dictionary invites a playful reading. It challenges anyone to sit down with it in an idle moment only to find an hour gone by without being bored. Recently I noticed an advertisement for a dictionary as a wonder book. "Astonished Actually Means Thunderstruck" was the headline, written obviously in the hope that the prospective buyer would be thunderstruck, or wonderstruck, enough to look further. And the rest of the ad listed such tidbits as a "*disaster* literally means the stars are against you!" or "to tantalize is to torment with the punishment of Tantalus as told in Greek mythology."

While do not think astonishment is the dictionary's main mission in life, It cannot resist reporting some of the things It learned accidentally while thumbing its pages, in the course of writing this article. It discovered, that the word "solecism" derives from Soli, the name of a Greek colony in Cilicia, whose inhabitants were thought by the Athenians to speak bad Greek; hence, "solecism" was probably the equivalent in Greek slang for a Bostonian's contemptuous reference to "New Yorkese." I learned that "coal" originally meant charred wood.

It was then applied to mineral coal when this was first introduced, under such names as "sea-coal" and "pitcoal." Now that mineral coal is the more common variety, we redundantly refer to charred wood as "charcoal." I was edified by the fact that the drink "Tom and Jerry" derives its name from the two chief characters in Evan's "Life of London", that in England a low beer joint is called a "Tom and Jerry Shop," and, that indulgence in riotous behaviour is called "to tom and jerry."

It was always thought that a forlorn hope was really a hope on the verge of turning into despair, but it seems that it isn't a hope at all, "Hope" here is a misspelling of the Dutch word "hoop" meaning heap. A forlorn hope is a storming party, a band of heroes who willing to end up in a heap for their country's cause. And most shocking of all was the discovery that one theory about the origin of the magician's "hocus pocus" accounts for it as a corruption of "*hoc est corous*" — the sacred words accompanying the sacrament of the Eucharist.

This, together with the reversal in meaning of "dunce" — from the proper name of Duns Scotus, the subtlest doctor of the Church, to naming a numbskull provides a two-word commentary on the transition from the Middle Ages to modern times.

The staid modern dictionary is full of such wit even when it doesn't try to be funny, as Dr. Johnson did when he defined "oats" as "a grain which in England is generally given to horses, but in Scotland supports the people." Look up "Welsh rabbit," for example, or "scotch capon" or "swiss steak," and you will discover gentle jokes about national shortcomings in diet.

What interests me most of all are the shifts in meaning of common words in daily use. From meaning an attendant on horses, "marshall" has come to mean a leader of men; though also originating in the stable, "constable" has gone in the reverse direction from signifying an officer of highest rank to denoting a policeman; "boon" has done an about-face by becoming the gift which answers a petition, having been the prayer which asked for it; "magistrate" and "minister" have changed places with each other in the ups and downs of words, for in current political usage, "magistrate" usually names a minor official, whereas "minister" refers to a major diplomatic or cabinet post.

It is often hard to remember that a minister is a servant of the people, and harder, still to recall the precise point of religious controversy which caused the substitution of "minister" for "priest" as the name for one who served in the performance of sacerdotal functions. And readers of our Constitution should have their attention called to a shift in the word "citizen" from meaning any one who, by birth or choice, owes allegiance to the state, to the narrower designation of those who are granted the right to vote. Similarly, "commerce" has narrowed in meaning; like "trade," it once meant every dealing in merchandise, but now is distinguished from industry according to the difference between distributing commodities and producing them.

The word "commerce" reminds me of one other sort of incidental inquiry the dictionary lures you into. You discover that "commerce" and "mercenary" have the same root in "*mercis,*" wares, and that leads you to the closely related root "*merces,*" pay or reward, which is embodied in the word "mercy." If you start this game of research, you will find such roots as "*spec*" from "*spectare*" meaning to look at or see, which generates a family of English words (species, speculate, specimen, specify, spectacle, inspect, respect, aspect, etc.); or *"press"* from *"primo"*; meaning to squeeze, which has an equally large family (impress, repress, pressing, compress, suppress, oppress, depress, express, etc.).

It is almost as hard to stop writing about the dictionary in this way as to stop reading one when you are in hot pursuit of the mysteries of human speech. But, over and above such fascinations, the dictionary has its sobre uses. To make the most of these one has to know how to read the special sort of book a dictionary is. But, before I state the rules, let me see if I can explain why most people today don't use dictionaries in a manner befitting the purpose for which they were originally created.

In its various sizes and editions, the dictionary is an unlisted bestseller on every season's list. To be able to get along without one would be a sign of supreme literacy – of complete competence as a reader and writer. The dictionary exists, of course, because there is no one in that condition. But, if the dictionary is the necessity we all acknowledge, why is it so infrequently used by the man who owns one? And even when we do consult it, why do most of us misuse the dictionary or use it poorly?

The answer to both questions may be that few of us make efforts at reading or writing anything above the present level of our literary competence. The books – or maybe it is just the newspapers and magazines – we read, and the things we write, don't send us to the dictionary for help. Our vocabularies are quite adequate, because the first rule in most contemporary writing is the taboo against strange words, or familiar words in strange senses.

Of course, there are always people (not-excluding college graduates) who have difficulty with spelling or pronouncing even the common words in daily discourse. That, by the way, is the source of the most frequent impulse to go to the dictionary. There is nothing wrong about this! The dictionary is there to render this simple service – in fact, Noah Webster began his career as the compiler of a spelling book which sold in the millions. But my point remains – the dictionary has other and more important uses, and the reason we do not generally avail ourselves of these services is not our superiority, but rather our lack of need as the life of letters is currently lived.

The history of dictionaries, I think, will bear me out on this point. The Greeks did not have a dictionary, even though "lexicon" is the Greek word for it. They had no need for foreign language dictionaries because there was no literature in a foreign language they cared to read. They had no need for a Greek word-book because the small educated class already knew what such a book would contain. This small group of literate men would have been, like the modern French Academy, the makers of the dictionary, the arbiters of good usage. But at a time when so sharp a line separated the learned from the lewd (which, in an obsolete usage, means*unlettered*), there was no occasion for the few men who could make a dictionary to prefer one for the others.

George Santayana's remark about the Greeks — that they were the uneducated people in European history — has a double significance. The masses were, of course, uneducated, but even the learned few were not educated in the sense that they had to sit at the feet of foreign masters. Education, in that sense, begins with the Romans, who went to school to Greek pedagogues, and became cultivated through contact with Greek culture. It is not surprising, therefore, that the first dictionaries were glossaries of Homeric words. The earliest lexicon which is still extant is such a glossary, prepared by a Greek, Apollonius, in the fifth century of our era, obviously intended to help Romans read the "Iliad" and "Odyssey" of Homer, as well as other Greek literature which employed the Homeric vocabulary. Most of us today need similar glossaries to read Shakespeare well.

There were dictionaries in the Middle Ages — a famous Latin one by the Spaniard, Isidore of Seville, which was really a philosophical work, a sort of encyclopedia of worldly knowledge accomplished by discussions of the most important technical terms occurring in learned discourse. There were foreign-language dictionaries in the Renaissance made necessary by the fact that the *humane letters* which dominated the education of the period were from the ancient languages. Even when the vulgar tongues – English, French, or Italian – gradually displaced Latin as the language of learning, the pursuit of learning was still the privilege of the few. Under such circumstances, dictionaries were intended for a limited audience, mainly as an aid to reading the most worthy literature. In attempting to compile a standard dictionary, that is would furnish a guide to others who tried to read them, or who tied to write as well.

The beginning the educational motive dominated the making of dictionaries, though, as in the case of Dr. Johnson, and the work of the French and Italian Academies, there was also an interest in preserving the purity and order of the language. As against the latter interest, the English Dictionary, was a new departure, in that it did not try to dictate the best usage but rather to present an accurate historical record of every type of usage – the worst as well as the best, taken from popular as well as stylish writing. But this conflict between the mission of the lexicographer as self-appointed arbiter and his function as historian can regarded as a side-issue, for the dictionary, however constructed, is primarily an educational instrument. And the problem is whether that instrument is currently well used.

Noah Webster is in a sense the hero of the story. Alarmed by the state into which learning had fallen after the Revolutionary War, Webster sought to make a one volume dictionary which would serve in the self-education of the semi-literate masses. He was concerned with the masses, not the elite, and with selfeducation, at a time when this country had not yet become democratic enough to regard the public education of all its children as a primary obligation of the state. The Webster dictionary was probably one of the first self-help books to become a popular bestseller. And the paradox is that now, with public education widely established in this country, with literacy as universal as suffrage, the self-help potentialities of a dictionary are seldom realized by the millions who own one. I am not thinking merely of children from progressive schools who cannot use a dictionary because they do not know the alphabet. I am thinking of all the products of contemporary education who, not being taught or inspired to read the great and difficult books, have little use for the dictionary. *How much better educated was the self-read man whom Webster helped!*

This brief history of dictionaries is relevant to the rules for reading and using them well. One of the first rules as to how to read a book is to know what sort of book it is. That means knowing what the author's intention was and what sort of thing you can expect to find in his work. If you look upon a dictionary merely as a spelling book or a guide to pronunciation, you will use it accordingly. If you realise that it contains a wealth of historical information, crystallized in the growth of language; you will pay attention, not merely to the variety of meanings which are listed under each word, but to their order.

And above all if you are interested in advancing your own education, you will use a dictionary according to its primary intention – as a help in reading hooks that might otherwise be too difficult because their vocabulary includes technical words, archaic words, literary allusions or even familiar words used in now obsolete senses. The number of words in a man's vocabulary is as definite as the number of dollars he has in the bank; equally definite is the number of senses in which a man is able to use any given word. But there is this difference: a man cannot draw upon-the public treasury when his bank-balance is overdrawn, but we can all draw upon the dictionary to get the coin we need to carry on the transaction of reading anything we want to read.

Let be sure that it not misunderstood, not saying that a dictionary is all you need in order to move anywhere in the realms of literature. There are many problems to be solved, in reading a book well, other than those arising from the author's vocabulary. And even with respect to vocabulary, the dictionary's primary service is on those occasions when you are confronted with a technical word or with a word that is wholly new to you – such as "costard" (an apple), or "hontzin" (a South American bird), or "rabato" (a kind of flaring collar). More frequently the problem of interpretation arises because a relatively familiar word seems to be used in a strange sense. Here the dictionary will help, but it will not solve the problem. The dictionary may suggest the variety of senses in which the troublesome word can be used, but it can never determine how the author you are reading used it. That you must decide by wrestling with the context.

More often, than not; especially with distinguished writers, the word may be given a special, an almost unique, shade of meaning. The growth of your own vocabulary, in the important dimension of multiple meanings, as well as in mere quantity of words will depend, first of all, upon the character of the books you read, and secondly, upon the use you make of the dictionary as a guide. You will misuse it – you will stultify rather than enlighten yourself – if you substitute the dictionary for the exercise of your own interpretative judgment in reading.

This suggests several other rules as to how *not* to read a dictionary. There is no more irritating fellow than the man who tries to settle an argument about communism, or justice, or liberty, by quoting from Webster. Webster and all his fellow lexicographers may be respected as authorities on word-usage, but they are not the ultimate founts of wisdom.

They are no Supreme Court to which we can appeal for a decision of those fundamental controversies which, despite the warnings of semanticists, get us involved with abstract words. It is well to remember that the dictionary's authority can, for obvious reasons, be surer in the field of concrete words, and even in the field of the abstract technical words of science, than it ever can be with respect to philosophical words. Yet these words are indispensable if we are going to talk, read, or write about the things that matter most.

Another negative rule is: Don't swallow the dictionary. Don't try to get word-rich quick, by memorizing a lot of fancy words whose meanings are unconnected with any actual experience. Merely verbal knowledge is almost worse than no knowledge at all. If learning consisted in nothing but knowing the meanings of words, we could abolish all our courses of study, and substitute the dictionary for every other sort of book. But no one except a pedant or a fool would regard it as profitable or wise to read the dictionary from cover to cover.

In short, don't forget that the dictionary is a book about words, not about things. It can tell you how men have used words, but it does not define the nature of the things the words name. A Scandinavian university undertook a "linguistic experiment" to prove that human arguments always reduce to verbal differences: Seven lawyers were given seven dictionary definitions of truth and asked to defend them.

They soon forgot to stick to the "verbal meanings" they had been assigned, and became vehemently involved in defending or opposing certain fundamental views about the nature of truth. The experiment showed that discussions may start about the meanings of words, but that, when interest in the problem is aroused, they seldom end there. Men pass from words to things, from names to natures. The dictionary can start an argument, but only thought or research can end it.

If we remember that a dictionary is a book about words, we can derive from that fact all the rules for reading a dictionary intelligently. Words can be looked at in four ways:

1. *Words are physical things*: Writable marks and speakable sounds. There must, therefore, be uniform ways of spelling and pronouncing them, though the uniformity is often spoiled by variations.
2. *Words are parts of speech:* Each single word plays a grammatical role in the more complicated structure of a phrase or a sentence. According to the part it plays, we classify it as a certain part of speech — noun or verb, adjective or adverb, article or preposition. The same word can vary in different usages, shifting from one part of speech to another, as when we say "Man the boat" or "Take the jump." Another sort of grammatical variation in words arises from their inflection, but in a relatively uninflected language like English, we need pay attention only to the conjugation of the verb

(infinitive, participle, past tense, etc.), the case of the noun, (singular and plural), and the degree of the adjective (especially the comparative and superlative).

3. *Words are signs:* They have meanings, not one but many. These meanings are related in various ways: Sometimes they shade from one into another; sometimes one word will have two or more sets of totally unrelated meanings. Through their meanings words are related to one another — as synonyms sharing in the same meaning even though they differ in its shading; or as antonyms through opposition or contrast of meanings. Furthermore, it is in their capacity as signs that we distinguish words as proper or common names (according as they name just one thing or many which are alike in some respect); and as concrete or abstract names (according as they point to some thing which we can sense, or refer to some aspect of things which we can understand by thought but not observe through our senses).
4. *Finally, words are conventional:* They mean or signify natural things, but they themselves are not natural. They are man-made signs. That is why every word has a history, just as everything else man makes has a time and place of origin, and a cultural career, in which it goes through certain transformations. The history of words is given by their etymological derivation from original word-roots, prefixes, and suffixes; it includes the account of their physical change, both in spelling and pronunciation; it tells of their shifting meanings, and which among them are archaic and obsolete, which are current and regular, which are idiomatic, colloquial, or slang.

A good dictionary will answer all your questions about words under these four heads. The art of reading a dictionary (as any other book) consists in knowing what questions to ask about words and how to find the answers. Ii has suggested the questions. The dictionary itself tells you how to find the answers. In this respect, it is a perfect self-help book, because it tells you what to pay attention to and how to interpret the various abbreviations and symbols it uses in giving you the four varieties of information about words. Anyone who fails to consult the explanatory notes and the list of abbreviations at the beginning of a dictionary can blame only himself for not being able to read the dictionary well. Unfortunately, many people fail here, as in the case of other books, because they insist upon neglecting the prefatory matter — as if the author were just amusing himself by including it.

These suggestions about how to read, and how not to misuse, a dictionary are easy to follow. But like all other rules they will be followed well only by the man who is rightly motivated in the first place. And, in the last place, they will be wisely applied only by the man who remembers that we are both *free* and *bound* in all our dealing with language, whether as writers or readers.

GUIDE TO USE DICTIONARY

When reading this guide, if you are in doubt as to which part of speech is which, consult the Grammar, where each word class is presented separately in tabular form.

The guide assumes your familiarity with a number of terms. If you are not acquainted with them you may find the following, radically simplified, definitions helpful:

Case: The specification of the syntactic function of a noun, pronoun or adjective by means of an inflectional ending. In Icelandic the cases comprise the nominative (for subject and subjective completions, etc.), the genitive (for possession, with certain prepositions, and certain verbs, etc.), the accusative (with many verbs for the direct object, but also with certain prepositions, etc.), and the dative (for indirect object, with certain verbs and prepositions, etc.)

Compound: A word composed of two or more words or word elements joined together

Inflection: The systematic alteration of word forms (usually by the addition or alteration of an ending) to indicate differences of meaning or syntactic function, as in: I go, she goes; girl, girls; he, him; sing, sang, sung

Morphology: The inflectional system of a given word

The contains the headword, information on word class, and morphological details.

THE HEADWORD

Order of Entries

All headwords are printed in bold and presented in the alphabetical order that is now standard for Modern Icelandic:

a, á, b, d, ð, e, é, f, g, h, i, í, j, k, l, m,

n, o, ó, p, r, s, t, u, ú, v, x, y, ý, þ, æ, ö

This means, for example, that all words beginning with i- are listed before words beginning with í-.

Consequently, when two headwords are distinguished only by the presence or absence of an accent over a vowel, the form without the accent is placed first.

hlið *f*

hlíð *f*

When headwords with the same spelling (homonyms) introduce successive entries, they are distinguished by means of superscript numbers.

á·líka *adj indecl*

á·líka *adv*

Presentation of Headwords

A headword is often divided into parts: by means of a dot or by means of a slash/.

A dot marks a division of a compound word into constituent parts. Only one such division is noted.

tilviljunar·kenndur

A slash in a headword marks the point at which any inflectional endings given later in the lemma should be added.

borð/a *v* (*acc*) **(-aði)**

indicates that the preterite of borða is **borðaði;**

stelp/a *f* (**-u, -ur**)

Indicates that the genitive singular of **stelpa** is **stelpu** and that the nominative plural is **stelpur**.

In the case of a compound word whose second segment displays the effects of mutation, this segment is separated from the first by the slash rather than by the dot.

hólm/ganga *f* (**-göngu, -göngur**)

Lemmas that Consist of Cross-references

A headword can take the form of a reference from an inflected form with a different spelling.

hættir -> háttur

A headword can be a reference from a second word with an exactly similar meaning.

einskis virði *adj indecl*

= einskisverður

First elements of Compound Words

A headword can consist purely of the first element of a compound word followed by suggestions as to how the element is to be understood in compound words that are not included in the dictionary.

meðal- *in compounds*

average

PARTS OF SPEECH

The following main distinctions are commonly made: *adj* = adjective, *adv* = adverb, *conj* = conjunction, *interj*= interjection, *num* = numeral, *prep* = preposition, *pron* = pronoun, *v* = verb. Dual function is sometimes indicated as follows:

ótal *adj / adv*

Nouns

Nouns are not identified as such. Instead, their gender is

given (*m* for masculine, *f* for feminine, *n* for neuter), and where relevant they are given additional markers to show that they are registered only in the plural form or are indeclinable.

land *n*

sifjar *f pl*

var ·kárni *f indecl*

Verbs

Verbs are identified by the marker *v*. Note also *v refl* for a verb used in the reflexive form, and *v impers* for a verb that is always used in impersonal constructions.

éta *v* (*acc*)

fast/a *v*

á ·girn/ast *v refl*

lang/a *v impers*

Case markers. In the preceding example the first instance, **éta,** has the additional information (*acc*) after the verb marker. This indicates that the verb in question *can* be used transitively and that in transitive use the object of the verb is in the accusative case (as opposed to the dative (*dat*) or genitive (*gen*)).

The absence of a case marker indicates that the verb in question is registered only in an intransitive sense or senses. Case markers are never given for reflexive verb forms, but case usage is usually indicated by an example.

á ·girn/ast *v refl* **(-tist, -st)**

desire, crave

~~ **e-ð**

crave sth

Some verbs are frequently used with double objects, one in the accusative (the direct object), the other in the dative (the indirect object). A typical example of this is **bjóða e-m e-ð** 'offer sby sth' where in Icelandic the sby (**e-m**) is in the dative and the sth (**e-ð**) in the accusative. Verbs of this type are marked (*dat+acc*).

Adjectives

Where adjectives are indeclinable this is shown by the marker *adj indecl*, and when an adjective in origin is the past participle of a verb its source is often identified.

búinn *adj*

< búa

Where an adjective governs the dative case in its noun phrase, it is shown as follows:

[2]líkur *adj* (*dat*)

similar, resembling, like

vera ~ e-m

be like sby

INFLECTED FORMS

Inflectional endings or inflected forms of nouns, pronouns, verbs and adjectives are given in bold type in round brackets immediately after the indication of word class. In cases where there is mutation the portion of the word that includes the vowel (or the whole of the word) is presented in its entirety in the round brackets.

[1]höll *f* **(hallar, hallir)**

fé/lag *n* **(-lags, -lög)**

Some words occur with alternative endings for a given case; these are separated by *or*. Thus in the following example the genitive singular of **liður** appears both as **liðs** and **liðar**.

lið/ur *m* **(-s** *or* **-ar, -ir)**

Nouns

For nouns, the endings usually given are the genitive singular and the nominative plural. If only one ending is given it is always the genitive singular, and the absence of the plural form indicates that plural usage is unknown or extremely rare.

and úð *f* **(-ar)**

antipathy

Where the dative singular of a noun has a vowel change, this form is entered as a headword with a cross-reference.

ketti -> köttur

Verbs

For verbs that belong to the strong declension, the third person singular present (followed by a semicolon) is only given if the vowel differs from the vowel of the infinitive (the headword); otherwise only the third person singular preterite, the third person preterite plural, and the past participle are given, separated by commas.

bjóða *v* (*dat+acc*) **(býður ; bauð, buðu, boðið)**

bera *v* (*acc*) **(bar, báru, borið)**

For most classes of weak verbs only the third person singular preterite and the past participle are given. For the largest and most regular class of weak verbs (Class 1, those marked like **borg/a** *v* **(-aði)**) the past participle is, however, not given, since it is formed completely regularly by the addition of a final **-ð** to the infinitive (thus**borgað, kallað,** etc.).

Where the preterite subjunctive of a verb has a vowel change, the form is entered as a headword with a cross-reference.

byði *subj*

-> bjóða

Adjectives

For adjectives, mutated forms (feminine singular) are given (this form is the same as the neuter plural). Further details on the inflection of adjectives is to be found in the Grammar.

ban eitr/aður *adj* (*f* **-uð**)

DEFINITION

The primary spelling and usage of the definitions represent standard North American English. Spelling and usage variants in British English are also given, preceded by the marker (*UK*).

These variants are to be regarded purely as the *preferred* British form, and it is not necessarily implied that they cannot be used in American English./ (*UK*) introduces a British variant within a phrase.

gefa í botn

step on the gas (*UK*) accelerate

erfið/a *v* **(-aði)**

work hard, toil, labour (*UK*) labour

það er orðið ~

it has gotten light/ (*UK*) got light

There is a deliberate bias toward everyday speech in the English renderings; thus contracted forms such as 'couldn't' (rather than 'could not') are frequently found.

Basic form of Definition

The basic form of definition is used for an Icelandic word for which a single meaning is registered and for which one or more English equivalents are provided.

háðung *f* **(-ar)**

shame, disgrace, ignominy

Within a definition, round brackets may be used to enclose part of an explanation that is optional in English (often dependent on the context).

kyn·þroska *adj indecl*

(sexually) mature

Collocations/illustrative Phrases

The English equivalents of the Icelandic headword may be supplemented by collocations or illustrative phrases. They are printed in bold type and followed by a translation. Collocations ('fixed phrases') often demonstrate idiomatic usage;

fanta·brögð *n pl*

dirty tricks

beita ~um

hit below the belt

illustrative phrases, on the other hand, demonstrate how an Icelandic word is used in one or more of its senses, and the translation shows how the phrase in which it appears can be conveniently rendered into English:

fern *adj*

four (of a type)

~ar buxur

four pairs of pants/(*UK*) trousers

Especially in the representation of phrases there is a tendency in this as in any dictionary of Icelandic to use masculine grammatical forms as illustrative material. This is done to avoid introducing variations to the headwords which, where applicable, in accordance with tradition are given in the masculine form. Grammatical gender is arbitrary (its roots are too deeply embedded in the history of language for us to be able to see any logic in it) and it has no sexist connotations.

hugsa um e-n

care for sby, care to sby's needs

Use of the tilde (~). In the Icelandic phrases incorporated in the definitions the sign ~ (single tilde) and ~~(double tilde) are used as abbreviations for all or part of the headword.

~ is used to represent the whole of a headword that is not broken up by slash.

iðinn *adj*

diligent, industrious

~ við kolann (= iðinn við kolann)

persevering

í grip *n pl*

gera e-ð í ~um (= gera e-ð í ígripum)

do sth on the side

~ is also used to represent the part of the headword that precedes the slash.

ímugust/ur *m*

hafa ~ á e-m (= hafa ímugust á e-m)

dislike sby

~~ is used where the headword is broken up by a vertical slash but both parts (the whole of the divided headword) are to be inserted in the example.

kynn/ast *v refl* **(-tist, -st)**

~~ e-m

get acquainted with sby, get to know sby

Round brackets are used to enclose part of an Icelandic phrase that is optional and may therefore be missing in a specific occurrence.

þol rif *n pl*

reyna (á) ~in í e-m

put sby to the test

The slash is used to indicate alternatives in collocations and phrases.

fisk/ur *m* **(-s, -ar)**

fish

e-ð/e-r er ekki upp á marga ~a

sth/sby is not up to much

Collocations on Own

When use of a headword outside a particular collocation or phrase is not registered in this dictionary, only the collocation itself (introduced by a colon) and its translation are given.

þrándur *m*

vera e-m ~ í götu

be an obstacle to sby

Complex entries for Words with Multiple Meanings

Many of the Icelandic headwords in the dictionary have

more than one meaning. Where this is the case the different senses are numbered separately, and as a rule the numbered definitions are distinguished from each other for the Icelandic user by means of a semantic indicator written in Icelandic and italicized in parenthesis.

ná·kvæmur *adj*

1. (*áreiðanlegur*) exact, precise
2. (*gaumgæfilegur*) thorough, thoroughgoing
3. (*vandlegur*) careful

A phrase may also be placed in an individually numbered section.

reynd *f* **(-ar, -ir)**

1. (*reynsla*) experience
2. (*veruleiki*) reality
3. í ~ in practice

Where the headword is registered in many phrases, they are grouped together in a separate numbered section marked *phrases.* Within this numbered section, the instances are arranged in roughly alphabetical order, usually according to the prepositions or adverbs incorporated in the phrases.

kast/a *v* (*dat*) **(-aði)**

1. (*varpa*) throw, fling, hurl
2. (*ala afkvæmi*) foal
3. *phrases*

~~ **eign sinni á e-ð**

claim sth as one's own

~~ **kveðju á e-n**

greet sby briefly

~~ **rýrð á e-ð**

belittle sth

~~ **af sér vatni**

make water, take a leak

~~ **aftur**

reflect

~~ e-u fram

throw out a remark

~~ fram vísu

make up a quatrain on the spot

~~ mæðinni

take a breather

~~ upp

vomit, throw up

Entries for Complex Verbs

Numbered divisions in verb entries may be introduced by grammatical markers, such as *impers* for impersonal, *refl* for reflexive, *pp* for past participle, *prp* for present participle, where meanings or groups of usages are associated with these grammatical forms.

dett/a *v* **(datt, duttu, dottið)**

1. (*hrapa*) fall, drop

2. (*missa fótanna*) fall, stumble and fall

3. *impers*

mér ~ur e-ð í hug

sth occurs to me

það datt yfir mig

I was amazed. . .

Reflexive or middle-voice usages of verbs are often presented in this manner.

leita. . .

2. *refl*

~~st við

try

Where a verb changes its meaning in accordance with which grammatical case it governs, the entry is divided accordingly.

ausa *v* (*dat/acc*) **(eys ; jós, jusu, ausið)**

A. (*dat*) (*taka með ausu*) scoop, ladle

~ skömmum yfir e-n

pour abuse on sby

B. (*acc*)

1. (~ *bát*) bail

2. ~ **barn vatni**

baptize a child. . .

The introduction of the division into parts **A.** and **B.** may give rise to further grammatical divisions in a manner similar to that described in the following example **C.** *impers* and **D.**

hen/da *v* (*dat/acc*) (**-ti, -t**)

A. (*dat*)

1. (*kasta*) throw

2. (*fleygja*) throw away, discard

B. (*acc*)

1. (*grípa*) catch

~~ e-ð á lofti

catch sth in midair

2. *phrases*

~~ reiður á e-u

grasp (the significance of) sth

~~ gaman að e-m

make fun of sby

C. *impers*

það ~ti mig

it happened to me

D. *refl* dash, rush

Entries for Prepositions

Prepositions in Icelandic usually also function as adverbs. The entries for these words are divided up in a manner similar to that described above for verbs. Thus the structure for the entry for the preposition **í** is as follows:

í *prep / adv*

A. *prep* (*acc*)

  1., etc.

B. *prep* (*dat*)

  1., etc.

C. *adv*

RESTRICTIVE MARKERS

It is the deliberate policy of this dictionary to keep the number of markers and labellings concerning usage to a minimum. English speakers will come to the dictionary with questions occasioned by encountering a given word in a particular context. We expect that this context will supply the information necessary to determine the word's specific application and stylistic level.

Usage

Some explanation, often concerning sphere of usage, is occasionally given in brackets after the English equivalent.

reit/ur . . .

  3. (~~ *á taflborði*) square (in chess, etc)

Figurative Meanings

Figurative meanings (as opposed to literal) are not usually given a separate marker. A clearly differentiated figurative usage will sometimes be apparent either by the introduction of a new numbered section with its corresponding Icelandic semantic indicator and translation:

yfir·bragð *n* (-s)

  1. (*útlit*) appearance

  2. (*yfirskin*) pretext, excuse

or by the inclusion of a phrase demonstrating the figurative sense:

tugg/a *f* (-u, -ur)

  chewed mouthful

gömul ~~

cliché

Colloquialisms

Colloquial words and phrases in Icelandic are rendered as far as possible by English equivalents which are equally colloquial. No special marking is given.

Idiomatic or highly colloquial English equivalents of Icelandic phrases (equivalents which are not exact translations but unabashed 'renderings') are enclosed by single quotation marks.

fíl/a *v* (*acc*) **(-aði)**

~~ e-ð vel, ~~ e-ð í botn

'be really into sth'

Slang

No specific marker is used for slang or 'vulgar' speech.

Poetic or Archaic Vocabulary

Poetic or archaic vocabulary is readily incorporated in everyday Icelandic. Such words are marked *poet* for 'poetic'.

fold *f* **(-ar)**

poet ground, land

Chapter 2

English Usage: Dictionary

a : ad. one; any; each
able : v. having the power to do something
about : ad. almost ("about half"); of or having a relation to ("We talk about the weather.")
above : ad. at a higher place
accept : v. to agree to receive
accident : n. something that happens by chance or mistake; an unplanned event
accuse : v. to say a person is responsible for an act or crime; to make a statement against someone
across : ad. from side to side; to the other side
act : v. to do something
activist : n. one who seeks change through action
actor : n. someone acting in a play or show
add : v. to put (something) with another to make it larger; to say more
administration: n. the executive part of a government, usually headed by a president or prime minister
admit : v. to accept ("admitted to the United Nations"); to express one's guilt or responsibility ("He admitted that what he did was wrong.")
adult : n. a grown person
advise : v. to help with information, knowledge or ideas in making a decision
affect : v. to produce an effect on; to influence ("A lack of sleep affected the singer's performance.")
afraid : ad. feeling fear

after	:	ad. later; behind
again	:	ad. another time; as before
against	:	ad. opposed to; not agreeing with something
age	:	n. how old a person or thing is
agency	:	n. an organization that is part of a larger group ("an agency of the United Nations")
aggression	:	n. an attack against a person or country; the violation of a country's borders
ago	:	ad. of time past; before now
agree	:	v. to have the same belief as someone; to be willing to do something
agriculture	:	n. farming
aid	:	v. to help; to support; n. help, assistance
aim	:	v. to point a gun at; n. a goal or purpose
air	:	n. the mixture of gases around the earth, mostly nitrogen and oxygen, that we breathe
air force	:	n. a military organization using airplanes
airplane	:	n. a vehicle with wings that flies
airport	:	n. a place where airplanes take off and land
album	:	n. a collection of recorded music
alcohol	:	n. a strong, colorless liquid, usually made from grain, used as a drug or in industrial products
alive	:	ad. having life; not dead
all	:	ad. everything; everyone; the complete amount
ally	:	n. a nation or person joined with another for a special purpose
almost	:	ad. a little less than completely
alone	:	ad. separated from others
along	:	ad. near or on ("along the road")
already	:	ad. before now; even now
also	:	ad. added to; too
although	:	conj. even if it is true that
always	:	ad. at all times; every time
ambassador	:	n. a nation's highest diplomatic representative (to another government)
amend	:	v. to add to or to change (a proposal or law)
ammunition	:	n. the bullets or shells fired from guns
among	:	ad. in or part of (a group)

amount	:	n. the number, size or weight of anything
anarchy	:	n. a lack of order; lawlessness
ancestor	:	n. a family member from the past
ancient	:	ad. very old; long ago
and	:	conj. also; in addition to; with
anger	:	n. a strong emotion against someone or something
animal	:	n. a living creature that moves, such as a dog or cat
anniversary	:	n. a yearly celebration or observance of an event that happened in the past
announce	:	v. to make known publicly; to declare officially
another	:	ad. one more; a different one
answer	:	n. a statement produced by a question; v. to make a statement after being asked a question
any	:	ad. one or more of no special kind
apologize	:	v. to express regret for a mistake or accident for which one accepts responsibility
appeal	:	v. to take to a higher court, person or group for a decision; to call on somebody for help
appear	:	v. to show oneself; to come into sight; to seem
appoint	:	v. to name; to choose ("appoint a judge")
approve	:	v. to agree with; to agree to support
archeology	:	n. the scientific study of past human life and activities
area	:	n. any place or part of it
argue	:	v. to offer reasons for or against something; to dispute; to disagree
arms	:	n. military equipment; weapons
army	:	n. military ground forces
around	:	ad. on every side (of)
arrest	:	v. to seize a person for legal action; to take as a prisoner
arrive	:	v. to come to a place, especially at the end of a trip
art	:	n. expressions or creations by humans, such as paintings, music, writing or statues
artillery	:	n. big guns

as	:	conj. equally ("as fast as"); when; while
ash	:	n. the part left after something burns
ask	:	v. to question; to say something is wanted ("We ask the teacher questions every day.")
assist	:	v. to help
astronaut	:	n. a person who travels in space
astronomy	:	n. the scientific study of stars and the universe
asylum	:	n. political protection given by a government to a person from another country
at	:	prep. in or near ("at the edge"); where ("look at"); when ("at noon")
atmosphere	:	n. the gases surrounding any star or planet
attach	:	v. to tie together; to connect
attack	:	n. a violent attempt to damage, injure or kill; v. to start a fight
attempt	:	v. to work toward something; to try; to make an effort
attend	:	v. to be present at
automobile	:	n. a vehicle with wheels used to carry people; a car
autumn	:	n. the time of the year between summer and winter
average	:	n. something (a number) representing the middle; ad. common; normal
avoid	:	v. to stay away from
awake	:	ad. not sleeping
award	:	n. an honour or prize for an act or service
away	:	ad. not near
baby	:	n. a newly born creature
back	:	n. the part behind the front; ad. the other way from forward
bad	:	ad. wrong; acting against the law; not good
balance	:	v. to make two sides or forces equal
ball	:	n. something round
balloon	:	n. a device of strong, light material that rises when filled with gas lighter than air
ballot	:	n. a piece of paper used for voting
ban	:	v. to not permit; to stop; n. an official restriction

bank	:	n. an organization that keeps and lends money
bar	:	v. to prevent or block
barrier	:	n. anything that blocks or makes an action difficult
base	:	n. a military centre; v. to establish as a fact ("Her research was based on experiments.")
battle	:	n. a fight between opposing armed forces
be	:	v. to live; to happen; to exist
beat	:	v. to hit again and again
beauty	:	ad. that which pleases the eye, ear or spirit
because	:	prep. for the reason that ("He left because he was sick.")
become	:	v. to come to be
bed	:	n. a sleeping place
before	:	prep. earlier
begin	:	v. to do the first part of an action; to start
behind	:	ad. at the back of; in back of
believe	:	v. to think; to feel sure of; to accept as true; to trust
bell	:	n. an instrument that makes a musical sound ("a church bell")
belong	:	v. to be owned by; to be a member of
below	:	ad. lower than
best	:	ad. the most good
betray	:	v. to turn against; to be false to
better	:	ad. more good than
between	:	ad. in the space or time that separates; from one to the other ("talks between two nations")
big	:	ad. of great size; not small
bill	:	n. a legislative proposal
biology	:	n. the scientific study of life or living things in all their forms
bird	:	n. a creature that flies
bite	:	v. to cut with the teeth
black	:	ad. dark; having the colour like that of the night sky
blame	:	v. to accuse; to hold responsible
blanket	:	n. a cloth cover used to keep warm

bleed	:	v. to lose blood
blind	:	ad. not able to see
block	:	v. to stop something from being done; to prevent movement
blood	:	n. red fluid in the body
blow	:	v. to move with force, as in air ("The wind blows.")
blue	:	ad. having the colour like that of a clear sky
boat	:	n. something built to travel on water that carries people or goods
body	:	n. all of a person or animal; the remains of a person or animal
boil	:	v. to heat a liquid until it becomes very hot
bomb	:	n. a device that explodes with great force; v. to attack or destroy with bombs
bone	:	n. the hard material in the body
book	:	n. a long written work for reading
border	:	n. a dividing line between nations
born	:	v. to come to life; to come into existence
borrow	:	v. to take as a loan
both	:	ad. not just one of two, but the two together
bottle	:	n. a container, usually made of glass, to hold liquid
bottom	:	ad. the lowest part of something
box	:	n. something to put things into; a container, usually made of paper or wood
boy	:	n. a young male person
boycott	:	v. to refuse to take part in or deal with
brain	:	n. the control centre of thought, emotions and body activity of all creatures
brave	:	ad. having no fear
bread	:	n. a food made from grain
break	:	v. to divide into parts by force; to destroy
breathe	:	v. to take air into the body and let it out again
bridge	:	n. a structure built over a waterway, valley or road so people and vehicles can cross from one side to the other
brief	:	ad. short; not long

bright : ad. giving much light; strong and clear in colour
bring : v. to come with something
broadcast : v. to send information, stories or music by radio or television; n. a radio or television programme
brother : n. a male with the same father or mother as another person
brown : ad. having the colour like that of coffee
budget : n. a spending plan
build : v. to join materials together to make something
building : n. anything built for use as a house, factory, office, school, store or place of entertainment
bullet : n. a small piece of metal shot from a gun
burn : v. to be on fire; to destroy or damage by fire
burst : v. to break open suddenly
bury : v. to put into the ground and cover with earth
bus : n. a public vehicle to carry people
business : n. one's work; buying and selling to earn money; trade
busy : ad. doing something; very active
but : conj. however; other than; yet
buy : v. to get by paying something, usually money
by : conj. near; at; next to ("by the road"); from ("a play by William Shakespeare"); not later than ("by midnight")
cabinet : n. a group of ministers that helps lead a government
call : v. to give a name to ("I call myself John."); to ask for or request ("They called for an end to the fighting.")
calm : ad. quiet; peaceful; opposite tense
camera : n. a device for taking pictures
camp : n. a place with temporary housing
campaign : n. a competition by opposing political candidates seeking support from voters; a connected series of military actions during a war
can : v. to be able to; to have the right to; n. a container used to hold liquid or food, usually made of metal

cancel	:	v. to end; to stop
cancer	:	n. a disease in which dangerous cells grow quickly and destroy parts of the body
candidate	:	n. a person who seeks or is nominated for an office or an honour
capital	:	n. the official centre of a government; the city where a country's government is
capitalism	:	n. an economic system in which the production of most goods and services is owned and operated for profit by private citizens or companies
capture	:	v. to make a person or animal a prisoner; to seize or take by force; to get control of
car	:	n. a vehicle with wheels used to carry people; an automobile; a part of a train
care	:	v. to like; to protect; to feel worry or interest
careful	:	ad. acting safely; with much thought
carry	:	v. to take something or someone from one place to another
case (court)	:	n. a legal action
case (medical)	:	n. an incident of disease ("There was only one case of chicken pox at the school.")
cat	:	n. a small animal that often lives with humans
catch	:	v. to seize after a chase; to stop and seize with the hands
cause	:	v. to make happen; n. the thing or person that produces a result
cease-fire	:	n. a halt in fighting, usually by agreement
celebrate	:	v. to honour a person or event with special activities
centre	:	n. the middle of something; the place in the middle; a place that is the main point of an activity
century	:	n. one hundred years
ceremony	:	n. an act or series of acts done in a special way established by tradition
chairman	:	n. a person leading a meeting or an organized group

champion	:	n. the best; the winner
chance	:	n. a possibility of winning or losing or that something will happen
change	:	v. to make different; to become different
charge	:	v. to accuse someone of something, usually a crime; n. a statement in which someone is accused of something
chase	:	v. to run or go after someone or something
cheat	:	v. to get by a trick; to steal from
cheer	:	v. to shout approval or praise
chemical	:	n. elements found in nature or made by people; substances used in the science of chemistry
chemistry	:	n. the scientific study of substances, what they are made of, how they act under different conditions, and how they form other substances
chief	:	n. the head or leader of a group; ad. leading; most important
child	:	n. a baby; a boy or girl
children	:	n. more than one child
choose	:	v. to decide between two or more
circle	:	n. a closed shape that has all its points equally distant from the centre, like an "O"
citizen	:	n. a person who is a member of a country by birth or by law
city	:	n. any important large town
civilian	:	ad. not military
civil rights	:	n. the political, economic and social rights given equally to all people of a nation
claim	:	v. to say something as a fact
clash	:	n. a battle; v. to fight or oppose
clean	:	v. to make pure; ad. free from dirt or harmful substances ("clean water")
clear	:	ad. easy to see or see through; easily understood
clergy	:	n. a body of officials within a religious organization
climate	:	n. the normal weather conditions of a place
climb	:	v. to go up or down something by using the feet and sometimes the hands

clock : n. a device that measures and shows time
close : v. to make something not open; ad. near to
cloth : n. a material made from plants, chemicals, animal hair and other substances
clothes : n. what people wear
cloud : n. a mass of fog high in the sky
coal : n. a solid black substance used as fuel
coalition : n. forces, groups or nations joined together
coast : n. land on the edge of the ocean
coffee : n. a drink made from the plant of the same name
cold : ad. not warm; having or feeling great coolness or a low temperature
collect : v. to bring or gather together in one place; to demand and receive ("collect taxes")
college : n. a small university
colony : n. land controlled by another country or government
colour : n. the different effects of light on the eye, making blue, red, brown, black, yellow and others
combine : v. to mix or bring together
come : v. to move toward; to arrive
command : v. to order; to have power over something
comment : v. to say something about; to express an opinion about something
committee : n. a group of people given special work
common : ad. usual; same for all ("a common purpose")
communicate : v. to tell; to give or exchange information
community : n. a group of people living together in one place or area
company : n. a business organized for trade, industrial or other purposes
compare : v. to examine what is different or similar
compete : v. to try to do as well as, or better than, another or others
complete : ad. having all parts; ended or finished
complex : ad. of or having many parts that are difficult to understand; not simple

compromise : n. the settlement of an argument where each side agrees to accept less than first demanded

computer : n. an electronic machine for storing and organizing information, and for communicating with others

concern : n. interest, worry ("express concern about"); v. to fear ("to be concerned")

condemn : v. to say a person or action is wrong or bad

condition : n. something declared necessary to complete an agreement; a person's health

conference : n. a meeting

confirm : v. to approve; to say that something is true

conflict : n. a fight; a battle, especially a long one

congratulate : v. to praise a person or to express pleasure for success or good luck

Congress : n. the organization of people elected to make the laws of the United States (the House of Representatives and the Senate); a similar organization in other countries

connect : v. to join one thing to another; to unite; to link

conservative : n. one who usually supports tradition and opposes great change

consider : v. to give thought to; to think about carefully

constitution : n. the written general laws and ideas that form a nation's system of government

contain : v. to hold; to include

container : n. a box, bottle or can used to hold something

continent : n. any of the seven great land areas of the world

continue : v. to go on doing or being

control : v. to direct; to have power over

convention : n. a large meeting for a special purpose

cook : v. to heat food before eating it

cool : ad. almost cold

cooperate : v. to act or work together

copy : v. to make something exactly like another; n. something made to look exactly like another

corn : n. a food grain

correct	:	ad. true; free from mistakes; v. to change to what is right
cost	:	n. the price or value of something ("The cost of the book is five dollars."); v. to be valued at ("The book costs five dollars.")
cotton	:	n. a material made from a plant of the same name
count	:	v. to speak or add numbers
country	:	n. a nation; the territory of a nation; land away from cities
court	:	n. where trials take place; where judges make decisions about law
cover	:	v. to put something over a person or thing; n. anything that is put over a person or thing
cow	:	n. a farm animal used for its milk
crash	:	v. to fall violently; to hit with great force
create	:	v. to make; to give life or form to
creature	:	n. any living being; any animal or human
credit	:	n. an agreement that payments will be made at a later time
crew	:	n. a group of people working together
crime	:	n. an act that violates a law
criminal	:	n. a person who is responsible for a crime
crisis	:	n. an extremely important time when something may become much better or worse; a dangerous situation
criticize	:	v. to say what is wrong with something or someone; to condemn; to judge
crop	:	n. plants that are grown and gathered for food, such as grains, fruits and vegetables
cross	:	v. to go from one side to another; to go across
crowd	:	n. a large number of people gathered in one place
crush	:	v. to damage or destroy by great weight; to defeat completely
cry	:	v. to express or show sorrow or pain
culture	:	n. all the beliefs, traditions and arts of a group or population

cure : v. to improve health; to make well ("The doctor can cure the disease."); n. something that makes a sick person well ("Antibiotics are a cure for infection.")

curfew : n. an order to people to stay off the streets or to close their businesses

current : n. movement of air, water or electricity; ad. belonging to the present time ("She found the report in a current publication.")

custom : n. a long-established belief or activity of a people

customs : n. taxes on imports

cut : v. to divide or injure with a sharp tool; to make less; to reduce

dam : n. a wall built across a river to hold back flowing water

damage : v. to cause injury or destruction; n. harm; hurt or injury, usually to things

dance : v. to move the body and feet to music; n. a series of steps, usually to music

danger : n. a strong chance of suffering injury, damage or loss

dark : ad. having little or no light ("The room was dark.")

date : n. an expression of time; a day, month and year

daughter : n. a person's female child

day : n. twenty-four hours; the hours of sunlight

dead : ad. not living

deaf : ad. not able to hear

deal : v. to have to do with ("The talks will deal with the problem of pollution."); to buy or sell ("Her company deals in plastic.")

debate : v. to argue for or against something; n. a public discussion or argument

debt : n. something that is owed; the condition of owing

decide : v. to choose; to settle; to judge

declare : v. to say; to make a statement

decrease : v. to make less in size or amount

deep	:	ad. going far down; a long way from top to bottom
defeat	:	v. to cause to lose in a battle or struggle; n. a loss; the condition of having lost
defend	:	v. to guard or fight against attack; to protect
deficit	:	n. a shortage that results when spending is greater than earnings, or imports are greater than exports
define	:	v. to give the meaning of; to explain
degree	:	n. a measure of temperature
delay	:	v. to decide to do something at a later time; to postpone; to cause to be late
delegate	:	n. one sent to act for another; one who represents another
demand	:	v. to ask by ordering; to ask with force
democracy	:	n. the system of government in which citizens vote to choose leaders or to make other important decisions
demonstrate	:	v. to make a public show of opinions or feelings ("The crowd demonstrated in support of human rights."); to explain by using examples ("The teacher demonstrated the idea with an experiment.")
denounce	:	v. to accuse of being wrong or evil; to criticize severely
deny	:	v. to declare that something is not true; to refuse a request
depend	:	v. to need help and support
deplore	:	v. to regret strongly; to express sadness
deploy	:	v. to move forces or weapons into positions for action
depression	:	n. severe unhappiness; a period of reduced business and economic activity during which many people lose their jobs
describe	:	v. to give a word picture of something; to give details of something
desert	:	n. a dry area of land
design	:	v. to plan or create plans for

desire	:	v. to want very much; to wish for
destroy	:	v. to break into pieces; to end the existence of
detail	:	n. a small part of something; a small piece of information
develop	:	v. to grow; to create; to experience progress
device	:	n. a piece of equipment made for a special purpose
dictator	:	n. a ruler with complete power
die	:	v. to become dead; to stop living; to end
diet	:	n. usual daily food and drink
different	:	ad. not the same
difficult	:	ad. not easy; hard to do, make or carry out
dig	:	v. to make a hole in the ground
dinner	:	n. the main amount of food eaten at a usual time ("The family had its dinner at noon."); a special event that includes food ("The official dinner took place at the White House.")
diplomat	:	n. a person who represents his or her government in dealing with another government
direct	:	v. to lead; to aim or show the way ("He directed me to the theater."); ad. straight to something; not through some other person or thing ("The path is direct.")
direction	:	n. the way (east, west, north, south); where someone or something came from or went to
dirt	:	n. earth or soil
disappear	:	v. to become unseen; to no longer exist
disarm	:	v. to take away weapons; to no longer keep weapons; to make a bomb harmless by removing its exploding device
discover	:	v. to find or learn something
discuss	:	v. to talk about; to exchange ideas
disease	:	n. a sickness in living things, often caused by viruses, germs or bacteria
dismiss	:	v. to send away; to refuse to consider
dispute	:	v. to oppose strongly by argument; n. an angry debate

dissident	:	n. a person who strongly disagrees with his or her government
distance	:	n. the amount of space between two places or objects ("The distance from my house to your house is two kilometers.")
dive	:	v. to jump into water head first
divide	:	v. to separate into two or more parts
do	:	v. to act; to make an effort
doctor	:	n. a person trained in medicine to treat sick people
document	:	n. an official piece of paper with facts written on it, used as proof or support of something
dog	:	n. a small animal that often lives with humans
dollar	:	n. United States money, one hundred cents
door	:	n. an opening for entering or leaving a building or room
down	:	ad. from higher to lower; in a low place
dream	:	v. to have a picture or story in the mind during sleep; n. a picture or story in the mind during sleep; a happy idea about the future
drink	:	v. to take liquid into the body through the mouth
drive	:	v. to control a moving vehicle
drop	:	v. to fall or let fall; to go lower
drown	:	v. to die under water
drug	:	n. anything used as a medicine or in making medicine; a chemical substance used to ease pain or to affect the mind
dry	:	ad. not wet; without rain
during	:	ad. through the whole time; while (something is happening)
dust	:	n. pieces of matter so small that they can float in the air
duty	:	n. one's job or responsibility; what one must do because it is right and just
each	:	ad. every one by itself
early	:	ad. at or near the beginning, especially the beginning of the day; opposite late
earn	:	v. to be paid in return for work done

earth	:	n. the planet we all live on; the ground or soil
earthquake	:	n. a sudden, violent shaking of the earth's surface
ease	:	v. to reduce; to make less difficult
east	:	n. the direction from which the sun rises
easy	:	ad. not difficult; not hard to do
eat	:	v. to take food into the body through the mouth
ecology	:	n. the scientific study of the environment and links among living and material things
economy	:	n. the system by which money, industry and trade are organized
edge	:	n. the line where something ends or begins
education	:	n. the act of teaching
effect	:	n. the result or change caused by something ("The storm had a serious effect on the economy.")
effort	:	n. an attempt; the work necessary to do something
egg	:	n. the rounded object containing unborn young produced by female birds, fish or reptiles; a single cell in a female person or animal that can develop into a baby
either	:	ad. one of two, but not the other
elect	:	v. to choose by voting
electricity	:	n. a form of energy that flows through wires to provide heat and light, and power to machines
embassy	:	n. the offices of an ambassador and his or her assistants
emergency	:	n. an unexpected and dangerous situation demanding quick action
emotion	:	n. a strong feeling such as love, hate, fear or sadness
employ	:	v. to give work in return for wages
empty	:	ad. having nothing inside; v. to remove everything
end	:	v. to stop; to finish; n. the part which comes last
enemy	:	n. a person opposing or hating another; a person or people of the other side in a war

energy	:	n. power used to do work, usually with machines; the ability and willingness to be active
enforce	:	v. to make something be done
engine	:	n. a machine that uses energy to cause movement or to do work
engineer	:	n. a person who designs engines, machines, roads, bridges or railroads
enjoy	:	v. to be pleased or satisfied by something
enough	:	ad. as much as necessary; pro. the amount needed
enter	:	v. to come or go into
environment	:	n. all surrounding things, conditions and influences that affect life; the natural world of land, sea, air, plants and animals
equal	:	ad. the same in amount, size, weight or value; having the same rights
equipment	:	n. things, tools or machines needed for a purpose or activity
escape	:	v. to get free; to get away from; to get out of
especially	:	ad. more than others ("We liked the food, especially the fish.")
establish	:	v. to bring into existence; to create
estimate	:	v. to form an opinion about a value, size or amount using less than complete information
ethnic	:	ad. of or concerning people belonging to a large group because of their race, religion, language, tribe or where their ancestors lived
evaporate	:	v. to change from a liquid into a gas
even	:	ad. in a way not thought possible ("They survived, even though the building was destroyed.")
event	:	n. that which happens, especially something of importance
ever	:	ad. at any time
every	:	ad. each one; all
evidence	:	n. material or facts that prove something; a reason for believing
evil	:	ad. not good; extremely bad

exact : ad. having no mistakes; correct in every detail
examine : v. to study closely
example : n. a part that shows what the rest of a thing or group is like
excellent : ad. extremely good
except : prep. but for
exchange : v. to trade; to give or receive one thing for another
excuse : v. to take away blame; to pardon; to forgive; n. a reason (sometimes false) for an action
execute : v. to kill
exercise : n. an activity or effort for the purpose of improving the body or to stay in good health
exile : v. to force a person to leave his or her country; to expel; n. a person who is forced to leave his or her country
exist : v. to be; to live
expand : v. to make larger; to grow larger
expect : v. to think or believe that something will happen; to wait for an event
expel : v. to force out; to remove from; to send away
experience : v. to live through an event, situation or condition ("She experienced great pain."); n. something that one has done or lived through ("The experience caused her great pain.")
experiment : v. to test; n. a test or trial carried out to prove if an idea is true or false, or to discover something
expert : n. a person with special knowledge or training
explain : v. to give reasons for; to make clear; to tell about; to tell the meaning
explode : v. to break apart violently with a loud noise, like a bomb
explore : v. to travel in a place that is not well known to learn more about it; to make a careful search; to examine closely
export : v. to send to another country; n. something sent to another country, usually for sale
express : v. to say clearly

extend : v. to stretch out in area or length; to continue for a longer time

extra : ad. more than normal, expected or necessary

extreme : ad. more than the usual or accepted

extremist : n. a person with strong religious or political beliefs who acts in an extreme or violent way

face : n. the front of the head:eyes, nose, mouth; v. to look toward; to turn toward; to have before you, such as a problem or danger

fact : n. something known or proved to be true

factory : n. a building or group of buildings where goods are made

fail : v. to not succeed; to not reach a goal

fair : ad. just; honest; what is right

fall : v. to go down quickly; to come down; to drop to the ground or a lower position

false : ad. not true; not correct

family : n. the group that includes children and their parents

famous : ad. known very well to many people

far : ad. at, to or from a great distance

farm : n. land used to grow crops and animals for food

fast : ad. moving or working at great speed; quick

fat : n. tissue in the bodies of humans and animals used to store energy and to keep warm; ad. thick; heavy

father : n. the male parent; a man who has a child or children

fear : v. to be afraid; to worry that something bad is near or may happen ("He feared falling down."); n. a strong emotion when there is danger or trouble ("He had a fear that he would fall down.")

federal : ad. of or having to do with a national or central government

feed : v. to give food to

feel : v. to have or experience an emotion; to know by touching

female	:	n. a woman or girl; the sex that gives birth; ad. of or about women
fence	:	n. something around an area of land to keep animals or people in or out
fertile	:	ad. rich in production of plants or animals; producing much
few	:	ad. not many; a small number of
field	:	n. an area of open land, usually used to grow crops or to raise animals
fierce	:	ad. extremely strong; violent; angry
fight	:	v. to use violence or force; to attempt to defeat or destroy an enemy; n. the use of force; a battle
fill	:	v. to put or pour something into a container until there is space for no more
film	:	v. to record something so it can be seen again; to make a motion picture or movie; n. a thin piece of material for making pictures with a camera; a movie
final	:	ad. at the end; last
financial	:	ad. of or about the system that includes the use of money, credit, investments and banks
find	:	v. to discover or learn something by searching or by accident; to decide a court case ("The jury finds the man guilty of murder.")
fine	:	n. a payment ordered by a court to punish someone for a crime; ad. very good; very small or thin
finish	:	v. to complete; to end
fire	:	v. to shoot a gun; n. the heat and light produced by something burning
firework	:	n. rockets producing bright fire in the sky, used in holiday celebrations
firm	:	ad. not easily moved or changed ("She is firm in her opinion.")
first	:	ad. coming before all others
fish	:	n. a creature that lives and can breathe in water
fit	:	v. to be of the correct size or shape ("These shoes fit my feet.")

fix	:	v. to make good or right again
flag	:	n. a piece of colored cloth used to represent a nation, government or organization
flat	:	ad. smooth; having no high places
flee	:	v. to run away from
float	:	v. to be on water without sinking; to move or be moved gently on water or through air
flood	:	v. to cover with water; n. the movement of water out of a river, lake or ocean onto land
floor	:	n. the bottom part of a room for walking on ("The book fell to the floor."); the level of a building ("The fire was on the first floor.")
flow	:	v. to move like a liquid
flower	:	n. the colored part of plants that carry seeds
fluid	:	n. any substance that can flow, such as a liquid
fly	:	v. to move through the air with wings, like a bird or airplane; to travel in an airplane or flying vehicle
fog	:	n. a mass of wet air that is difficult to see through; a cloud close to the ground
follow	:	v. to come or go after; to accept the rule or power of; to obey
food	:	n. that which is taken in by all living things for energy, strength and growth
fool	:	v. to make someone believe something that is not true; to trick; n. a person who is tricked easily
foot	:	n. the bottom part of the leg; the part of the body that touches the ground when a person or animal walks
for	:	prep. because of ("He is famous for his work."); in exchange ("Give me one dollar for the book."); through space or time ("They travelled for one hour."); representative of ("I speak for all people."); to be employed by ("She works for a computer company.")
force	:	v. to make someone do something or make something happen by using power; n. power, strength; strength used against a person or

		object; military power of a nation; a military group
foreign	:	ad. of, about or from another nation; not from one's own place or country
forest	:	n. a place of many trees
forget	:	v. to not remember
forgive	:	v. to pardon; to excuse; to remove guilt
form	:	v. to make; to start; to shape ("They formed a swim team."); n. a kind ("Swimming is a form of exercise.")
former	:	ad. earlier in time; not now
forward	:	ad. the direction in front of; toward the front
free	:	v. to release; ad. not controlled by another or by outside forces; not in prison; independent; not limited by rules; without cost
freedom	:	n. the condition of being free
freeze	:	v. to cause or to become very cold; to make or to become hard by cold
fresh	:	ad. newly made or gathered; recent
friend	:	n. a person one likes and trusts
frighten	:	v. to cause great fear
from	:	prep. having a person, place or thing as a beginning or cause ("It is a message from the president."); at a place distant, not near ("The school is five kilometers from my home."); because of ("He is suffering from cancer.")
front	:	n. the forward part; the opposite of back; the beginning; the first part
fruit	:	n. food from trees and plants
fuel	:	n. any substance burned to create heat or power
full	:	ad. containing as much as a person or thing can hold; complete
fun	:	n. anything that is pleasing and causes happiness
funeral	:	n. a ceremony held in connection with the burial or burning of the dead
future	:	n. time after now ("We can talk about it in the

		future."); ad. in the time to come ("All future meetings will be held in this room.")
gain	:	v. to get possession of; to get more; to increase
game	:	n. an activity with rules in which people or teams play or compete, usually sports
gas	:	n. any substance that is not solid or liquid; any substance that burns to provide heat, light or power
gather	:	v. to bring or come together into a group or place; to collect
general	:	n. a high military leader; ad. without details; affecting or including all or almost all
gentle	:	ad. soft; kind; not rough or violent
get	:	v. to receive; to gain; to go and bring back; to become; to become the owner of
gift	:	n. something given without cost
girl	:	n. a young female person
give	:	v. to present to another to keep without receiving payment
glass	:	n. a hard, clear material that is easily broken, used most often for windows or for containers to hold liquids
go	:	v. to move from one place to another; to leave
goal	:	n. that toward which an effort is directed; that which is aimed at; the end of a trip or race
god	:	n. the spirit that is honored as creator of all things ("They believe in God."); a spirit or being believed in many religions to have special powers
gold	:	n. a highly valued yellow metal
good	:	ad. pleasing; helpful; kind; correct; not bad
goods	:	n. things owned or made to be sold
govern	:	v. to control; to rule by military or political power
government	:	n. a system of governing; the organization of people that rules a country, city or area
grain	:	n. the seed of grass plants used for food, such as wheat, rice and corn; those plants that produce the seeds

granddaughter	:	n. the daughter of a person's daughter or son
grandfather	:	n. the father of a person's father or mother
grandmother	:	n. the mother of a person's father or mother
grandson	:	n. the son of a person's daughter or son
grass	:	n. a plant with long, narrow, green leaves
gray	:	ad. having the colour like that made by mixing black and white
great	:	ad. very large or more than usual in size or number; very good; important
green	:	ad. having the colour like that made by mixing yellow and blue; having the colour like that of growing leaves and grass
grind	:	v. to reduce to small pieces by crushing
ground	:	n. land; the earth's surface; soil
group	:	n. a number of people or things together; a gathering of people working for a common purpose
grow	:	v. to develop or become bigger; to increase in size or amount
guarantee	:	v. to promise a result; to promise that something will happen
guard	:	v. to watch and protect a person, place or thing ("He guards the president."); n. a person or thing that watches or protects ("He is a prison guard.")
guerrilla	:	n. a person who fights as part of an unofficial army, usually against an official army or police
guide	:	v. to lead to; to show the way; n. one who shows the way
guilty	:	ad. having done something wrong or in violation of a law; responsible for a bad action
gun	:	n. a weapon that shoots bullets
hair	:	n. the fine material that grows from the skin, especially from the head
half	:	n. one of two equal parts of something
halt	:	v. to come or cause to come to a stop; to stop
hang	:	v. to place something so the highest part is supported and the lower part is not; to kill by hanging

happen	:	v. to become a fact or event; to take place
happy	:	ad. pleased; satisfied; feeling good; not sad
hard	:	ad. not easily cut or broken; solid; difficult to do or understand; needing much effort or force
harm	:	v. to injure; to damage; n. damage; hurt
harvest	:	v. to gather crops; n. the crop after it is gathered
hat	:	n. a head cover
hate	:	v. to have strong emotions against; to consider as an enemy; opposite love
have	:	v. to possess; to own; to hold
he	:	pro. the boy or man who is being spoken about
head	:	v. to lead; to command; n. leader; chief; the top part of something; the highest position
headquarter	:	n. the centre from which orders are given; the main offices of a business or organization
heal	:	v. to return to good health; to cure; to become well
health	:	n. the general condition of the body and mind; the condition of being free from sickness or disease
hear	:	v. to receive sound through the ears; to receive news about
heat	:	v. to make hot or warm; n. great warmth; that which is produced by burning fuel; energy from the sun
heavy	:	ad. having much weight; not easy to lift; of great amount or force
helicopter	:	n. a machine without wings that can fly up or down or remain in one place above the ground
help	:	v. to give support; to assist; to make easier; n. support; aid
here	:	ad. in, to or at this place
hero	:	n. a person honored for being brave or wise
hide	:	v. to prevent from being seen or found; to make secret
high	:	ad. tall; far up; far above the ground; important; above others
hijack	:	v. to seize or take control of a vehicle by force
hill	:	n. a small mountain

history	:	n. the written record or description of past events; the study of the past
hit	:	v. to strike; to touch with force
hold	:	v. to carry or support, usually in the hands or arms; to keep in one position; to keep as a prisoner; to contain; to possess; to occupy; to organize and be involved in ("The two sides hold talks this week.")
hole	:	n. an opening; a torn or broken place in something
holiday	:	n. a day when one does not work; a day on which no work is done to honour or remember a person or event
holy	:	ad. greatly honored in religion
home	:	n. the building where a person lives, especially with family; the place where one was born or comes from; the area or country where one lives
honest	:	ad. truthful; able to be trusted
honour	:	v. to obey; to show strong, good feelings for ("to honour one's parents"); n. an award; an act of giving special recognition ("He received many honors for his efforts to help others.")
hope	:	v. to expect; to believe there is a good chance that something will happen as wanted; to want something to happen
horrible	:	ad. causing great fear; terrible
horse	:	n. a large animal often used for racing, riding or farm work
hospital	:	n. a place where sick or injured people are given medical care
hostage	:	n. a person captured and held as a guarantee that a demand or promise will be honored
hostile	:	ad. ready to fight; ready for war
hot	:	ad. having or feeling great heat or a high temperature
hotel	:	n. a building with rooms, and often food, for travellers
hour	:	n. a measure of time; sixty minutes

house	:	n. a building in which people live; a country's parliament or lawmaking group ("House of Representatives")
how	:	ad. in what way; to what amount
however	:	conj. yet; but
huge	:	ad. very big; of great size
human	:	ad. of or about people
humour	:	n. the ability to understand, enjoy or express what makes people laugh
hunger	:	n. the need for food
hunt	:	v. to search for animals to capture or kill them; to seek; to try to find
hurry	:	v. to do or go fast
hurt	:	v. to cause pain, injury or damage
husband	:	n. a man who is married
I	:	pro. the person speaking
ice	:	n. frozen water
idea	:	n. a thought or picture in the mind; a belief
identify	:	v. to recognize someone or something and to say who or what they are
if	:	conj. on condition; provided that ("I will go if you go.")
illegal	:	ad. not legal; in violation of a law
imagine	:	v. to make a picture in the mind; to form an idea
immediate	:	ad. without delay; very near in time or place
import	:	v. to bring from another country; n. something brought from another country, usually for sale
important	:	ad. having great meaning, value or power
improve	:	v. to make better; to become better
in	:	prep. inside; held by; contained by; surrounded by; during
incident	:	n. an event or something that happens
incite	:	v. to urge or cause an action or emotion, usually something bad or violent
include	:	v. to have; to make a part of
increase	:	v. to make more in size or amount
independent	:	ad. not influenced by or controlled by another or others; free; separate

individual : n. one person

industry : n. any business that produces goods or provides services; the work and related activity in factories and offices; all organizations involved in manufacturing

infect : v. to make sick with something that causes disease

inflation : n. a continuing rise in prices while the value of money goes down

influence : v. to have an effect on someone or something; to cause change

inform : v. to tell; to give knowledge to

information : n. knowledge; facts

inject : v. to force a fluid into, such as putting medicine or drugs into the body through the skin

injure : v. to cause harm or damage to a person or animal

innocent : ad. not guilty of a crime; not responsible for a bad action

insane : ad. mentally sick

insect : n. a very small creature, usually with many legs and sometimes with wings

inspect : v. to look at something carefully; to examine, especially by an expert

instead : ad. in the place of; taking the place of

instrument : n. a tool or device designed to do something or to make something

insult : v. to say something or to do something that makes another person angry or dishonored

intelligence : n. the ability to think or learn; information gathered by spying

intelligent : ad. quick to understand or learn

intense : ad. very strong; extremely serious

interest : n. what is important to someone ("He acted to protect his interests." "She had a great interest in painting."); a share in owning a business; money paid for the use of money borrowed

interfere : v. to get in the way of; to work against; to take

		part in the activities of others, especially when not asked to do so
international	:	ad. of or about more than one nation or many nations; of the whole world
intervene	:	v. to come between; to come between in order to settle or solve
invade	:	v. to enter an area or country by force with an army
invent	:	v. to plan and make something never made before; to create a new thing or way of doing something
invest	:	v. to give money to a business or organization with the hope of making more money
investigate	:	v. to study or examine all information about an event, situation or charge; to search for the truth
invite	:	v. to ask someone to take part in or join an event, organization or gathering
involve	:	v. to take part in; to become a part of; to include
iron	:	n. a strong, hard metal used to make machines and tools
island	:	n. a land area with water all around it
issue	:	n. an important problem or subject that people are discussing or arguing about
it	:	pro. a thing, place, event or idea that is being spoken about ("The sky is blue, but it also has a few white clouds.")
jail	:	n. a prison for those waiting to be tried for a crime or for those serving sentences for crimes that are not serious
jewel	:	n. a valuable stone, such as a diamond or emerald
job	:	n. the work that one does to earn money
join	:	v. to put together or come together; to become part of or a member of
joint	:	ad. shared by two or more
joke	:	n. something done or said to cause others to laugh
judge	:	v. to form an opinion about; to decide a question,

		especially a legal one; n. a public official who decides problems of law in a court
jump	:	v. to push down on the feet and move up quickly into the air
jury	:	n. a group of people chosen to decide what is true in a trial
just	:	ad. only ("Help me for just a minute."); very shortly before or after the present ("He just left."); at the same time ("He left just as I came in."); what is right or fair ("The law is just, in my opinion.")
keep	:	v. to possess; to have for oneself
kick	:	v. to hit with the foot
kidnap	:	v. to seize and take away by force
kill	:	v. to make dead; to cause to die
kind	:	n. sort ("What kind of dog is that?"); ad. gentle; caring; helpful
kiss	:	v. to touch with the mouth to show love or honour
knife	:	n. a tool or weapon used to cut
know	:	v. to understand something as correct; to have the facts about; to recognize someone because you have met and talked together before
knowledge	:	n. that which is known; learning or understanding
labour	:	n. work; workers as a group
laboratory	:	n. a room or place where experiments in science are done
lack	:	v. to be without; n. the condition of needing, wanting or not having
lake	:	n. a large area of fresh water surrounded by land
land	:	v. to come to the earth from the air ("Airplanes land at airports."); n. the part of the earth not covered by water; the ground
language	:	n. words and their use; what people speak in a country, nation or group
large	:	ad. big; being of more than usual size, amount or number; opposite small

last	:	v. to continue ("The talks will last three days."); ad. after all others; the only one remaining ("She is the last person in line.")
late	:	ad. after the correct time; near the end; opposite early
laugh	:	v. to make sounds to express pleasure or happy feelings
launch	:	v. to put into operation; to begin; to send into the air or space
law	:	n. all or any rules made by a government
lead	:	v. to show the way; to command; to control; to go first
leak	:	v. to come out of or to escape through a small opening or hole (usually a gas or liquid)
learn	:	v. to get knowledge about; to come to know a fact or facts
leave	:	v. to go away from; to let something stay where it is
left	:	ad. on the side that is toward the west when one is facing north; opposite right
legal	:	ad. of or in agreement with the law
legislature	:	n. a government lawmaking group
lend	:	v. to permit someone to use a thing temporarily; to make a loan of money
less	:	ad. smaller in amount; not as much
let	:	v. to permit to do or to be; to make possible
letter	:	n. a message written on paper; a communication in writing sent to another person
level	:	n. the amount or height that something reaches or rises to; the position of something or someone
liberal	:	ad. one who usually supports social progress or change
lie	:	v. to have one's body on the ground or other surface; to say something that one knows is not true
life	:	n. the time between being born and dying; opposite death; all living things
lift	:	v. to take or bring up to a higher place or level

light	:	n. a form of energy that affects the eyes so that one is able to see; anything that produces light; ad. bright; clear; not heavy
lightning	:	n. light produced by electricity in the air, usually during a storm
like	:	v. to be pleased with; to have good feelings for someone or something; ad. in the same way as; similar to
limit	:	v. to restrict to a number or amount; n. the greatest amount or number permitted
line	:	n. a long, thin mark on a surface; a number of people or things organized; one after another; the edge of an area protected by military forces
link	:	v. to connect; to unite one thing or event with another; n. a relation between two or more things, situations or events
liquid	:	n. a substance that is not a solid or gas, and can move freely, like water
list	:	v. to put in writing a number of names of people or things; n. a written series of names or things
listen	:	v. to try to hear
literature	:	n. all the poems, stories and writings of a period of time or of a country
little	:	ad. not tall or big; a small amount
live	:	v. to have life; to exist; ad. having life; alive
load	:	v. to put objects on or into a vehicle or container; n. that which is carried
loan	:	n. money borrowed that usually must be returned with interest payments; something borrowed
local	:	ad. about or having to do with one place
lonely	:	ad. feeling alone and wanting friends; visited by few or no people ("a lonely man")
long	:	ad. not short; measuring from beginning to end; measuring much; for much time
look	:	v. to turn the eyes toward so as to see; to search or hunt for; to seem to be
lose	:	v. to have no longer; to not find; to fail to keep; to be defeated

loud : ad. having a strong sound; full of sound or noise

love : v. to like very much; to feel a strong, kind emotion (sometimes involving sex); n. a strong, kind emotion for someone or something; opposite hate

low : ad. not high or tall; below the normal height; close to the ground

loyal : ad. showing strong friendship and support for someone or something

luck : n. something that happens by chance

machine : n. a device with moving parts used to do work

magazine : n. a publication of news, stories, pictures or other information

mail : n. letters, papers and other things sent through an official system, such as a post office

main : ad. the most important or largest

major : ad. great in size, importance or amount

majority : n. the greater number; more than half

make : v. to produce; to create; to build; to do something or to carry out an action; to cause to be or to become

male : n. a man or boy; the sex that is the father of children; ad. of or about men

man : n. an adult male human

manufacture : v. to make goods in large amounts

many : ad. a large number or amount of

map : n. a picture of the earth's surface or a part of it

march : v. to walk in a group like soldiers; to walk together in a large group to protest about something

mark : v. to make a sign or cut on something

market : n. a place or area where goods are sold, bought or traded; an economic system in which the prices of things are decided by how many there are and how much money people are willing to pay for them

marry : v. to join a man and woman together as husband and wife; to become husband and wife (usually in a religious or civil ceremony)

mass	:	n. an amount of matter having no special form and usually of a large size
mate	:	v. to bring together a male and a female to create another creature
material	:	n. the substance, substances or matter of which something is made or from which something can be made, such as wood, cloth or stone; anything that can be made into something else
mathematics	:	n. the science dealing with amounts, sizes and shapes, as explained by numbers and signs
matter	:	n. anything that can be seen or felt; what things are made of
may	:	v. a word used with an action word to mean permit or possible ("May I go?" "They may leave tomorrow.")
mayor	:	n. the chief official of a city or town government
meal	:	n. food eaten to satisfy hunger, such as dinner
mean	:	v. to want to; to give the idea of; to have the idea of
measure	:	v. to learn the amount, size or distance of something; n. an action taken; a legislative proposal
meat	:	n. the part of a dead animal used for food
media	:	n. all public information organizations, including newspapers, television and radio
medicine	:	n. a substance or drug used to treat disease or pain; the science or study of treating and curing disease or improving health
meet	:	v. to come together with someone or something at the same time and place
melt	:	v. to make a solid into a liquid by heating it
member	:	n. one of a group
memorial	:	n. something done or made to honour the memory of a person or event
memory	:	n. a picture in the mind of past events; the ability to remember; a thing remembered
mental	:	ad. about or having to do with the mind
mercy	:	n. kindness toward those who should be punished; the power to be kind or to pardon

message	:	n. written or spoken news or information; a note from one person to another person or group
metal	:	n. a hard substance such as iron, steel or gold
method	:	n. the way something is done
microscope	:	n. a device used to make very small things look larger so they can be studied
middle	:	n. the centre; a place or time of equal distance from both sides or ends; ad. in the centre
militant	:	n. someone active in trying to cause political change, often by the use of force or violence
military	:	n. the armed forces of a nation or group; ad. of or about the armed forces
milk	:	n. the white liquid produced by female animals to feed their young
mind	:	n. the thinking, feeling part of a person
mine	:	v. to dig useful or valuable substances out of the earth; n. a place in the earth where such substances are found; a bomb placed under the ground or under water so it cannot be seen
mineral	:	n. a substance found in nature that is not an animal or a plant, such as coal or salt
minister	:	n. a member of a cabinet; a high government official ("prime minister,"foreign minister")
minor	:	ad. small in size; of little importance
minority	:	n. the smaller number; opposite majority
minute	:	n. a measure of time; one of the sixty equal parts of an hour; sixty seconds
miss	:	v. to fail to hit, see, reach or meet
missile	:	n. any weapon that can be thrown or fired through the air and explodes when it reaches its target
missing	:	ad. lost; not found
mistake	:	n. a wrong action or decision; an action done without the knowledge that it was wrong
mix	:	v. to put different things together to make one thing
mob	:	n. a large group of wild or angry people

model	: n. an example; something, usually small, made to show how something will look or work
moderate	: ad. not extreme
modern	: ad. of the present or very recent time; the most improved
money	: n. pieces of metal or paper used to pay for things
month	: n. one of the twelve periods of time into which a year is divided
moon	: n. the bright object often seen in the night sky that orbits the earth about every twenty-nine days
moral	: ad. concerning what is right or wrong in someone's actions
more	: ad. greater in size or amount
morning	: n. the early part of the day, from sunrise until noon
most	: ad. greatest in size or amount
mother	: n. the female parent; a woman who has a child or children
motion	: n. a movement; a continuing change of position or place
mountain	: n. a part of the earth's surface that rises high above the area around it
mourn	: v. to express or feel sadness
move	: v. to change position; to put or keep in motion; to go
movement	: n. the act of moving or a way of moving; a series of acts or efforts to reach a goal
movie	: n. a motion picture; a film
much	: ad. great in amount
murder	: v. to kill another person illegally; n. the crime of killing another person
music	: n. the making of sounds by singing or using a musical instrument
must	: v. a word used with an action word to mean necessary ("You must go to school.")
mystery	: n. something that is not or cannot be explained or understood; a secret

name : v. to appoint; to nominate; to give a name to; n. a word by which a person, animal or thing is known or called

narrow : ad. limited in size or amount; not wide; having a short distance from one side to the other

nation : n. a country, together with its social and political systems

native : n. someone who was born in a place, not one who moved there

natural : ad. of or about nature; normal; common to its kind

nature : n. all the plants, animals and other things on earth not created by humans; events or processes not caused by humans

navy : n. the part of a country's military force trained to fight at sea

near : ad. not far; close to

necessary : ad. needed to get a result or effect; required

need : v. to require; to want; to be necessary to have or to do

negotiate : v. to talk about a problem or situation to find a common solution

neither : ad. not one or the other of two

neutral : ad. not supporting one side or the other in a dispute

never : ad. at no time; not ever

new : ad. not existing before; not known before; recently made, built, bought or grown; another; different

news : n. information about any recent events, especially as reported by the media

next : ad. coming immediately after; nearest

nice : ad. pleasing; good; kind

night : n. the time between when the sun goes down and when it rises, when there is little or no light

no : ad. used to reject or to refuse; not any; not at all

noise : n. sound, especially when loud

nominate : v. to name someone as a candidate for an

election; to propose a person for an office or position

noon : n. the middle of the day; twelve o'clock in the daytime

normal : n. the usual condition, amount or form; ad. usual; what is expected

north : n. the direction to the left of a person facing the rising sun

not : ad. a word showing that something is denied or untrue ("She is not going.")

note : v. to talk about something already known; n. a word or words written to help a person remember; a short letter

nothing : n. not anything; no thing

now : ad. at this time; immediately

nowhere : ad. not in, to or at any place

nuclear : ad. of or about the energy produced by splitting atoms or bringing them together; of or about weapons that explode by using energy from atoms

number : n. a word or sign used to show the order or amount of things

obey : v. to act as one is ordered to act

object : v. to show that one does not like or approve; to protest; n. something not alive that can be seen or touched

observe : v. to watch; to look at carefully; to celebrate or honour something ("They will observe the anniversary of the day she was born.")

occupy : v. to take and hold or to control by force

ocean : n. the area of salt water that covers almost seventy-five per cent of the earth's surface; any of the five main divisions of this water

of : prep. made from; belonging to; about; connected to; included among

off : ad. away; at a distance; condition when something is no longer operating or continuing; not on; not connected

offensive	:	n. a military campaign of attack; ad. having to do with attacking
offer	:	v. to present or propose; n. the act of presenting or proposing; that which is presented or proposed
office	:	n. a room or building where business or work is done; a public position to which one is elected or appointed
officer	:	n. a person in the military who commands others; any person who is a member of a police force
official	:	n. a person with power in an organization; a representative of an organization or government; ad. of or about an office; approved by the government or someone in power
often	:	ad. many times
oil	:	n. a thick liquid that does not mix with water and that burns easily; a black liquid taken from the ground and used as fuel
old	:	ad. not young or new; having lived or existed for many years
on	:	prep. above and held up by; touching the upper surface of ("The book is on the table."); supported by ("He is on his feet."); about ("The report on the meeting is ready."); at the time of ("He left on Wednesday.")
once	:	ad. one time only
only	:	ad. being the single one or ones; no more than ("We have only two dollars.")
open	:	v. to start ("They opened talks."); ad. not closed; not secret
operate	:	v. to do work or a job; to cut into the body for medical reasons
opinion	:	n. a belief based on one's own ideas and thinking
oppose	:	v. to be against; to fight against
opposite	:	ad. different as possible; completely different from; exactly the other way ("North is the opposite direction from south.")

oppress	:	v. to make others suffer; to control by the use of unjust and cruel force or power
or	:	conj. giving another of two choices; giving the last of several choices
orbit	:	v. to travel in space around a planet or other object; n. the path or way an object travels in space around another object or planet
order	:	v. to give a command; to tell someone what to do; n. a command; the correct or normal way things are organized; a peaceful situation in which people obey laws
organize	:	v. to put in order; to put together into a system
other	:	ad. different; of another kind; the remaining one or ones of two or more ("That man is short; the other is tall.")
our	:	ad. of or belonging to us
oust	:	v. to force to leave; to remove by force
out	:	ad. away from the inside; opposite of in
over	:	conj. above; covering; across, in or on every part of ("all over the world")
overthrow	:	v. to remove from power; to defeat or end by force
owe	:	v. to pay or have to repay (usually money) in return for something received
own	:	v. to have or possess for oneself
pain	:	n. a hurt or suffering somewhere in the body
paint	:	v. to cover with a liquid colour; to make a picture with liquid colors; n. a colored liquid used to cover or protect a surface
pan	:	n. a metal container used for cooking
paper	:	n. a thin, flat material made from plants or cloth often used for writing
parachute	:	n. a device that permits a person or thing to fall slowly from an airplane or helicopter to the ground
parade	:	n. a group of people and vehicles moving together to celebrate a special event or anniversary

pardon : v. to forgive for a crime and release from punishment

parent : n. a father or mother

parliament : n. a government lawmaking group

part : n. something less than the whole; not all of something

party : n. a group of people working together for a political purpose; a group of people or friends gathered together for enjoyment

pass : v. to go by or move around something; to move along; to cause or permit to go

passenger : n. a person travelling by airplane, train, boat or car who is not the pilot or driver

passport : n. a document permitting a person to travel to another country

past : n. the time gone by; the time before; ad. recent; immediately before; former

path : n. a narrow way for walking; a way along which something moves

patient : n. a person being treated by a doctor for a health problem

pay : v. to give money for work done or for something bought

peace : n. the condition of freedom from war, fighting or noise; rest; quiet

people : n. any group of persons; all the persons of a group, race, religion or nation ("the American people")

per cent : n. a part of every hundred ("Ten is ten per cent of one hundred.")

perfect : ad. complete or correct in every way; completely right or good; without mistakes

perform : v. to speak, dance or sing in front of others

period : n. an amount of time within events, restrictions or conditions

permanent : ad. never changing; lasting for a very long time or for all time

permit : v. to let; to make possible

person : n. a man, woman or child

physical : ad. of the body

physics : n. the study of motion, matter and energy

picture : n. something that shows what another thing looks like; an idea or representation of something as seen by the eye; a painting; what is made with a camera

piece : n. a part of something larger

pig : n. a farm animal used for its meat

pilot : n. one who guides or flies an airplane or helicopter

pipe : n. a long, round piece of material used to move liquid or gas

place : v. to put something somewhere; n. an area or a part of an area; space where a person or thing is; any room, building, town or country

plan : v. to organize or develop an idea or method of acting or doing something ">("They plan to have a party."); n. an organized or developed idea or method ("The plan will not work.")

planet : n. a large object in space that orbits the sun ("Earth is a planet.")

plant : v. to put into the ground to grow; n. a living growth from the ground which gets its food from air, water and earth

plastic : n. a material made from chemicals that can be formed and made into things

play : v. to have fun; to not work; to take part in a sport; to make music on an instrument; n. a story acted in a theater

please : v. to make one happy; to give enjoyment

plenty : n. all that is needed; a large enough amount

plot : v. to make secret plans; n. a secret plan to do something wrong or illegal

poem : n. words and their sounds organized in a special way to express emotions

point : v. to aim one's finger toward; to aim; n. the sharp end of something poison : n. a substance that can destroy life or damage health

police : n. a government agency responsible for guarding the public, keeping order, and making sure people obey the law; members of that agency

policy : n. an established set of plans or goals used to develop and make decisions in politics, economics or business

politics : n. the activities of government and of those who are in public office

pollute : v. to release dangerous or unpleasant substances into the air, soil or water

poor : n. people with little or no money; ad. lacking money or goods; of bad quality

popular : ad. liked by many people; generally approved by the public

population : n. all the people in a place, city or country

port : n. a city where ships load or unload goods; a place on a coast where ships can be safe from a storm

position : n. a place; the way of holding the body; the way a thing is set or placed; a job (or level of a job) in an organization

possess : v. to have; to own; to control or be controlled by

possible : ad. able to be done; can happen or is expected to happen

postpone : v. to delay action until a later time

pour : v. to flow; to cause to flow

power : n. the ability to control or direct others; control; strength; ruling force; force or energy used to do work ("Water power turns the wheel.")

praise : v. to say good things about; to approve

pray : v. to make a request to a god or spirit; to praise a god or spirit

pregnant : ad. carrying a child within the body before it is born; expecting to give birth to a baby

present : v. to offer for consideration ("We will present our idea to the committee."); n. a gift ("I gave them a present for their anniversary."); now ("The present time is a good time."); ad. to be at a place ("I was present at school yesterday.")

president : n. the chief official of a country that is a republic; the leader of an organization

press : v. to urge strongly; n. newspapers, magazines and other publications

pressure : n. the force produced when something is pushed down or against something else

prevent : v. to keep or stop from going or happening

price : n. the amount of money for which anything is bought, sold or offered for sale

prison : n. a place where a person is kept as punishment for a crime

private : ad. of or about a person or group that is secret; opposite public

prize : n. something offered or won in a competition; something of value that one must work hard for to get

probably : ad. a good chance of taking place; a little more than possible

problem : n. a difficult question or situation with an unknown or unclear answer

process : n. an operation or series of changes leading to a desired result

produce : v. to make; to create; to cause something to be; to manufacture

profession : n. a job that requires special training

professor : n. a teacher at a college or university

profit : n. money gained from a business activity after paying all costs of that activity

programme : n. a plan of action; the different events or parts of a meeting or show

progress : n. movement forward or toward improvement or a goal

project : n. a planned effort to do something

propaganda : n. ideas or information used to influence opinions

property	:	n. anything owned by someone such as land, buildings or goods
propose	:	v. to present or offer for consideration
protect	:	v. to guard; to defend; to prevent from being harmed or damaged
protest	:	v. to speak against; to object
prove	:	v. to show to be true
provide	:	v. to give something needed or wanted
public	:	ad. of or about all the people in a community or country; opposite private
publication	:	n. something that is published such as a book, newspaper or magazine
publish	:	v. to make public something that is written; to include something in a book, newspaper or magazine
pull	:	v. to use force to move something toward the person or thing using the force; opposite push
pump	:	v. to force a gas or liquid up, into or through
punish	:	v. to cause pain, suffering or loss for doing something bad or illegal
purchase	:	v. to buy with money or with something of equal value; n. that which is bought
pure	:	ad. free from anything that is different or that reduces value; clean
purpose	:	n. the reason or desired effect for doing something; goal
push	:	v. to use force to move something away from the person or thing using the force; opposite pull
put	:	v. to place; to set in position
quality	:	n. that which something is known to have or be ("An important quality of steel is its strength."); amount of value or excellence ("Their goods are of the highest quality.")
question	:	v. to ask; to express wonder or disbelief; n. a sentence or word used in asking for information; a problem; an issue to be discussed
quick	:	ad. fast

quiet	:	ad. with little or no noise; having little or no movement; calm
race	:	v. to run; to take part in a competition to decide who or what can move fastest; to take part in a campaign for political office; n. one of the major groups that humans can be divided into because of a common physical similarity, such as skin colour
radar	:	n. a device that uses radio signals to learn the position or speed of objects that may be too far away to be seen
radiation	:	n. waves of energy from something that produces heat or light; energy from a nuclear substance, which can be dangerous
radio	:	n. the system of sending and receiving signals or sounds through the air without wires
raid	:	v. to make a sudden attack; n. a sudden attack carried out as an act of war, or for the purpose of seizing or stealing something
railroad	:	n. a road for trains; a company that operates such a road and its stations and equipment
rain	:	n. water falling from the sky
raise	:	v. to lift up; to move to a higher position; to cause to grow; to increase
rare	:	ad. not common; not usual; not often
rate	:	n. speed; a measure of how quickly or how often something happens; the price of any thing or service that is bought or sold
reach	:	v. to put a hand toward; to arrive at; to come to
react	:	v. to act as a result of or in answer to
read	:	v. to look at and understand the meaning of written words or numbers
ready	:	ad. prepared; completed; organized; willing
real	:	ad. true; truly existing; not false
realistic	:	ad. in agreement with the way things are
reason	:	n. the cause for a belief or act; purpose; something that explains
reasonable	:	ad. ready to listen to reasons or ideas; not extreme; ready or willing to compromise

rebel : v. to act against a government or power, often with force; to refuse to obey; n. one who opposes or fights against the government of his or her country

receive : v. to get or accept something given, offered or sent

recent : ad. a short time ago

recession : n. a temporary reduction in economic activity, when industries produce less and many workers lose their jobs

recognize : v. to know or remember something or someone that was known, known about or seen before; to accept another nation as independent and establish diplomatic ties with its government

record : v. to write something in order to have it for future use; to put sound or pictures in a form that can be kept and heard or seen again; n. a writing that shows proof or facts about something

recover : v. to get again something that was lost, stolen or taken away ("The police recovered the stolen money."); to return to normal health or normal conditions She is expected to recover from the operation.")

red : ad. having the colour like that of blood

reduce : v. to make less or smaller in number, size or amount; to cut

reform : v. to make better by changing; to improve; n. a change to a better condition

refugee : n. a person who has been forced to flee because of unjust treatment, danger or war

refuse : v. to reject; to not accept, give or do something

regret : n. a feeling of sadness or sorrow about something that is done or that happens

reject : v. to refuse to accept, use or believe

relation : n. understandings or ties between nations; members of the same family; people connected by marriage or family ties

release	v. to free; to permit to go; to permit to be known or made public
religion	n. a belief in, or the honoring of, a god or gods
remain	v. to stay in a place after others leave; to stay the same
remains	n. a dead body
remember	v. to think about the past; opposite forget
remove	v. to take away or take off; to put an end to; to take out of a position or office
repair	n. work done to fix something
repeat	v. to say or do again
report	v. to tell about; to give the results of a study or investigation; n. the story about an event; the results of a study or investigation; a statement in which the facts may not be confirmed
represent	v. to act in the place of someone else; to substitute for; to serve as an example
repress	v. to control or to restrict freedoms by force
request	v. to ask for; n. the act of asking for
require	v. to need or demand as necessary
rescue	v. to free from danger or evil
research	n. a careful study to discover correct information
resign	v. to leave a position, job or office
resist	v. to oppose; to fight to prevent
resolution	n. an official statement of agreement by a group of people, usually reached by voting
resource	n. anything of value that can be used or sold
responsible	ad. having a duty or job to do ("He is responsible for preparing the report."); being the cause of ("They were responsible for the accident.")
rest	v. to sit, lie down or sleep to regain strength; n. that which remains; the others
restrain	v. to keep controlled; to limit action by a person or group
restrict	v. to limit; to prevent from increasing or becoming larger
result	v. to happen from a cause; n. that which follows or is produced by a cause; effect

retire	:	v. to leave a job or position because one is old or in poor health
return	:	v. to go or come back; to bring, give, take or send back
revolt	:	v. to protest violently; to fight for a change, especially of government
rice	:	n. a food grain
rich	:	ad. having much money or goods; having plenty of something
ride	:	v. to sit on or in and be carried along; to travel by animal, wheeled vehicle, airplane or boat
right	:	n. what a person legally and morally should be able to do or have ("It is their right to vote."); ad. agreeing with the facts; good; correct; opposite wrong; on the side that is toward the east when one is facing north; opposite left
riot	:	v. to act with many others in a violent way in a public place; n. a violent action by a large group of people
rise	:	v. to go up; to go higher; to increase; to go from a position of sitting or lying to a position of standing
risk	:	n. the chance of loss, damage or injury
river	:	n. a large amount of water that flows across land into another river, a lake or an ocean
road	:	n. a long piece of hard ground built between two places so people can walk, drive or ride easily from one place to the other
rob	:	v. to take money or property secretly or by force; to steal
rock	:	n. a hard piece of mineral matter
rocket	:	n. a device shaped like a tube that moves through air or space by burning gases and letting them escape from the back or bottom, sometimes used as a weapon
roll	:	v. to turn over and over; to move like a ball
room	:	n. a separate area within a building with its own walls

root	:	n. the part of a plant that is under the ground and takes nutrients from the soil
rope	:	n. a long, thick piece of material made from thinner pieces of material, used for tying
rough	:	ad. not flat or smooth; having an uneven surface; violent; not made well
round	:	ad. having the shape of a ball or circle
rub	:	v. to move something over the surface of another thing
rubber	:	n. a substance made from the liquid of trees with the same name, or a similar substance made from chemicals
ruin	:	v. to damage severely; to destroy
rule	:	v. to govern or control; to decide; n. a statement or an order that says how something must be done
run	:	v. to move quickly by steps faster than those used for walking
sabotage	:	v. to damage or destroy as an act against an organization or nation ("The rebels sabotaged the railroad.")
sacrifice	:	v. to do without something or to suffer a loss for a belief, idea, goal or another person
sad	:	ad. not happy
safe	:	ad. away from harm or danger
sail	:	v. to travel by boat or ship
sailor	:	n. a person involved in sailing a boat or ship
salt	:	n. a white substance found in sea water and in the ground, used to affect the taste of food
same	:	ad. not different; not changed; like another or others
sand	:	n. extremely small pieces of crushed rock found in large amounts in deserts and on coasts
satellite	:	n. a small object in space that moves around a larger object; an object placed in orbit around the earth
satisfy	:	v. to give or provide what is desired, needed or demanded

save	:	v. to make safe; to remove from harm; to keep for future use
say	:	v. to speak; to express in words
school	:	n. a place for education; a place where people go to learn
science	:	n. the study of nature and the actions of natural things, and the knowledge gained about them
sea	:	n. a large area of salt water, usually part of an ocean
search	:	v. to look for carefully
season	:	n. one of the four periods of the year that is based on the earth's position toward the sun (spring, summer, autumn, winter); a period of time based on different weather conditions ("dry season", "rainy season"); a period during the year when something usually happens ("baseball season")
seat	:	n. a thing to sit on; a place to sit or the right to sit there ("a seat in parliament")
second	:	ad. the one that comes after the first
secret	:	n. something known only to a few and kept from general knowledge; ad. hidden from others; known only to a few
security	:	n. freedom from danger or harm; protection; measures necessary to protect a person or place ("Security was increased in the city.")
see	:	v. to know or sense through the eyes; to understand or know
seed	:	n. the part of a plant from which new plants grow
seek	:	v. to search for ("They are seeking a cure for cancer."); to try to get ("She is seeking election to public office."); to plan to do ("Electric power companies are seeking to reduce their use of coal.")
seem	:	v. to appear to be ("She seems to be in good health.")
seize	:	v. to take quickly by force; to take control of quickly; to arrest

self X : n. all that which makes one person different from others

sell : v. to give something in exchange for money

Senate : n. the smaller of the two groups in the governments of some countries, such as in the United States Congress

send : v. to cause to go; to permit to go; to cause to be carried, taken or directed to or away from a place

sense : v. to come to know about by feeling, believing or understanding; n. any of the abilities to see, hear, taste, smell or feel

sentence : v. to declare the punishment for a crime; n. the punishment for a crime

separate : v. to set or keep people, things or ideas away from or independent from others; ad. not together or connected; different

series : n. a number of similar things or events that follow one after another in time, position or order

serious : ad. important; needing careful consideration; dangerous

serve : v. to work as an official; to be employed by the government; to assist or help

service : n. an organization or system that provides something for the public ("Schools and roads are services paid for by taxes."); a job that an organization or business can do for money; military organizations such as an army, navy or air force; a religious ceremony

set : v. to put in place or position; to establish a time, price or limit

settle : v. to end (a dispute); to agree about (a problem); to make a home in a new place

several : ad. three or more, but not many

severe : ad. not gentle; causing much pain, sadness or damage

sex : n. either the male or female group into which all

		people and animals are divided because of their actions in producing young; the physical activity by which humans and animals can produce young
shake	:	v. to move or cause to move in short, quick movements
shape	:	v. to give form to; n. the form of something, especially how it looks
share	:	v. to give part of something to another or others; n. a part belonging to, given to or owned by a single person or a group; any one of the equal parts of ownership of a business or company
sharp	:	ad. having a thin edge or small point that can cut or hurt; causing hurt or pain
she	:	pro. the girl or woman who is being spoken about
sheep	:	n. a farm animal used for its meat and hair
shell	:	v. to fire artillery; n. a metal container that is fired from a large gun and explodes when it reaches its target; a hard outside cover
shelter	:	v. to protect or give protection to; n. something that gives protection; a place of safety
shine	:	v. to aim a light; to give bright light; to be bright; to clean to make bright
ship	:	v. to transport; n. a large boat
shock	:	v. to cause to feel sudden surprise or fear; n. something that greatly affects the mind or emotions; a powerful shake, as from an earthquake
shoe	:	n. a covering for the foot
shoot	:	v. to cause a gun or other weapon to send out an object designed to kill; to use a gun
short	:	ad. lasting only for a small period of time; not long; opposite tall
should	:	v. used with another verb (action word) to show responsibility ("We should study."), probability ("The talks should begin soon."), or that something is believed to be a good idea ("Criminals should be punished.")

shout : v. to speak very loudly
show : v. to make something be seen; to make known; n. a play or story presented in a theater, or broadcast on radio or television, for enjoyment or education; something organized to be seen by the public
shrink : v. to make or become less in size, weight or value
sick : ad. suffering physically or mentally with a disease or other problem; not in good health
sickness : n. the condition of being in bad health
side : n. the outer surfaces of an object that are not the top or bottom; parts away from the middle; either the right or left half of the body
sign : v. to write one's name; n. a mark or shape used to mean something; evidence that something exists or will happen; a flat piece of material with writing that gives information
signal : v. to send a message by signs; n. an action or movement that sends a message
silence : v. to make quiet; to stop from speaking or making noise; n. a lack of noise or sound
silver : n. a valued white metal
similar : ad. like something else but not exactly the same
simple : ad. easy to understand or do; not difficult or complex
since : prep. from a time in the past until now ("I have known her since we went to school together.")
sing : v. to make music sounds with the voice
single : ad. one only
sink : v. to go down into water or other liquid
sister : n. a female with the same father or mother as another person
sit : v. to rest on the lower part of the body without the support of the legs; to become seated
situation : n. the way things are during a period of time
size : n. the space occupied by something; how long, wide or high something is

skeleton	:	n. all the bones of a human or other animal together in their normal positions
skill	:	n. the ability gained from training or experience
skin	:	n. the outer covering of humans and most animals
sky	:	n. the space above the earth
slave	:	n. a person owned or controlled by another
sleep	:	v. to rest the body and mind with the eyes closed
slide	:	v. to move smoothly over a surface
slow	:	v. to reduce the speed of; ad. not fast in moving, talking or other activities
small	:	ad. little in size or amount; few in number; not important; opposite large
smash	:	v. to break or be broken into small pieces by force; to hit or move with >force
smell	:	v. to sense through the nose; n. something sensed by the nose ("the smell of food cooking")
smoke	:	v. to use cigarettes or other tobacco products by burning them and breathing in the smoke; n. that which can be seen rising into the air like a cloud from something burning
smooth	:	ad. having a level surface; opposite rough
snow	:	n. soft, white pieces of frozen water that fall from the sky, usually in winter or when the air temperature is very cold
so	:	ad. in such a way that ("He held the flag so all could see it."); also; too ("She left early, and so did we."); very ("I am so sick."); as a result ("They were sick, so they could not come."); conj. in order that; for the purpose of ("Come early so we can discuss the plans.")
social	:	ad. of or about people or a group
soft	:	ad. not hard; easily shaped; pleasing to touch; not loud
soil	:	n. earth in which plants grow
soldier	:	n. a person in the army
solid	:	ad. having a hard shape with no empty spaces inside; strong; not in the form of a liquid or gas

solve : v. to find an answer; to settle

some : ad. of an amount or number or part not stated; not all

son : n. a person's male child

soon : ad. not long after the present time; quickly

sort : n. any group of people or things that are the same or are similar in some way; a kind of something

sound : n. fast-moving waves of energy that affect the ear and result in hearing; that which is heard

south : n. the direction to the right of a person facing the rising sun

space : n. the area outside the earth's atmosphere where the sun, moon, planets and stars are; the area between or inside things

speak : v. to talk; to say words with the mouth; to express one's thoughts to others and exchange ideas; to give a speech to a group

special : ad. of a different or unusual kind; not for general use; better or more important than others of the same kind

speech : n. a talk given to a group of people

speed : v. to make something go or move faster; n. the rate at which something moves or travels; the rate at which something happens or is done

spend : v. to give as payment; to use ("He spends much time studying.")

spill : v. to cause or permit liquid to flow out, usually by accident

spirit : n. the part of a human that is not physical and is connected to thoughts and emotions; the part of a person that is believed to remain alive after death

split : v. to separate into two or more parts; to divide or break into parts

sport : n. any game or activity of competition involving physical effort or skill

spread	:	v. to become longer or wider; to make or become widely known
spring	:	n. the time of the year between winter and summer
spy	:	v. to steal or get information secretly; n. one who watches others secretly; a person employed by a government to get secret information about another country
square	:	n. a flat shape having four equal sides
stab	:	v. to cut or push into or through with a pointed weapon
stand	:	v. to move into or be in a position in which only the feet are on a surface; to be in one position or place
star	:	n. a mass of gas that usually appears as a small light in the sky at night, but is not a planet; a famous person, usually an actor or singer
start	:	v. to begin; to make something begin
starve	:	v. to suffer or die from a lack of food
state	:	v. to say; to declare; n. a political part of a nation
station	:	n. a place of special work or purpose ("a police station"); a place where passengers get on or off trains or buses; a place for radio or television broadcasts
statue	:	n. a form of a human, animal or other creature usually made of stone, wood or metal
stay	:	v. to continue to be where one is; to remain; to not leave; to live for a time ("They stayed in New York for two years.")
steal	:	v. to take without permission or paying
steam	:	n. the gas that comes from hot water
steel	:	n. iron made harder and stronger by mixing it with other substances
step	:	v. to move by lifting one foot and placing it in a new position; n. the act of stepping; one of a series of actions designed to reach a goal
stick	:	v. to attach something to another thing using a substance that will hold them together; to

		become fixed in one position so that movement is difficult ("Something is making the door stick."); n. a thin piece of wood
still	:	ad. not moving ("The man was standing still."); until the present or a stated time ("Was he still there?"); even so; although ("The job was difficult, but she still wanted to do it.")
stone	:	n. a small piece of rock
stop	:	v. to prevent any more movement or action; to come or bring to an end
store	:	v. to keep or put away for future use; n. a place where people buy things
storm	:	n. violent weather, including strong winds and rain or snow
story	:	n. the telling or writing of an event, either real or imagined
stove	:	n. a heating device used for cooking
straight	:	ad. continuing in one direction without turns
strange	:	ad. unusual; not normal; not known
street	:	n. a road in a city, town or village
stretch	:	v. to extend for a distance; to pull on to make longer or wider
strike	:	v. to hit with force; to stop work as a way to seek better conditions, more pay or to make other demands
strong	:	ad. having much power; not easily broken, damaged or destroyed
structure	:	n. the way something is built, made or organized; a system that is formed or organized in a special way; a building
struggle	:	v. to try with much effort; to fight with; n. a great effort; a fight
study	:	v. to make an effort to gain knowledge by using the mind; to examine carefully
stupid	:	ad. not able to learn much; not intelligent
subject	:	n. the person or thing being discussed, studied or written about
submarine	:	n. an underwater ship

substance : n. the material of which something is made (a solid, liquid or gas)

substitute : v. to put or use in place of another; n. a person or thing put or used in place of another

subversion : n. an attempt to weaken or destroy a political system or government, usually secretly

succeed : v. to reach a goal or thing desired; to produce a planned result

such : ad. of this or that kind; of the same kind as; similar to

sudden : ad. not expected; without warning; done or carried out quickly or without preparation

suffer : v. to feel pain in the body or mind; to receive or experience hurt or sadness

sugar : n. a sweet substance made from liquids taken from plants

suggest : v. to offer or propose something to think about or consider

summer : n. the warmest time of the year, between spring and autumn

sun : n. the huge star in the sky that provides heat and light to earth

supervise : v. to direct and observe the work of others

supply : v. to give; to provide; n. the amount of something that can be given or sold to others

support : v. to carry the weight of; to hold up or in position; to agree with others and help them reach a goal; to approve

suppose : v. to believe, think or imagine ("I suppose you are right."); to expect ("It is supposed to rain tonight.")

suppress : v. to put down or to keep down by force; to prevent information from being known publicly

sure : ad. very probable; with good reason to believe; true without question

surface : n. the outer side or top of something ("The rocket landed on the surface of the moon.")

surplus : n. an amount that is more than is needed; extra;

		("That country has a trade surplus. It exports more than it imports.")
surprise	:	v. to cause a feeling of wonder because something is not expected; n. something not expected; the feeling caused by something not expected
surrender	:	v. to give control of oneself or one's property to another or others; to stop fighting and admit defeat
surround	:	v. to form a circle around; to be in positions all around someone or something
survive	:	v. to remain alive during or after a dangerous situation
suspect	:	v. to imagine or believe that a person is guilty of something bad or illegal; n. a person believed to be guilty
suspend	:	v. to cause to stop for a period of time
swallow	:	v. to take into the stomach through the mouth
swear in	:	v. to put an official into office by having him or her promise to carry out the duties of that office ("The chief justice will swear in the president.")
sweet	:	ad. tasting pleasant, like sugar
swim	:	v. to move through water by making motions with the arms and legs
sympathy	:	n. a sharing of feelings or emotions with another person, usually feelings of sadness
system	:	n. a method of organizing or doing something by following rules or a plan; a group of connected things or parts working together for a common purpose or goal
take	:	v. to put a hand or hands around something and hold it, often to move it to another place; to carry something; to seize; to capture; to begin to be in control ("The president takes office tomorrow.")
talk	:	v. to express thoughts in spoken words; n. a meeting for discussion
tall	:	ad. higher than others; opposite short
tank	:	n. a large container for holding liquids; a heavy military vehicle with guns

target	:	n. any person or object aimed at or fired at
taste	:	v. to sense through the mouth ("The fruit tastes sweet.")
tax	:	n. the money a person or business must pay to the government so the government can provide services
tea	:	n. a drink made from the plant of the same name
teach	:	v. to show how to do something; to provide knowledge; to cause to understand
team	:	n. a group organized for some purpose, often for sports
tear	:	v. to pull apart, often by force
tears	:	n. the fluid that comes out of the eyes while crying
technical	:	ad. involving machines, processes and materials in industry, transportation and communications; of or about a very special kind of subject or thing ("You need technical knowledge to understand how this system works.")
technology	:	n. the use of scientific knowledge and methods to produce goods and services
telephone	:	n. a device or system for sending sounds, especially the voice, over distances
telescope	:	n. a device for making objects that are far away appear closer and larger
television	:	n. a device that receives electronic signals and makes them into pictures and sounds; the system of sending pictures and sounds by electronic signals over a distance so others can see and hear them on a receiver
tell	:	v. to give information; to make known by speaking; to order; to command
temperature	:	n. the measurement of heat and cold
temporary	:	ad. lasting only a short time
tense	:	ad. having fear or concern; dangerous; opposite calm
term	:	n. a limited period of time during which someone does a job or carries out a responsibility

		("He served two terms in Congress."); the conditions of an agreement that have been accepted by those involved in it
terrible	:	ad. very bad; causing terror or fear
territory	:	n. a large area of land
terror	:	n. extreme fear; that which causes great fear
terrorist	:	n. a person who carries out acts of extreme violence as a protest or a way to influence a government
test	:	v. to attempt to learn or prove what something is like or how it will act by studying or doing ("The scientists will test the new engine soon."); n. an attempt to learn or prove what something is like or how it will act by studying or doing ("The test of the new engine takes place today."); a group of questions or problems used to find out a person's knowledge ("The students did well on the language test.")
than	:	conj. connecting word used to link things that may be similar, but are not equal ("My sister is taller than I am.")
thank	:	v. to say that one has a good feeling toward another because that person did something kind ("I want to thank you for helping me.")
that	:	ad. showing the person, place or thing being spoken about ("That man is a soldier."); pro. the person, place or thing being spoken about ("The building that I saw was very large.")
the	:	pro. used in front of a name word to show that it is a person or thing that is known about or is being spoken about
theater	:	n. a place where movies are shown or plays are performed
them	:	pro. other people being spoken about
then	:	ad. at that time; existing; and so
theory	:	n. a possible explanation of why something exists or how something happens using experiments or ideas, but which is not yet

proven ("Other scientists are debating his theory about the disappearance of dinosaurs.")

there : ad. in that place or position; to or toward that place

these : pro. of or about the people, places or things nearby that have been spoken about already

they : pro. those ones being spoken about

thick : ad. having a large distance between two opposite surfaces ("The wall is two meters thick."); having many parts close together ("The forest is very thick."); almost solid, such as a liquid that does not flow easily; opposite thin

thin : ad. having a small distance between two opposite surfaces; not fat; not wide; opposite thick

thing : n. any object

think : v. to produce thoughts; to form ideas in the mind; to consider; to believe

third : ad. coming after two others

this : pro. of or about the person, place or thing nearby that has been spoken about already

threaten : v. to warn that one will do harm or cause damage

through : prep. in at one end and out at the other; from front to back; from top to bottom; with the help of; by

throw : v. to cause to go through the air by a movement of the arm

tie : v. to join or hold together with some material; n. anything that joins or unites; links or connections ("The two nations have strong trade ties.")

time : n. that which is measured in minutes, hours, days and years; a period that can be identified in hours and minutes and is shown on a clock; a period when an event should or will take place

tired : ad. having less strength because of work or exercise; needing sleep or rest

to : prep. showing the direction of an action; showing the person or place toward which an action is directed; showing a goal or purpose

today	:	n. this day
together	:	ad. in one group; at the same time or place; in cooperation
tomorrow	:	n. the day after today
tonight	:	n. this night
too	:	ad. also; as well as; more than is necessary
tool	:	n. any instrument or device designed to help one do work
top	:	n. the upper edge or surface; the highest part; the cover of something
torture	:	v. to cause severe pain; n. the act of causing severe pain in order to harm, to punish or to get information from
total	:	n. the complete amount
touch	:	v. to put the hand or fingers on
toward	:	prep. in the direction of; leading to
town	:	n. a centre where people live, larger than a village but not as large as a city
trade	:	v. to buy and sell or exchange products or services; n. the activity of buying, selling or exchanging products or services
tradition	:	n. a ceremony, activity or belief that has existed for a long time
traffic	:	n. the movement of people, vehicles or ships along a street, road or waterway
tragic	:	ad. extremely sad; terrible
train	:	v. to teach or learn how to do something; to prepare for an activity; n. an engine and the cars connected to it that move along a railroad
transport	:	v. to move goods or people from one place to another
transportation	:	n. the act or business of moving goods or people
trap	:	v. to catch or be caught by being tricked; to be unable to move or escape; n. a device used to catch animals
travel	:	v. to go from one place to another, usually for a long distance

treason	:	n. the act of fighting against one's own country or of helping its enemies
treasure	:	n. a large collection of money, jewels or other things of great value
treat	:	v. to deal with; to act toward in a special way; to try to cure
treatment	:	n. the act of treating; the use of medicine to try to cure or make better
treaty	:	n. a written agreement between two or more nations
tree	:	n. a very tall plant that is mostly wood, except for its leaves
trial	:	n. an examination in a court of a question or dispute to decide if a charge is true
tribe	:	n. a group of families ruled by a common chief or leader
trick	:	v. to cheat; to fool a person so as to get something or make him or her do something
trip	:	n. a movement from one place to another, usually a long distance
troop	:	n. a number of soldiers in a large controlled group
trouble	:	n. that which causes concern, fear, difficulty or problems
truce	:	n. a temporary halt in fighting agreed to by all sides involved
truck	:	n. a heavy vehicle used to carry goods
true	:	ad. correct; not false
trust	:	v. to believe that someone is honest and will not cause harm
try	:	v. to make an effort; to take court action against a person to decide if he or she is guilty or innocent of a crime
tube	:	n. a long, round structure through which liquids or gases can flow; a long, thin container in which they can be kept
turn	:	v. to change direction; to move into a different position; to change colour, form or shape

under	:	prep. below; below the surface of; less than; as called for by a law, agreement or system ("The river flows under the bridge." "Such action is not permitted under the law.")
understand	:	v. to know what is meant; to have knowledge of
unite	:	v. to join together
universe	:	n. all of space, including planets and stars
university	:	n. a place of education that usually includes several colleges and research organizations
unless	:	conj. except if it happens; on condition that ("I will not go, unless the rain stops.")
until	:	conj. up to a time; before
up	:	ad. to, in or at a higher position or value
urge	:	v. to advise strongly; to make a great effort to get someone to do something
urgent	:	ad. needing an immediate decision or action
us	:	pro. the form of the word "we" used after a preposition ("He said he would write to us.") or used as an object of a verb ("They saw us yesterday.")
use	:	v. to employ for a purpose; to put into action
usual	:	ad. as is normal or common; as is most often done, seen or heard
valley	:	n. a long area of land between higher areas of land
value	:	n. the quality of being useful, important or desired; the amount of money that could be received if something is sold
vegetable	:	n. a plant grown for food
vehicle	:	n. anything on or in which a person or thing can travel or be transported, especially anything on wheels; a car or truck
version	:	n. the form of something with different details than earlier or later forms
very	:	ad. extremely ("He was very late.")
veto	:	v. to reject or refuse to approve
vicious	:	ad. bad; dangerous; showing harm or hate
victim	:	n. someone or something that is injured, killed or made to suffer; someone who is tricked

victory	:	n. a success in a fight or competition
village	:	n. a very small town
violate	:	v. to fail to obey or honour; to break (an agreement)
violence	:	n. the use of force to cause injury, death or damage
visit	:	v. to go to or come to a place for a short time for friendly or business reasons
voice	:	n. the sound made by creatures, especially humans, for speaking
volcano	:	n. a hill or mountain around a hole in the earth's surface that can explode, sending hot, melted rock and ash into the air
vote	:	v. to choose a candidate in an election; n. a choice or decision expressed by the voice, by hand or by writing
wage	:	n. money received for work done
wait	:	v. to delay acting; to postpone
walk	:	v. to move by putting one foot in front of the other
wall	:	n. the side of a room or building formed by wood, stone or other material; a structure sometimes used to separate areas of land
want	:	v. to desire; to wish for; to need
war	:	n. fighting between nations, or groups in a nation, using weapons
warm	:	ad. almost hot; having or feeling some heat
warn	:	v. to tell of possible danger; to advise or inform about something bad that may happen
wash	:	v. to make clean, usually with water
waste	:	v. to spend or use without need or care; to make bad use of; n. a spending of money, time or effort with no value gained or returned; something thrown away as having no value; the liquid and solid substances that result from body processes and are passed out of the body
watch	:	v. to look at; to observe closely; to look and wait for

water	:	n. the liquid that falls from the sky as rain or is found in lakes, rivers and oceans
wave	:	v. to move or cause to move one way and the other, as a flag in the wind; to signal by moving the hand one way and the other; n. a large mass of water that forms and moves on the surface of a lake or ocean
way	:	n. a path on land or sea or in the air; how something is done; method
we	:	pro. two or more people, including the speaker or writer ("He and I will go together, and we will return together.")
weak	:	ad. having little power; easily broken, damaged or destroyed; opposite strong
wealth	:	n. a large amount of possessions, money or other things of value
weapon	:	n. anything used to cause injury or to kill during an attack, fight or war
wear	:	v. to have on the body, as clothes
weather	:	n. the condition of the atmosphere resulting from sun, wind, rain, heat or cold
week	:	n. a period of time equal to seven days
weigh	:	v. to measure how heavy someone or something is
welcome	:	v. to express happiness or pleasure when someone arrives or something develops
well	:	ad. in a way that is good or pleasing; in good health; n. a hole in the ground where water, gas or oil can be found
west	:	n. the direction in which the sun goes down
wet	:	ad. covered with water or other liquid; not dry
what	:	pro. used to ask about something or to ask for information about something ("What is this?"); ad. which or which kind ("He wants to know what you would like to drink.")
wheat	:	n. a grain used to make bread; the plant that produces the grain
wheel	:	n. a round structure that turns around a centre

when	:	ad. at what time; at any time ("When will she come home?"); conj. during or at the time ("I studied hard when I was in school.")
where	:	ad., conj. at, to or in what place ("Where is his house?" "The house where he lives is in the old part of the city.")
which	:	pro. used to ask about what one or what ones of a group of things or people ("Which programme do you like best?" "Which students will take the test?")
while	:	n. a space of time ("Please come to my house for a while."); conj. at or during the same time ("It may not be a good idea to eat while you are running.")
white	:	ad. having the colour like that of milk or snow
who	:	pro. what or which person or persons that ("Who wants to go?"); the person or persons ("They are the ones who want to go.")
whole	:	ad. the complete amount; all together; not divided; not cut into pieces
why	:	ad. for what cause or reason ("Why did she do it?"); conj. the reason for which ("I do not know why she did it.")
wide	:	ad. having a great distance from one side to the other; not limited
wife	:	n. a woman who is married
wild	:	ad. living and growing in natural conditions and not organized or supervised by humans; angry; uncontrolled
will	:	v. a word used with action words to show future action ("They will hold talks tomorrow.")
willing	:	ad. being ready or having a desire to ("They are willing to talk about the problem.")
win	:	v. to gain a victory; to defeat another or others in a competition, election or battle
wind	:	n. a strong movement of air
window	:	n. an opening in a wall to let in light and air, usually filled with glass

winter	:	n. the coldest time of year, between autumn and spring
wire	:	n. a long, thin piece of metal used to hang objects or to carry electricity or electronic communications from one place to another
wise	:	ad. having much knowledge and understanding; able to use knowledge and understanding to make good or correct decisions
wish	:	v. to want; to express a desire for
with	:	prep. along or by the side of; together; using ("He fixed it with a tool."); having ("the house with the red door")
withdraw	:	v. to take or move out, away or back; to remove
without	:	prep. with no; not having or using; free from; not doing
woman	:	n. an adult female human
wonder	:	v. to ask oneself; to question ("She wonders if it is true."); n. a feeling of surprise
wonderful	:	ad. causing wonder; especially good
wood	:	n. the solid material of which trees are made
word	:	n. one or more connected sounds that form a single part of a language
work	:	v. to use physical or mental effort to make or do something; n. the effort used to make or to do something; that which needs effort; the job one does to earn money
world	:	n. the earth; the people who live on the earth
worry	:	v. to be concerned; to continue thinking that something, possibly bad, can happen
worse	:	ad. more bad than
worth	:	n. value measured in money
wound	:	v. to injure; to hurt; to cause physical damage to a person or animal; n. an injury to the body of a human or animal in which the skin is usually cut or broken
wreck	:	v. to damage greatly; to destroy; n. anything that has been badly damaged or broken

wreckage	:	n. what remains of something severely damaged or destroyed
write	:	v. to use an instrument to make words appear on a surface, such as paper
wrong	:	ad. not correct; bad; not legal; opposite right
year	:	n. a period of time equal to twelve months
yellow	:	ad. having the colour like that of gold or the sun
yes	:	ad. used to express agreement or to permit
yesterday	:	n. the day before today
yet	:	ad. at some time before now ("Have they arrived yet?"); now; at this time ("I cannot tell you about it yet."); conj. however ("The sun was shining, yet it was cold.")
you	:	pro. the person or persons being spoken to
young	:	ad. in the early years of life; not old
zero	:	n. the number meaning none or nothing
zoo	:	n. a place where animals are kept for the public to look at and study

Chapter 3

English Usage: Idioms

abide by (something)

- to follow the rules of something
  The cleaning staff must abide by the rules of the school.

able to breathe easily again

- to be able to relax and recover from a stressful time or event
  My friend was able to breathe easily again when his company did not go bankrupt.

able to do (something) blindfolded

- to be able to do something easily and quickly
  The car was easy to fix and we were able to do it blindfolded.

able to do (something) standing on one's head

- to be able to do something easily and quickly
  The boy is good at fixing his bicycle. He can do it standing on his head.

able to take a joke

- to be able to let others laugh and joke about you
  Our boss is not able to take a joke. We must be careful what we say to him.

about time

- to be something that should have happened earlier
  "It is about time that you returned that book to me."

about to (do something)

- to be on the point of doing something

I was about to leave my house when the phone rang.

above all else

- most importantly of all
  Above all else, I plan to go to the Natural History Museum when I visit the city.

above and beyond

- to be more than is required
  The work that the man did on our house was above and beyond what was required.

above reproach

- to be not deserving of blame or criticism
  The actions of the police officer were above reproach.

above suspicion

- to be very honest so that nobody will suspect you
  The man's actions are always above suspicion.

absent-minded

- to be forgetful
  My grandfather is very absent-minded and he often forgets his keys.

according to Hoyle

- doing something strictly by the rules, doing something the usual and correct way
  "According to Hoyle, we should not use this room but probably nobody will complain if we do use it."

according to (someone or something)

- as said or told by someone, in agreement with something, in the order of something, in proportion to something
  According to our teacher, there will be no class next week.
  We did everything according to the terms of our agreement.

account for (something)

- to provide an answer/explanation for something
  The bad weather accounts for the fact that only a few people came to the meeting.

acid test

- a test where the conclusions are beyond doubt
  The problem was an acid test of our faith in the new manager.

add up

- to total up to a certain amount
  I plan to add up the money that I owe to my father.

add up (to something)

- to mean something, to result in something
  The things that my friend said about his boss do not add up.

advise against (something)

- to suggest that something should not be done
  We were advised against swimming in the river.

afraid of one's own shadow

- to be easily frightened
  The small dog is afraid of his own shadow.

after a fashion

- poorly, barely adequate
  The cleaning staff cleaned the room after a fashion but not very well.

after all

- in spite of what was expected
  I have decided to take swimming lessons after all.

after all

- because of the reason given, something needs to be considered
  "You don't need to phone him. After all, he never phones you."

after all is said and done

- finally, when everything is settled
  After all is said and done the mayor of our city is doing a very good job.

after hours

- after the regular closing or finishing time
  The library has a place to return books after hours.

after the fact

- after something has happened

The man said that he was sorry but it was after the fact. He had already caused many problems.

against one's will

- to be without a person's consent or agreement
  The police took the man to jail against his will.

against the clock

- to hurry to do something before a particular time
  We worked against the clock to finish the project.

ahead of one's time

- to have ideas or attitudes that are more advanced than those of others
  The ideas of the politician were ahead of his time.

ahead of schedule

- before the time on a schedule that has been decided
  We finished our work ahead of schedule.

ahead of the game

- to have done more than necessary
  We worked hard all week in order to be ahead of the game on Monday morning.

ahead of time

- earlier than arranged or planned
  We started the meeting ahead of time so that we could go home early.

aim at (something)

- to plan or try to reach a target
  We are aiming at a big increase in sales next year.

air one's dirty laundry/linen in public

- to make public something embarrassing that should be a secret
  The dinner party became uncomfortable when the host began to air his colleague's dirty laundry in public.

air one's grievances

- to complain (often publicly)
  We aired our grievances during the monthly meeting.

air (something) out

- to freshen something by putting it in the open air

We put the blankets outside in order to air them out.

alive and kicking

- to be well and healthy
  My aunt is 87 years old and she is very much alive and kicking.

alive and well

- to be well and healthy
  The worker is alive and well after the accident.

all along

- all the time, throughout
  I knew all along that my friend would not get the promotion.

all at once

- suddenly, without warning
  All at once the fire alarm rang and we had to leave the building.

all in all

- in summary, after considering everything
  We had a few problems but all in all the meeting was successful.

all in one piece

- safely, without damage
  Our furniture arrived all in one piece after we moved.

all or nothing

- everything, one hundred per cent of something
  It is all or nothing. If I cannot fully participate in the meeting I will not attend.

all-out-effort

- a very good and thorough effort
  We are making an all-out-effort to finish our work.

all over but the shouting

- to be decided and finished
  It was all over but the shouting for the football fans after their team moved to another city.

all over the place

- everywhere
  We traveled all over the place on our holiday.

all right

- okay, satisfactory
  I think that it will be all right for me to bring my friend to the party.

all set

- to be ready to begin, to be okay
  We were all set so we began the meeting.

all the time

- always, continually
  My sister asks for money all the time but I never give it to her.

all thumbs

- to have difficulty fixing things or working with one's hands, to be clumsy
  My friend is all thumbs when he fixes things around his house.

all to the good

- for the best, for one's benefit
  It was all to the good that my sister quit her job.

all told

- including everything/everyone, everything counted
  All told, there were at least twelve candidates for the job.

allow for (someone or something)

- to plan to have enough of something, to plan on the possibility of something
  We must allow for enough time to go to the stadium.

along with (someone or something)

- in addition to someone or something
  I went to the concert along with my friend.

amount to (something)

- to total something, to result in something
  The small amounts of time later amounted to much time.

amount to (something)

- to become successful
  The boy will never amount to anything if he does not change his behaviour.

amount to the same thing

- to be the same or have the same effect as something
  Going by taxi or by bus amounts to the same thing. We will still be late for the concert.

answer to (someone)

- to explain or justify one's actions to someone
  The manager had to answer to the company president about the financial problems.

any number of (someone or something)

- a large number of people or something
  I had any number of reasons not to buy the computer.

argue for the sake of arguing/argument

- to argue only to be different
  My friend's brother always argues for the sake of arguing.

arm and a leg

- a large amount of money
  The man's new car cost him an arm and a leg.

arm in arm

- to be joined together by the arms
  The young girls walked arm in arm to school.

armed and dangerous

- to have a weapon that may be used (usually used for a criminal)
  The criminal was armed and dangerous when the police arrested him.

armed to the teeth

- to be armed with many weapons
  The police were armed to the teeth during the raid.

around the clock

- all day and all night
  We worked around the clock to prepare the store to open.

arrive on the scene

- to appear in a certain place
  When the fire department arrived on the scene the fire was finished.

as a last resort

- if everything else fails
  As a last resort we decided to borrow some money to buy the car.

as a matter of fact

- actually
  "As a matter of fact, we have been to the art gallery many times."

as a result of (something)

- because of something that has happened
  As a result of a car accident my friend could not work for several months.

as a rule

- usually, as a habit
  As a rule, I get up at 7:00 every morning.

as dull as dishwater

- very uninteresting
  The speakers at the conference were as dull as dishwater.

as far as

- to the extent or degree of something
  As far as I know the movie will start next week.

as far as possible

- as much as possible
  We went as far as possible with the project before we had to stop.

as for

- with regard to, concerning
  "As for me, I think that I will go home now."

as good as one's word

- to be dependable if one promises something
  My friend is as good as his word. You can always trust him.

as if

- in the same way that something would be, that
  The drink tastes as if it were made with orange juice.
  It seemed as if the whole town came to the concert.

as is

- in whatever condition something happens to be
  We bought the old sofa as is. It was very cheap.

as long as

- provided that, on condition that
  "As long as you promise to be very careful you can borrow my car."

as luck would have it

- by chance
  As luck would have it, I was able to borrow some clothes for the party.

as usual

- most of the time, following the usual pattern
  As usual, the girl forgot to bring her book to class.

as well

- in addition, also, too
  I plan to take a computer course this summer as well.

as well as

- in addition to
  "Please bring your swimming suit as well as your towel."

as yet

- until now, up to the present
  As yet, our secretary has not talked about her plans to leave the company.

ask for the moon

- to ask for too much
  The woman is asking for the moon. She will never get what she wants.

ask for trouble

- to behave in a way that will likely cause trouble
  The boy is asking for trouble if he misses another class.

ask (someone) out

- to ask a person for a date
  My friend finally asked the woman at the bank out.

asleep at the switch

- to not be alert to an opportunity

I was asleep at the switch. I did not know about the job so I did not apply for it.

assault and battery

- a criminal charge where one violently attacks and beats someone
  The man was arrested for assault and battery after the fight.

at a loss

- in a state of uncertainty or bewilderment
  We were at a loss about what to do with the broken computer.

at a loss for words

- speechless, unable to speak
  I was at a loss for words when I met my friend after many years.

at a stretch

- continuously
  My friend sometimes works for three weeks at a stretch.

at all costs

- regardless of the cost or difficulty, no matter what
  The company wants to protect their product designs at all costs.

at any rate

- anyway
  "At any rate, I am not going to a movie tonight."

at bay

- at a distance
  We tried to keep the dog at bay when we entered the building.

at best

- under the most favorable circumstances
  The doctors said that the man had ten months at best to live.

at cross-purposes

- to have opposite ways of doing something, to have opposing goals
  The two men are always at cross purposes. They cannot agree about anything.

at death's door

- to be near death
  The young woman was at death's door after the accident.

at ease

- to be relaxed and comfortable
  The players felt at ease after the coach talked to them.

at hand

- within reach, nearby
  I stopped working because I did not have any tools at hand.

at heart

- basically, fundamentally
  The woman is a nice person at heart although many people dislike her.

at home

- in one's house
  I left my money at home so I had to borrow some.

at it again

- to be doing something again
  The two boys were at it again. We could hear them fighting.

at large

- to be free, to not be captured
  The criminal was at large for many months.

at last

- finally, after a long time
  I waited all morning for my friend's call until at last it came.

at least

- no less than
  There were at least 60,000 people in the stadium.

at length

- in detail, finally
  The speaker talked at length about the new product.

at loggerheads (with someone)

- to be having a quarrel or disagreement with someone, to oppose someone

We are at loggerheads with the company over their plans to build a new factory.

at loose ends

- restless and unsettled
  My friend's mother was at loose ends after her husband died.

at odds (with someone)

- in disagreement with someone
  The man has been at odds with his boss over his new sales territory.

at once

- immediately
  The police came at once after we called them.

at one sitting

- at one time
  We finished the food at one sitting.

at peace

- peaceful, happy
  The woman was relaxed and at peace after her friend's funeral.

at random

- without sequence or order
  The members of the team were chosen at random from among the regular players.

at risk

- in danger
  The children were at risk of getting sick when the disease spread in the school.

at sea

- to be on the sea, to be away on a voyage on the ocean
  My grandfather was at sea for several months when he was a young man.

at sea (about something)

- to be confused about something, to be lost
  Most members of the class were at sea when the teacher tried to explain the difficult theory.

at sixes and sevens

- to be lost and bewildered

We were at sixes and sevens when the local grocery store closed.

at the latest

- no later than

  The tour will start at noon at the latest.

at the outset

- from the first or early stage

  At the outset of the meeting there were problems between some members of the group.

at the present time

- now, at present

  At the present time there are no extra helpers available.

at the top of one's lungs

- with a very loud voice

  I cried out for my friend at the top of my lungs.

at times

- sometimes, occasionally

  At times, our teacher is very nice but at other times she is not nice.

at will

- whenever one wants, freely

  The little boy was able to do what he wanted at will.

attract (someone's) attention

- to cause someone to notice you

  The strange behaviour of the man attracted the policeman's attention.

augur well for (someone or something)

- to predict good things for someone or something

  The poor business conditions do not augur well for the workers.

avoid (someone or something) like the plague

- to avoid someone or something totally

  The girls avoided the new student like the plague.

back and forth

- backwards and forwards, first one way and then the other way

The argument went back and forth before the judge made a decision.

back down (from someone or something)

- to fail to carry through on a threat to do something
  The government backed down from their plan to sell the national airline.

back in circulation

- to be available to the public again (a library book)
  The books were back in circulation after we returned them to the library.

back in circulation

- to be socially active again (after the breakup of a relationship between two people)
  My friend stopped seeing his girlfriend and he is now back in circulation.

back of beyond

- somewhere very remote
  Every summer we go to the back of beyond for a camping trip.

back off

- to retreat or move away (from a fight or argument or an object)
  The man wanted to start an argument but finally he backed off.

back on one's feet

- to return to good financial or physical health
  My friend is back on his feet after his company went out of business.

back out (of something)

- to withdraw from an agreement or promise
  The company backed out of the agreement with the foreign firm.

back the wrong horse

- to support someone or something that cannot win or succeed
  We backed the wrong horse in the election and our candidate lost badly.

back-to-back

- something follows immediately after something else, two people touching backs
  There were two back-to-back games today because of the rain last week.

back to square one

- to go back to the beginning of something
  The city was back to square one in their effort to build a new bridge.

back to the drawing board

- to go back and start a project or idea from the beginning
  The boss does not like our idea so we must go back to the drawing board.

back to the salt mines

- to return to work or return to something else that you do not want to do
  We finished our lunch and went back to the salt mines.

back up (someone or something)

- to support someone or something
  The doctor made a mistake and the hospital refused to back him up.

bad blood (between people)

- unpleasant feelings between people
  There was much bad blood between the three brothers.

bad-mouth (someone or something)

- to say bad things about someone or something
  The supervisor has the habit of bad-mouthing her boss.

bag of tricks

- a collection of special techniques or methods
  The teacher has a bag of tricks to keep her students occupied.

bail out (of something)

- to abandon a situation, to jump out of an airplane
  The plan to buy a summer home with our friends

was becoming too expensive so we decided to bail out.

bail (someone) out

- to pay a sum of money that allows someone to get out of jail while waiting for a trial
  The singer had to pay much money to bail himself out of prison.

bail (someone or something) out

- to help or rescue someone or something
  The government decided to bail out the troubled bank.

balance the books

- to check that all the money in a business is accounted for
  The accountant spent several days trying to balance the books of his company.

ball of fire

- an active and energetic person
  The woman is a ball of fire and is always busy doing something.

bang/beat one's head against the wall

- to try to do something that is hopeless
  I am banging my head against the wall when I try to ask my boss for something.

bank on (someone or something)

- to be sure of someone or something, to count on someone or something
  You can bank on my sister to help you.

baptism of fire

- a first experience of something (often difficult or unpleasant)
  We went through a baptism of fire when we had to learn how to operate the small business.

bargain for (something)

- to anticipate something, to take something into account
  The difficulty of the job was more than I had bargained for.

be a new one on (someone)

- to be something one has not heard before and something that is difficult to believe
  It was a new one on me when my friend said that he was studying Russian.

be all ears

- to listen eagerly and carefully
  The boy was all ears when the teacher described the circus.

be all things to all people

- to be everything that is wanted by all people
  The politician tries to be all things to all people and it is difficult to know what she really believes.

be curtains for (someone or something)

- to be the end or death for someone or something
  It was curtains for my old car when it finally broke down last week.

be game

- to be ready for action or agreeable to participate in something
  All of the students were game to go to the science exhibition.

be into (something)

- to be interested or involved in something
  My friend is very much into music and writing songs.

be of the persuasion that (something) is so

- to believe that something is true or exists
  My grandfather is of the persuasion that it is more important to work than to go to school.

be off

- to leave or depart
  I plan to be off very early tomorrow morning to go to the airport.

be off to a bad start

- to start something under bad circumstances
  The production of the play was off to a bad start when the lights did not work.

be off on the wrong foot

- to start something under bad circumstances
  I tried to talk to my new neighbour but it seems that we are off on the wrong foot already.

be that as it may

- even if what you say is true
  "Be that as it may, we are not going to permit the school dance to take place."

beat around the bush

- to speak indirectly or evasively
  "Stop beating around the bush and give us your final decision."

beat one's brains out

- to work very hard (to do something)
  We beat our brains out in order to think of a name for the new magazine.

beat one's head against the wall

- to waste one's time trying to do something that is hopeless
  I was beating my head against the wall to try and convince my friend to come to the restaurant.

beat (someone) to the punch/draw

- to do something before others
  My friend beat me to the punch and arrived at the interview first.

beat (something) into (someone's) head

- to force someone to learn something
  The teacher thinks that she must beat the material into the heads of the students.

beat the clock

- to finish something before the time is up
  The basketball team worked hard to beat the clock and win the game.

beat the living daylights out of (someone)

- to beat someone severely
  The two men beat the living daylights out of the man at the gas station.

beat the rap

- to escape conviction and punishment (for a crime)
  The man beat the rap and did not have to go to jail.

beat the tar out of (someone)

- to beat someone severely
  The older boy beat the tar out of the young boy in the schoolyard..

beat up (someone)

- to harm someone by hitting or beating them
  The young boys beat up one of the older students.

become engaged to (someone)

- to make a plan to marry someone
  My friend plans to become engaged to her boyfriend next month.

become engaged with (someone)

- to make a plan to marry someone
  The girl has recently become engaged with her boyfriend.

becoming on/to (someone)

- to make someone look good
  The red dress looked very becoming on my girlfriend.

(no) bed of roses

- a situation that is happy and comfortable (usually used in the negative)
  The new job was very difficult and certainly no bed of roses.

(have a) bee in one's bonnet

- to have an idea that continually occupies one's thoughts.
  My friend has a bee in her bonnet about going to Europe next year.

beef up (something)

- to make something stronger
  The police beefed up the security around the convention site.

before long

- soon

I had to wait a few minutes but before long my friend arrived to meet me.

beg the question

- to invite the question that follows

  The purchase of the expensive car begged the question of where the man got the money.

beside oneself (with something)

- to be very upset or excited about something

  The boy was beside himself with joy after winning the contest.

beside the point

- to be not relevant to the subject that you are considering or discussing

  "What you are saying is beside the point. We are not talking about salary now."

best/better part of (something)

- to be almost all of something

  We spent the best part of a day trying to fix the vacuum cleaner.

bet on the wrong horse

- to misjudge a coming event, to misread the future

  I think that he bet on the wrong horse by investing all of his money into the new stock.

bet one's bottom dollar

- to be very certain about something

  I would bet my bottom dollar that my friend will be late for the movie.

better off

- to be in a better situation than before

  He would be better off if he sold his old car and bought a new one.

between a rock and a hard place

- to be in a very difficult position

  We were between a rock and a hard place in our effort to solve the problem.

between the devil and the deep blue sea

- to be in a very difficult position

The mayor was between the devil and the deep blue sea when he tried to keep the two groups happy.

betwixt and between

- to be undecided, to be between two decisions
  We were betwixt and between in our effort to try and decide which school to send our child to.

beyond a shadow of a doubt

- to be completely without doubt
  Everyone believed beyond a shadow of a doubt that the man had stolen the money.

bid adieu to (someone or something)

- to say good-bye to someone or something
  Everybody gathered to bid adieu to the popular supervisor.

bide one's time

- to patiently wait for an opportunity to occur.
  The man is biding his time as he waits to become president of the company.

big frog/fish in a small pond

- an important person in a less important place
  The woman was a big fish in a small pond when she moved to the small town.

birds and the bees

- human sex and reproduction
  The father tried to tell his son about the birds and the bees.

birds-eye view

- a view from high above, a brief look at something
  We had a birds-eye view of the playing field from our seats high up in the stadium.

birthday suit

- a completely naked body
  The little boy was running down the street in his birthday suit.

bite off more than one can chew

- to try to do more than one is able to do
  I bit off more than I can chew by agreeing to do another assignment.

bite one's nails

- to be nervous or anxious about something
  The children were biting their nails as they waited for the results of the test.

bite one's tongue

- to try not to say something that you really want to say
  I had to bite my tongue and not tell our boss what had happened.

bite (someone's) head off

- to speak angrily to someone
  I am afraid to speak to my teacher when she is in a bad mood because she may bite my head off.

bite the bullet

- to endure a difficult situation, to face a difficult situation bravely
  I have decided to bite the bullet and begin to study for my Master's degree.

bite the dust

- to be killed, to break down, to be defeated
  I think that my car will bite the dust soon.

bite the hand that feeds you

- to harm or turn against someone who does good things for you
  He is biting the hand that feeds him when he criticizes and fights against his boss.

bitter pill to swallow

- an unpleasant fact that one must accept
  Losing the election was a bitter pill to swallow for the candidate.

black out

- to faint or pass out
  Suddenly the young woman blacked out while she was standing in front of the computer.

black sheep of the family

- the worst member of a family
  The boy was the black sheep of the family and nobody liked him.

blow a fuse

- to burn out a fuse, to become angry
  We quickly replaced the old fuse when our house blew a fuse last night.
  My friend blew a fuse when I told him that I had lost his book

blow one's own horn

- to praise oneself
  My friend is always blowing his own horn and is very annoying at times.

blow one's top/stack

- to become very angry
  The customer blew his stack when they refused to exchange his purchase at the store.

blow over

- to die down, to calm down
  The problem with the lost invoices has blown over and everybody is happy again.

blow (someone or something) off

- to avoid someone, to not attend something
  We blew off the chance to go to the general meeting.

blow (something)

- to fail at something, to ruin something
  I think that I blew the final math exam last week.

blow (something) out of all proportion

- to make a bigger issue about something than it really is
  The problem was very small but the manager blew it out of all proportion.

blow the lid off (something)

- to reveal something (often a wrongdoing)
  The government investigation blew the lid off the illegal activities.

blow the whistle (on someone)

- to report someone's wrongdoing to the police or other authorities
  The employee blew the whistle on the illegal practices of the company.

blow to smithereens

- to explode into tiny pieces
  The gas tanker was blown to smithereens during the accident.

blow up (at someone)

- to get angry, to lose one's temper
  The passenger who was waiting in the line blew up at the ticket agent.

blow up in (someone's) face

- to be ruined while one is working on it (a plan/ project etc.), to explode suddenly
  The secret plan blew up in our face when we discovered that everybody already knew about it.

.**blue blood**

- someone from a noble or aristocratic family
  The art exhibition attracted many of the blue bloods in the town.

blue in the face

- to be exhausted and speechless
  You can argue with him until you are blue in the face but you will never change his mind.

bog down

- to slow down, to become stuck
  I quickly became bogged down with all of the work that I had to do.

boggle (someone's) mind

- to confuse or overwhelm someone
  The amount of waste in the city programme really boggles my mind.

boil down to (something)

- to reduce something to its essential or main part
  The reason that we could not go on a holiday boiled down to the fact that we did not have enough money.

bone of contention

- a reason for quarrels, the subject of a fight
  The family cottage was a major bone of contention after the father died.

bone up (on something)

- to study or review (something)
  I decided to take a course at night to bone up on my Spanish.

bottom line

- the result or final outcome of something, the last figure on a financial statement
  Although I do not want to buy a new car, the bottom line is that I need a car for work.

bottom out

- to reach the lowest point
  The stock market bottomed out at its lowest level in many months.

bound and determined

- to be determined
  The man's wife is bound and determined to visit her sister this summer.

bound for somewhere

- to be on the way or planning to go somewhere
  My friend was bound for college when I last met him.

bound to (do something)

- to be certain to do something
  "If you ask your father he is bound to try and help you with your problem."

bow and scrape

- to be very humble and subservient
  I was forced to bow and scrape to get some money from my parents.

bow out

- to quit, to resign from something
  I wanted to join the tour but at the last minute I had to bow out.

bowl (someone) over

- to surprise or overwhelm someone
  The salesman bowled me over with his energetic sales talk.

brand-new

- absolutely new
  I was finally able to buy a brand-new car.

break a habit

- to end a habit
  My sister worked very hard to break her habit of eating too much chocolate.

break a law

- to fail to obey a law
  The young man broke the law when he drove his friend's car without a proper license.

break a record

- to set a new record that is better than an old one
  The team tried hard to break a record during the last week of the season.

break camp

- to close down a campsite and move on
  We decided to break camp and begin on our journey.

break down

- to lose control of one's emotions
  The woman broke down while the lawyer questioned her at the trial.

break down

- to stop working because of mechanical failure
  The car broke down on the lonely road and nobody knew about it.

break down (something)

- to analyse something
  We must break down these figures for further study.

break down (something)

- to divide into parts, to separate into simpler substances
  We tried to break down the sentence for further study.
  The sugar began to break down soon after it was swallowed.

break out in a cold sweat

- to perspire from fever or anxiety
  I usually break out in a cold sweat when I have to make a speech.

break out in (something)

- to erupt in a rash or pimples
  The girl always breaks out in a rash when she eats shrimp.

break out of (something)

- to escape from something
  Several prisoners tried to break out of prison last month.

break (someone's) fall

- to lessen the impact of a falling person
  The baby fell out of the window but thankfully the bushes broke her fall.

break the ice

- to relax and start a conversation in a formal situation
  Nobody was enjoying the party until the host was able to break the ice.

break the news (to someone)

- to tell someone some information first
  He is planning to break the news about his transfer tomorrow.

break up

- to separate, to divide into groups or pieces, to put an end to something
  Nobody wanted to break up their groups.
  We usually break up into small groups during our class.

break up (with someone)

- to end a relationship with someone
  My niece broke up with her boyfriend last June.

breath of fresh air

- a fresh and imaginative approach to something
  The manager's coaching style was a breath of fresh air compared to that of the previous coach.

breathe down (someone's) neck

- to watch someone closely, to try to make someone hurry
  The supervisor is always breathing down the necks of the employees.

breathe easy

- to relax after a stressful situation
  I was able to breathe easy after I found my lost wallet.

breathe one's last

- to die
  The woman breathed her last several days after she became ill.

brew a plot

- to make a plot
  The generals in the small country were brewing a plot to take control of the government.

bright and early

- very early
  The woman likes to get up bright and early every morning.

bright-eyed and bushy-tailed

- to be eager and cheerful
  Everybody was bright-eyed and bushy-tailed when we started out on the trip.

brimming with (something)

- to be full of some kind of happy behaviour
  The children were brimming with energy on the morning of the festival.

bring about (something)

- to make something happen
  The two company presidents worked hard to bring about the joining of their two companies.

bring around (someone)

- to bring someone for a visit
  I asked my friend to bring his new girlfriend around for a visit.

bring (someone) to

- to wake someone up, to bring someone to consciousness
  The medical doctor tried to bring the small boy to after he fell into the swimming pool.

bring (something) home to (someone)

- to cause someone to realise the truth of something
  The dry conditions are bringing home to the farmers the importance of saving water.

bring (something) into question

- to raise a question about something
  The actions of the government bring into question their interest in the case.

bring (something) off

- to make something happen
  The students tried hard to bring off a successful dance to collect money for their club.

bring to mind

- to recall something
  Her acting brought to mind some of the great actresses of the past.

bring up

- to introduce a subject into a discussion
  They brought up the subject at the meeting but nobody wanted to talk about it.

bring up

- to raise or care for a child
  My sister is bringing up three children.

bring up the rear

- to be at the end of the line or in the last position
  The runner from the other school was bringing up the rear in the school relay race.

to be broad in the beam

- to have wide hips or large buttocks
  The woman in the store was broad in the beam.

to be broke

- to have no money
  I spent all of my money on my holiday and now I am broke.

brush up on (something)

- to review something that one has already learned
  I am going to brush up on my English before my trip to New York.

a brush with the law

- a brief encounter or experience with the police because of a crime
  The man had a brush with the law when he was young but now he is totally honest.

buck for (something)

- to aim/try for a goal
  The soldier was bucking for a promotion.

buckle down (to something)

- to begin to work seriously at something
  I have to buckle down and study or I will fail the exam.

bug (someone)

- to irritate or bother someone
  The boy's rude behaviour is beginning to bug me.

build a fire under (someone)

- to stimulate someone to do something
  We keep trying to build a fire under our friend but he refuses to study or look for a job.

build castles in the air/in Spain

- to make plans that are impossible
  The girl is always building castles in the air and none of them have any chance to succeed.

build (something) to order

- to make something especially for a customer
  The family wanted to build their kitchen table and chairs to order.

build up (someone or something)

- to make someone or something bigger or stronger, to promote something
  The woman is always trying to build up her boss which makes her very well-liked by him.

build up to (something)

- to lead up to something
  Things were building up to be a very serious situation.

burn one's bridges behind one

- to do something that makes going back impossible
  He burned his bridges behind him and is unable to work in the same industry again.

burn (oneself) out

- to become very tired and almost sick from doing something for a long time or because of working too hard
  After working long hours for many months the woman finally burned herself out.

burn (someone) in effigy

- to burn a dummy that represents a hated person
  The crowd of people burned the Prime Minister in effigy.

burn the candle at both ends

- to work or play too hard without enough rest
  The man has been burning the candle at both ends with his work and he is now sick.

burn the midnight oil

- to study until very late at night
  We burned the midnight oil for three nights in order to study for the exam.

burn up

- to burn completely (usually things and not buildings)
  The uniforms burned up in the fire.

burst at the seams

- to explode with pride or laughter, to be full to the breaking point
  The train was bursting at the seams as it entered the station.

burst in on (someone or something)

- to enter a room and interrupt someone or some activity

The woman burst in on the meeting just as it started.

burst into flames

- to catch fire suddenly
  The curtains burst into flames after touching the small stove.

burst into tears

- to begin to cry suddenly
  The parents burst into tears of happiness when their daughter graduated.

burst onto the scene

- to appear suddenly in some location
  The young singer burst onto the scene when she was a teenager.

burst out laughing

- to begin to laugh suddenly
  We burst out laughing when the man screamed after seeing the mouse.

burst with joy

- to be full of happiness and feel that you will explode or burst
  My grandmother burst with joy when she saw her new baby granddaughter.

burst with pride

- to be full of pride and ready to burst
  The girl's parents were bursting with pride at the graduation ceremony.

bury/hide one's head in the sand

- to refuse to see something, to face or know something unpleasant
  He always buries his head in the sand and never wants to hear about family problems.

bury the hatchet

- to stop arguing and become friendly with someone
  He buried the hatchet with his brother and they are now friendly again.

business as usual

- to continue as usual

It was business as usual for the small stores soon after the fire destroyed the shopping area.

by all means

- certainly, yes
  "By all means, I will come to dinner next week."

by and by

- before long, after some time has passed
  By and by all of the family moved back to the city.

by and large

- on the whole, considering everything
  By and large we had a good meeting even though it was very short.

by any means

- by any way possible
  We decided to try to find a computer to use by any means.

by chance

- without planning
  By chance I saw my father's friend in the supermarket.

by leaps and bounds

- rapidly, by large movements forward
  The construction of the new airport is progressing by leaps and bounds.

by means of

- with the use of something
  We were able to enter the old building by means of a small window in the back.

by no means

- absolutely not
  By no means will I permit my child to play with the new video game.

by the book

- according to the rules
  The police officer does everything by the book when he arrests someone.

by the day

- one day at a time

My father was very sick but now he is getting better by the day.

by the dozen

- twelve at a time

  We usually buy bottles of water by the dozen.

by the handful

- in measurements equal to a handful

  We were eating fresh blueberries by the handful.

by the hour

- after each hour, one hour at a time

  We had to pay for our parking space by the hour.

by the month

- one month at a time

  The rent for our apartment is paid by the month.

by the same token

- similarly, moreover

  "By the same token, I don't want to go downtown again today."

by the seat of one's pants

- by luck and with very little skill

  I was able to complete the course by the seat of my pants.

by the skin of one's teeth

- by a very small margin, barely

  I arrived at the train station and was on time by the skin of my teeth.

by the sweat of one's brow

- by hard work

  He managed to make enough money to buy the farm by the sweat of his brow.

by the way

- incidentally

  "By the way, could you please bring your computer tomorrow."

by the week

- one week at a time

  We rented the car by the week.

by the year

- one year at a time
  The contract for the garbage pickup is renewed by the year.

by virtue of (something)

- because of something
  My father got his new job by virtue of his volunteer work in the community.

call a spade a spade

- to speak bluntly
  The supervisor called a spade a spade when he criticized the employee for being lazy.

call for (someone)

- to come and get someone
  "Could you please come and call for me before you go to the game."

call for (someone or something)

- to require something, to need the services of someone
  Our problems with the toilet call for a good plumber.

call it a day/night

- to quit work and go home
  I called it a day and decided to go home early.

call it quits

- to stop, to finish
  I called it quits and went home for the day.

call of nature

- the need to go to the toilet
  The driver stopped his truck to answer the call of nature.

call off (something)

- to cancel something
  The game was called off because of the rain.

call on (someone)

- to visit someone
  I plan to call on my brother during my holidays.

call on (someone)

- to ask someone to participate in something or contribute something
  The teacher called on me three times to answer questions in the class.

call out to (someone)

- to shout to someone
  We called out to our friend at the concert but she did not hear us.

call (someone) in

- to ask someone for help, to call for special advice
  We called in a special doctor to look at the patient.

call (someone or something) into question

- to dispute or cast doubt upon someone or something
  The lawyer called the man's statement about his neighbour into question.

call (someone) names

- to call a person unpleasant names
  The children began to call the new student names.

call (someone) on the carpet

- to call someone before an authority to be scolded or reprimanded
  The salesman was called on the carpet by his boss for losing the big sale.

call (someone's) bluff

- to challenge someone to prove that what they are saying is true
  I decided to call the man's bluff and I asked him to show me the evidence.

call (something) in

- to collect something for payment, to withdraw something from circulation
  The bank decided to call in the business loan.

call the shots

- to be in charge, to give orders
  The vice-president is now calling the shots and is in control of the company.

call up (someone)

- to telephone someone

  My friend said that he will call up his parents tomorrow night.

calm down

- to relax

  The woman finally calmed down after the accident.

cancel (something) out

- to destroy the effect of something

  The overeating by the girl cancelled out the benefits of her exercise.

can of worms

- a complicated situation or problem

  The lawsuit opened up a can of worms for the company.

can't do anything with (someone or something)

- to be unable to manage or control someone or something

  My sister is always complaining that she can't do anything with her daughter.

can't see the forest for the trees

- to be unable to understand the whole picture of something because you are only looking at small parts of it

  He has no understanding of most problems because he can't see the forest for the trees.

can't stand/stomach (someone or something)

- to dislike someone or something very much

  My uncle cannot stand his daughter's boyfriend.

card up one's sleeve

- a plan or argument that is kept back to be used later if needed

  I think that our boss has a card up his sleeve and he will be able to help us later.

cards are stacked against (someone)

- luck is against someone

  The cards have been stacked against the young boy since he was born.

(in) care of (someone)

- (send something) to one person at the address of another person
  I sent the parcel to my sister in care of her friend at the university.

carrot and stick

- a reward or a threat of punishment at the same time
  The trade negotiators took a carrot-and-stick approach to the automobile talks.

carried away

- to lose one's control or judgement due to strong feelings
  I got carried away and yelled at my friend for losing my textbook.

carry a lot of weight with (someone or something)

- to be very influential with someone or a group of people
  The man's education and experience carry a lot of weight in the university.

carry a tune

- to be able to sing accurately, to have musical ability
  The girl in the music class cannot carry a tune.

carry coals to Newcastle

- to bring something of which there is plenty, to duplicate something (Newcastle is a town in England where there is a lot of coal)
  Bringing extra food to the farmer's picnic was like bringing coals to Newcastle.

carry on

- to continue, to keep doing something as before
  We were permitted to carry on with the party after we talked to the apartment manager.

carry out (something)

- to do something, to put something (a plan) into action, to accomplish something
  We were able to carry out the move with no problems.

carry over (something)
- to save for another time or location
  The store will carry over the sale until next week.

carry the ball
- to be in charge of something
  The vice-president was forced to carry the ball while the president was away.

carry the day
- to win or be successful
  His fine performance in our company carried the day for us.

carry the torch
- to show loyalty to a cause or a person
  The man has been carrying the torch for the candidate for a long time.

carry the weight of the world on one's shoulders
- to appear to be burdened by all the problems of the world
  My aunt feels that she is working too hard and that she is carrying the weight of the world on her shoulders.

carry through with (something)
- to put a plan into action
  The company carried through with its plan to open a new factory.

a case in point
- an example that proves something or helps to make something clear
  What the man said is a case in point about what I have been saying all year.

a case of mistaken identity
- an incorrect identification of someone
  It was a case of mistaken identity when the police arrested the wrong person.

cash-and-carry
- a system where you pay cash for some goods and then carry them away
  The supermarkets in our city always operate on a cash-and-carry basis.

cash cow

- a good source of money
  His new business is a cash cow and he is making much money.

cash in (something)

- to exchange something for money
  We decided to cash in the coupons because we needed some money.

cash in on (something)

- to make a lot of money at something
  The small city cashed in on their success after the winter Olympics.

cash on the barrelhead

- to pay cash to buy something
  It was cash only at the store and we were forced to pay cash on the barrelhead for everything.

cast around/about for (someone or something)

- to look for someone or something
  We have been casting around for a new file clerk in our company.

cast aspersions on (someone)

- to make insulting remarks about someone
  The woman is always casting aspersions on he colleagues at work.

cast doubts on (someone or something)

- to cause someone or something to be doubted
  The first witness at the trial cast doubts on the testimony of the main witness.

cast in the same mold

- to be very similar
  The two sisters were cast in the same mold and were almost identical.

cast one's lot in with (someone)

- to join with someone and accept whatever happens
  The woman cast her lot in with the company and worked hard to keep the business going.

cast one's vote

- to vote

  We arrived early to cast our vote in the election.

catch a cold

- to become sick with a cold

  I caught a cold because of the rain and the cold weather.

catch-as-catch-can

- in any way possible

  We are in the middle of moving house so our meals are catch-as-catch-can.

catch fire

- to begin to burn

  We were very careful that the wooden house would not catch fire.

catch forty winks

- to get some sleep

  I was very tired so I stopped my car in order to catch forty winks.

catch on

- to understand something, to learn about something

  I was finally able to catch on and understand the math problem.

catch (someone) napping

- to find someone asleep, to find someone unprepared for something

  The boss caught the employee napping and became very angry.

catch (someone) off balance

- to surprise someone who is not prepared

  We were caught off balance when we discovered that our business license was no good.

catch (someone) off guard

- to catch a person at a time of carelessness

  I was caught off guard when the teacher asked me about my homework.

catch (someone) red-handed

- to find someone in the middle of doing something wrong
  The clerk caught the boy red-handed when he was stealing the candy.

catch up on (something)

- to do something that you have not had time to do, to learn about something (the daily news or news about old friends)
  I need to catch up on some of my reading this weekend.
  I met my friend and we caught up on some news.

catch up with (someone or something)

- to become even with someone (in a race or in schoolwork etc.)
  I think that it is too late to catch up with the rest of the class now.

caught in the middle/cross fire

- to be caught between two opposing people or groups so it is difficult to remain neutral
  I was caught in the middle when my friend and his girlfriend had a big fight.

caught short

- to not have enough of something (usually money) when you need it
  I was caught short last month and could not pay my credit card bill.

caught unaware

- to be surprised and unprepared for something
  Everybody was caught unaware by the sudden change in government policy.

cause a stir

- to cause people to become agitated and alarmed about something
  The soccer player caused a stir when he began to criticize the referee.

cause eyebrows to raise

- to shock people

I caused eyebrows to raise when I decided not to accept the award from my company.

cause tongues to wag

- to give people something to gossip about
  My sister caused tongues to wag when she came to the party without her husband.

cave in

- to weaken and be forced to give something up
  The company caved in to the union's demand for more money.

chalk (something) up to (something)

- to recognize something as the cause of something else
  We were able to chalk our success up to our new boat.

change horses in midstream

- to make new plans or choose a new leader in the middle of an important activity
  The company changed horses in midstream and totally changed their policy.

change of heart

- a change in the way one feels about something
  The woman had a change of heart and decided to let her child go to the circus.

change of pace

- the addition of some variety to one's life
  We decided to go to the lake for a change of pace and to get away from our busy schedules.

change one's tune

- to make a change in one's story/statement/opinion/policy
  Our supervisor has changed his tune recently and agrees that we need to do things differently.

change the subject

- to begin talking about something different
  I tried to change the subject when my friend began to talk about the money that I owed him.

in charge of something

- to be responsible for an activity or group of people
  Our teacher is in charge of selling tickets for the school dance.

cheat on (someone)

- to be unfaithful to someone
  The man began cheating on his wife which was the cause of their divorce.

cheek by jowl

- side by side, in close intimacy
  The fans entered the stadium cheek by jowl.

clean slate

- a record that shows no bad behaviour or other problems or past bad acts
  The man started off with a clean slate after he lost his previous job.

clean up one's act

- to improve one's performance
  The mayor will have to clean up his act if he wants to get elected again.

clear of (something)

- to be not touching something
  We checked that the ladder was clear of the electrical wires before we painted the house.

clear out (of somewhere)

- to leave, to get out (usually quickly or abruptly)
  We cleared out of the building as soon as our class was over.

clear out (something)

- to clean somewhere, to remove something
  We cleared out the room before we could start painting.

clear sailing

- to be an easy situation
  It was clear sailing when we finished work and began our journey.

clear (someone's) name

- to prove that someone is not guilty of something

The man tried very hard to clear his name regarding his past criminal activity.

clear the air

- to calm down and remove bad feelings
  We had a big argument but now it is time to clear the air.

clear the decks

- to clear away things and prepare for action, to get out of the way
  "Let`s clear the decks and get everyone out of the house so that we can begin work."

clear the table

- to remove the dishes and eating utensils from a table
  After we finished eating we quickly cleared the table.

clear up (something)

- to solve or explain (a problem etc.)
  We finally cleared up the problem that we were having with our computers.

cliffhanger

- a sports event/movie/election where the outcome is uncertain until the very end
  The playoff game was a cliffhanger and the most exciting game of the year.

climb the wall

- to be so bored that you become anxious and frustrated
  The woman began to climb the wall after only a few days at her new job.

clip joint

- a low-class business where people are cheated
  The men went into a clip joint near the bus station and had to pay a lot of money.

clip (someone's) wings

- to limit someone's activities or possibilities
  The company decided to clip the manager's wings and took away his expense account.

cloak-and-dagger

- involving secercy and plotting
  The agents were involved in cloak-and-dagger diplomacy over the spy scandal.

close at hand

- to be within reach
  The day that the new coach would be chosen was now close at hand.

close call/shave

- an accident that almost happens but does not happen
  I had a close call this morning when the truck almost hit me.

close in on (someone or something)

- to overwhelm or surround someone or something
  The soldiers quickly closed in on the enemy position.

close one's eyes to (something)

- to ignore something
  The teacher closed her eyes to the misbehavior of the students.

close ranks

- to come together for fighting, to unite and work together
  The political parties closed ranks and stopped arguing among themselves.

close the books (on someone or something)

- to put an end to something (like the books in accounting records)
  The owners of the team closed the books on the idea of building a new stadium.

close to home

- to be near to someone's personal feelings/wishes/interests
  My statement about the woman's work habits hit close to home and she became very quiet.

close to (someone)

- to be fond of someone
  The boy is very close to his grandfather.

cloud up

- to become cloudy

  It began to cloud up and soon started raining.

clue (someone) in

- to inform someone about something

  We tried to clue the principal in about why the students were absent.

the coast is clear

- no danger is in sight, no one can see you

  When the coast is clear we will try to enter the building.

cock-and-bull story

- a story that is not true

  The boys gave us a cock-and-bull story about the tire marks in front of our house.

cog in the machine

- a small and unimportant part of a large organization

  The employees felt like they were only cogs in the machine so the atmosphere at the company was not very good.

cold comfort

- no comfort at all

  The government offered money to the victims of the fire but it was cold comfort to those who had lost their families.

come a cropper

- to fail

  The man came a cropper in the chess tournament and that is why he is sad.

come a long way

- to make great progress

  The manager has come a long way and has learned many things about his new company.

come about

- to happen

  Everybody believes that the plans for the new community centre will never come about.

come across (someone or something)

- to find something or meet someone by chance
  I came across an interesting story in the newspaper last week.

Come again.

- Please repeat or say that again.
  "Come again. I did not hear you the first time."

come alive

- to brighten up and become active
  The girl finally came alive and began to enjoy the party.

come along

- to make progress, to thrive
  The work on our new house is coming along very well.

come around

- to finally agree to something, to return to consciousness or wake up
  My father finally came around and agreed to let me go to Germany to study.

come as no surprise

- to not be surprising
  It came as no surprise when the government decided to have an election.

come away empty-handed

- to return without anything
  Nobody came away empty-handed at the end of the birthday party.

come back

- to return to the place where you are now
  My cousin came back from her holidays last week.

come back (into fashion)

- to become popular again
  Recently bell-bottom pants have come back into fashion.

come back to (someone)

- to return to one's memory
  The strange events of last year are slowly coming back to me.

come between (two people)

- to disrupt the relationship between (two people)
  The mother's constant interfering finally came between the man and his wife.

come down with (something)

- to become sick with a cold etc.
  My mother came down with a cold so was unable to attend the dinner.

come from (somewhere)

- to be a native of a place
  Several of the new students come from Mexico.

come from far and wide

- to come from many different places
  The people came from far and wide to hear the new band.

come into (some money)

- to get possession of some money, to inherit some money
  The man came into a lot of money which he donated to charity.

come into fashion

- to become fashionable
  My sister says that although bell-bottom pants have come into fashion again she will never wear them.

come into one's own

- to begin to perform or work well because of good circumstances
  The player has come into his own as a basketball player since he changed positions.

come of age

- to be old enough to vote/marry/sign legal contracts etc.
  When the members of our class came of age everyone started to vote.

come off

- to be successful, to happen
  The party came off without any problems so everyone was very happy.

come on!

- please, hurry, go faster
  "Come on, I only have a few minutes before I must go."
  "Come on, stop doing that."

come on strong

- to overwhelm others with a strong personality
  The man came on too strong during the job interview and was unable to get the job.

come on the scene

- to appear in a certain area or place
  When the new DVD player came on the scene everybody wanted one.

come out ahead

- to improve one's situation
  Although our new car was expensive, we came out ahead as it is very cheap to operate.

come out for (someone or something)

- to announce one's support for (someone or something)
  The mayor recently came out for legal gambling in the city.

come out in the wash

- to work out all right
  Everything came out in the wash as the students worked out their problems.

come out of left field

- to come from an unexpected place
  The manager's new idea came out of left field and we have no idea what it means.

come out of nowhere

- to appear suddenly
  The eagle came out of nowhere and captured the small mouse.

come out of one's shell

- to become more friendly or sociable
  My sister's little boy came out of his shell and began to talk to everybody around him.

come out of the blue

- to appear suddenly (as if from the sky)
  My idea for making money suddenly came out of the blue.

come out of the closet

- to reveal one's secret interests, to reveal that one is gay
  Nobody was surprised when my cousin came out of the closet.

come to

- to regain consciousness
  The woman came to a few hours after the accident.

come to do/feel (something)

- to begin/learn to do or feel something
  At first I disliked the girl but recently I have come to accept her.

come to a bad end

- to have a disaster, to die
  The man and his family came to a bad end when they moved to the country.

come to a standstill

- to stop
  The circus came to a standstill when the elephant escaped from his cage.

come to blows

- to begin to fight
  The two men came to blows when they were trying to fix the car.

come to grief

- to have a bad accident or disappointment
  The man has recently come to much grief because of his son's problems with the police.

come to grips with (something)

- to struggle (successfully) with an idea or problem
  The woman has finally come to grips with her husband's gambling.

come to life

- to become alive or lively

The party came to life when the host and hostess entered the room.

come to light

- to be discovered, to become known

  It has come to light that the company recently lost millions of dollars.

come to mind

- to enter into one's consciousness

  Nothing came to mind when I tried to remember the names of the actors.

come to nothing/naught

- to end in failure

  All of my efforts to help my sister find a job came to nothing.

come to one's senses

- to begin to think clearly or act sensibly

  He came to his senses and decided to buy a cheap car rather than an expensive one.

come to pass

- to happen, to occur

  I do not know what will come to pass but for now the company has many financial problems.

come to terms with (someone or something)

- to reach an agreement with someone, to accept something

  We finally came to terms with the bank and were able to buy the house.

come to the fore

- to come into an important place or position, to come to the front

  Several members of the class came to the fore and decided to take important positions in the club.

come to the point

- to be direct

  His speech was interesting but he never really came to the point.

come true

- to actually happen

The young girl is working hard to make her dreams come true.

come unglued

- to lose emotional control
  The woman came unglued when she learned that she had lost her job.

come up

- to happen unexpectedly
  I know that I will not be able to go to the party if something comes up.

common touch

- a friendly manner with everyone
  He has a common touch and everyone likes him a lot.

con (someone) out of (something)

- to trick someone out of money or something valuable
  The man on the street corner tried to con the woman out of some money.

confide in (someone)

- to tell secrets or personal matters to someone
  I usually confide in my friend when I have a problem.

contrary to (something)

- in spite of something
  Contrary to what everybody thought, my friend had already quit his job.

control the purse strings

- to be in charge of the money
  My mother always used to control the purse strings in our family.

cook one's goose

- to ruin one's chances
  The girl cooked her goose and has no chance of getting the new job.

cook (something) up

- to invent something, to plan or plot something
  I do not know what kind of plan she is cooking up but it should be quite interesting.

cook the books

- to cheat in bookkeeping
  The accountant was fired when someone discovered that he was cooking the books.

cool as a cucumber

- to be very calm and brave, to be not worried or anxious
  The woman was as cool as a cucumber when her canoe turned over in the river.

cool off/down

- to let one's anger die away
  When the basketball players began to cool down they were allowed to play again.

cool one's heels

- to be kept waiting
  The man was forced to cool his heels in the waiting room before his boss would talk to him.

cop a plea

- to plead guilty to a crime in order to get a lesser penalty
  The man was forced to cop a plea when the evidence against him became too strong to dispute.

cop out

- to avoid doing something that you were planning to do
  My friend copped out from our plan to go to to the beach for the day.

a copycat

- someone who copies another person's work or actions
  The little boy was accused of being a copycat by the other children.

cost a pretty penny

- to cost a lot of money
  I believe that my aunt's new coat cost a pretty penny.

cost an arm and a leg

- to cost too much

The new motorcycle cost my brother an arm and a leg.

cough up

- to give something unwillingly
  The man finally coughed up enough money to pay for the bicycle.

a course of action

- the procedures that will be followed to do something
  We decided on our course of action before we told our boss about our decision.

cover a lot of ground

- to deal with much information or facts, to travel a great distance
  We covered a lot of ground in our history class at school.

cover for (someone)

- to make excuses for someone, to cover someone's errors
  I covered for my friend when the boss saw that she was away from her desk.

cover for (someone)

- to do someone else's work
  We always cover for each other when someone at work is sick.

cover one's tracks

- to hide where one has been, to hide what one has done
  The man was trying to cover his tracks but it was easy to see where he had been.

cover up (something)

- to hide something wrong or bad
  They tried to cover up the facts regarding the illegal election campaign funds.

cozy up to (someone)

- to try to be extra friendly to someone
  I do not know what my neighbour wants but recently he has been trying to cozy up to me.

crack a book

- to open a book to study
  I did not crack a book until the last week of classes.

crack a joke

- to tell a joke
  The man was a lot of fun at the party because he was always cracking jokes.

crack a smile

- to let a smile show on one's face
  Our boss never cracked a smile during the meeting.

crack down on (someone or something)

- to enforce laws or rules strictly
  The school principal decided to crack down on people running in the halls.

crack of dawn

- daybreak, early in the morning
  We got up at the crack of dawn to go fishing.

crack open a book

- to open a book to study
  I did not crack open a book during the weekend.

crack the whip

- to try to make someone work hard or obey you by threatening them
  We had to crack the whip in order to get the job finished before the weekend.

crack up

- to burst into laughter
  I cracked up when the man started talking about the incident with the taxi driver.

crackpot

- an eccentric person with ideas that do not make sense to others
  The man is a crackpot and you never know what he will do next.

cramp one's style

- to limit one's talk or action
  Working in the new department is beginning to cramp my style.

crank (something) out

- to produce or make something
  I was able to crank out two very good papers before the end of the year.

crash and burn

- to fail spectacularly
  We did not want to crash and burn so we were very careful about how we proceeded with the project.

a credit to (someone or something)

- to be invaluable or beneficial to someone or something
  The doctor was a credit to the hospital where he had trained.

the creeps

- a strong feeling of fear or disgust
  I get the creeps every time that I see a spider or snake.

creep up on (someone or something)

- to crawl quietly toward someone or something
  The thief crept up on the elderly woman in the supermarket.

cross one's heart and hope to die

- to promise that what you are saying is true
  "I promise that I will pay back the money next week. Cross my heart and hope to die."

cross one's mind

- to think of something, to occur to someone
  It crossed my mind that I would see him in the evening so I did not need to phone him.

cross out (something)

- to eliminate something by drawing a line through it
  I crossed out my name from the list of volunteers.

cross swords with (someone)

- to have an argument with someone
  I do not want to cross swords with the head teacher again.

cross the Rubicon

- to do something where you cannot go back (Julius Ceasar crossed the Rubicon and made a fight with the Roman Senate inevitable)
  The man crossed the Rubicon when he began on a course that he could never turn back from.

cross to bear/carry

- something that you must do or continue with even though you are suffering
  Looking after my sister's children is my cross to bear.

cut a fine figure

- to look good
  I plan to cut a fine figure when I go to the job interview next week.

cut a wide swath

- to attract a lot of attention
  The man cuts a wide swath when he enters a room.

a cut above (someone or something)

- a little better than someone or something
  The new principal is a cut above the previous one.

cut across

- to cross or go through something instead of going around it
  We decided to cut across the field because we were in a hurry to get to school.

cut and run

- to leave as quickly as possible
  We cut and run as soon as we had finished delivering the goods.

cut and dried

- to be previously decided, to be prearranged
  The decision was cut and dried and nobody asked for our opinion.

cut back on (something)

- to use fewer or use less of something
  We were forced to cut back on the number of people who were invited to the party.

cut both ways

- to serve both sides of an argument
  What the man said cuts both ways and we should carefully think about it.

cut class

- to not go to class
  I cut class last week and went to a movie.

cut one's losses

- to reduce one's losses
  We decided to cut our losses and sell our business before it lost too much money.

cut out for (something)

- to have a talent for something, to be suited for something
  I do not think that I am cut out for all of the travelling that is required for this job.

cut (someone) off

- to stop someone from saying something, to disconnect someone on the phone
  I tried to tell my father about the accident but he cut me off before I had a chance.

cut (someone) to the quick

- to hurt someone's feelings very badly
  The woman cut her friend to the quick when she criticized her new clothes.

cut the mustard

- to reach the required standard for something
  The man does not cut the mustard and he will never be able to work here.

cut to the chase

- to get to the important matter of something
  The lawyer cut to the chase and was able to get all of the information quickly.

daily grind

- the everyday work routine
  My father is tired of the daily grind of working and will retire soon.

dance to a different tune

- to changè one's behaviour or attitude
  Our boss began dancing to a different tune when his head salesman decided to quit.

dance with death

- to do something that is very risky
  The teenagers were dancing with death when they began to race their cars.

days running

- several days in a row
  There were concerts at the auditorium for six days running.

dead ahead

- to be directly ahead
  There was a truck dead ahead so we put on the car brakes suddenly.

dead as a doornail

- to be very dead
  The man was as dead as a doornail after the car accident.

dead centre

- the exact middle
  I easily hit the target dead centre.

dead duck

- a person or a thing in a hopeless situation
  The man is a dead duck and he has no hope of recovering his former position.

dead end

- the end of a road, an impasse
  The negotiations between the players and the owners have come to a dead end.

dead in one's/its tracks

- to be stopped exactly where someone or something is at the moment
  The police stopped the robber dead in his tracks.

dead letter

- a piece of mail that cannot be delivered or returned to the sender

The letter with no return address went back to the post office as a dead letter.

dead loss

- a total loss

  The money that I gave to my friend is a dead loss and none of it will be returned.

dead on one's feet

- to be exhausted

  I was dead on my feet after working all day in my garden.

deal in (something)

- to buy and sell something

  The man has been dealing in antiques for many years.

deal with (someone)

- to act in a specific way toward someone, to do business with someone

  The company is planning to deal with the late employee soon.

deal with (something)

- to be concerned with something, to take action about something

  We will deal with the boxes tomorrow.

decide in favour of (someone or something)

- to determine the winner of something, to decide who is right

  The city decided in favour of building a new bridge over the river.

decked out

- to be dressed in fancy clothes

  My sister was decked out in her best clothes for the party.

deem it to be necessary

- to believe that something is necessary

  The judge deemed it to be necessary to postpone the trial for a week.

deep-six (something)

- to throw away something, to dispose of something

I decided to deep-six the videos as I did not want them any longer.

deep water

- serious trouble or difficulty

  The boy will be in deep water if he does not tell us where he spent the money.

deliver the goods

- to do a good or successful job of something

  He is the best manager that we have had. He knows how to deliver the goods.

desert a sinking ship

- to leave a situation or place when things become difficult or unpleasant

  Many employees decided to desert a sinking ship when their company began to have problems.

devil of a job

- a very difficult job

  Everybody thought that unloading the truck was a devil of a job.

devil-may-care attitude

- an unworried attitude, an attitude where one does not care what happens

  The man has a devil-may-care attitude to his job and nothing bothers him.

diamond in the rough

- a good person or thing that is hidden by a rough exterior

  The man is a diamond in the rough and a very gentle person under his harsh exterior.

die down

- to come slowly to an end, to grow weaker

  When the sound of the music died down we were able to go to sleep.

die in one's boots

- to die fighting

  The soldiers died in their boots after fighting very hard.

the die is cast

- something has been decided and you cannot change the decision
  The die is cast and now that we have sold our house we must move.

dig (something) out

- to locate something
  I dug out last year's income tax forms to look at.

a dime a dozen

- common, easy to get and of little value
  Used books are a dime a dozen and it is dificult to sell them.

dip into (something)

- to borrow from a supply of something
  We had to dip into our savings to get enough money for a holiday.

dirt cheap

- to be extremely cheap
  The denim jackets were dirt cheap so I decided to buy two of them.

dispose of (something)

- to discard something, to destroy something, to get rid of something
  We must dispose of our old sofa before we buy a new one.

divide and conquer

- to split an opposing side into two groups so that you can win against them
  The government was trying to divide and conquer the opposition parties.

divide (something) fifty-fifty

- to divide something into two equal parts
  We divided the money that we won fifty-fifty.

do a double take

- to look again in surprise at someone or something
  The girl did a double take when she saw her old boyfriend with another woman.

do a job on (someone or something)

- to harm or damage someone or something
  We really did a job on the bookcase that we were trying to move.

do a land-office business

- to do much business in a short time
  The children are doing a land-office business by selling the cold drinks next to the stadium.

do a number on (someone or something)

- to hurt or damage someone or something
  The students did a number on the spectator stands during the soccer game.

do a snow job on (someone)

- to deceive or confuse someone
  The salesman tried to do a snow job on me but I did not believe him.

do something rash

- to take drastic action (usually without thinking)
  My friend is extremely angry and she may do something rash.

do the dishes

- to wash and dry some dishes
  We did the dishes soon after eating dinner.

do the honors

- to perform the duty of a host (when serving a drink etc.)
  "Would you like to do the honors and pour everybody a drink?"

do the trick

- to work well, to achieve a good or desired result
  I think that the new piece of equipment should do the trick and solve our problem.

do time

- to spend time in prison
  The man was doing time when we first heard about him.

do with (someone or something)

- to be acquainted/involved/associated with someone or something
  I did not have anything to do with the meeting this year.

do with (something)

- to benefit from (something)
  I have been working hard all day so now I could do with a cold drink.

do without (something)

- to manage without something
  We will have to do without sugar if there is none.

do wonders

- to produce excellent results
  If you begin to do some exercise it will do wonders for your health.

done for

- to be ruined/defeated/dying
  I think that our team is done for this season.

done in

- to be tired, to be exhausted
  I was done in so I went to bed early.

a dose of one's own medicine

- the same kind of treatment that one gives to other people
  The man got a dose of his own medicine when his boss began to treat him the same way that he treated others.

double back

- to turn back from where you are going or where you have been
  We decided to double back from the arena and return home for a few minutes.

double-check (something)

- to check again to be sure that something is correct
  I double-checked the price of the airplane ticket.

double-cross (someone)

- to deceive someone, to promise one thing and then do another

The man tried to double-cross his partner but was caught and sent to jail.

double-talk

- talk or words that appear to mean something but do not

  The speaker gave the audience much double-talk and nobody knew what he wanted to say.

double up

- to share a room with someone

  The passengers had to double up in hotel rooms when the plane landed because of the weather.

a doubting Thomas

- someone who needs strong proof to believe something

  My friend is a doubting Thomas and you must tell him many times before he will believe something.

down to earth

- to be sensible and practical

  My mother is very down to earth.

down to the last detail

- considering all of the details

  We fixed up everything on the boat, right down to the last detail.

down to the wire

- to be nearing a deadline, to be running out of time

  We went down to the wire but we were able to finish the job on time.

down with (an illness)

- to be ill, to be sick at home

  My sister was down with a cold so she could not go out for a few days.

drag in (someone or something)

- to insist on bringing someone or something into a discussion

  Th employee always drags in his personal problems when we talk about his job performance.

drag on

- to pass very slowly, to make something longer

The speech was dragging on so we decided to leave early.

a drag on (someone)

- a burden to someone
  The problems at work were a drag on my friend and he became sick because of them.

drag one's feet/heels

- to act slowly or reluctantly
  The man has been dragging his feet about whether or not to take the job.

draw a blank

- to get no response to something, to get a negative result
  The manager drew a blank when he went to the head office to get information about the merger.

draw a line betwen two things

- to separate two things
  We must draw a line between using the internet for work and using it for personal use.

draw blood

- to make a wound that bleeds, to anger someone
  The politician was very careful not to draw blood during the debate.

draw fire

- to receive criticism for something
  The government began to draw fire when they announced changes in the health care system.

draw fire

- to be a target, to attract or provoke shooting
  The soldiers drew fire when they entered the small village.

draw in one's horns

- to spend less money
  The company is not doing well so everybody must draw in their horns.

draw interest

- to appear interesting and attract someone's attention

The singers drew much interest when they performed at the festival.

draw interest

- to earn interest when money is deposited in a bank
  The money that we put in the bank draws interest every month.

draw lots/straws

- to choose from a group of things to decide who will do something
  We decided to draw lots to see who would wash the dishes.

draw (someone) out

- to make a person talk or tell something
  The girl was very quiet but we were able to draw her out and she began talking.

drop around

- to come for a visit
  My friend plans to drop around for a visit tomorrow.

drop back

- to move or step backwards, to retreat
  During the hike my foot began to get sore so I decided to drop back and rest for awhile.

drop by

- to visit someone
  My uncle dropped by after work for a visit.

drop by the wayside

- to give up or fail before the finish of something
  Many runners dropped by the wayside during the marathon.

drop dead

- to die suddenly
  The bus driver dropped dead while driving the bus.

Drop dead!

- Go away!, to stop bothering someone
  I told my brother to drop dead when he came into my room and now he is angry at me.

drop everything

- to stop doing what you are doing
  When the fire alarm rang we dropped everything and went outside.

drop in (on someone)

- to make a short or unplanned visit to someone
  I decided to drop in on my friend after I finished work for the day.

drop in one's tracks

- to collapse from exhaustion
  The runner dropped in his tracks during the last part of the race.

drown (someone) out

- to make so much noise that it is impossible to hear someone
  The team captain was drowned out by the cheering fans.

drum up (something)

- to encourage something by making an effort
  The company was able to drum up a lot of business during the summer.

drum (something) into (someone's) head

- to make someone learn something by force
  The teacher worked hard to drum the formulas into the heads of the students.

dry run

- an attempt or rehearsal for something
  The marriage ceremony was on Saturday so we had a dry run on Thursday night.

dry up

- to become dry
  The river began to dry up early in the summer.

duck soup

- easy, effortless
  "How was the test last week?"

"It was duck soup - no problem at all."

dumb bunny

- a stupid gullible person

He is a dumb bunny and you never know what he will do next.

Dutch auction

- an auction where you start off with a high price and then reduce it
  They always sell the flowers at a Dutch auction at the downtown market.

Dutch courage

- unusual or artificial courage (often because of alcohol)
  The man was full of Dutch courage when he began to criticize his boss.

Dutch treat

- a meal/movie etc. where each person pays his or her own way, to contribute equally to something
  When he goes out with his girlfriend it is always a Dutch treat as he does not have much money.

Dutch uncle

- someone who gives you advice like a parent or relative would
  My friend is like a Dutch uncle and he is always giving me advice about how I should act.

duty bound (to do something)

- to be forced by duty or honour to do something
  I was duty bound to talk to my friend about the money that I had lost.

dwell on (something)

- to think or talk about something all the time
  I wish that my friend would not dwell on his personal problems.

dyed-in-the-wool

- permanent, stubborn
  My father is a dyed-in-the-wool conservative and will never change.

dying to (do something or go somewhere)

- to be very anxious to do something or go somewhere
  I am dying to go and visit my friend in the country.

each and every

- every
  "I want each and every student to bring his or her textbook tomorrow."

eager beaver

- a person who is always eager to work hard or do extra work
  My colleague is an eager beaver and is always ready to work hard when we need him.

eagle eye

- an eye with sharp visual powers
  The woman watched her young child with an eagle eye.

an ear to the ground

- attention that is paid to the way things are going or the way people feel and think
  The president has an ear to the ground and knows everything that is going on in our company.

earn one's keep

- to earn one's pay or a place to live by doing some work
  I work hard in my uncle's garden in order to earn my keep when I stay with him.

ease off/up on (someone or something)

- to put less pressure on someone or something, to relax
  The president was asked to ease off on his efforts to cut staff in the company.

easier said than done

- to be easier to talk about than to do
  I would like to change jobs but it is easier said than done.

easy come, easy go

- something that you get easily can be lost easily
  My cousin does not care if he loses his job or not. For him everything is easy come, easy go.

easy does it

- doing something slowly or without sudden movements
  "Easy does it," I said as we moved the large piano.

easy-going

- to be tolerant and relaxed
  Our boss has a very easy-going management style.

easy to come by

- to be easy to find
  Money is not easy to come by for many people with no education.

eat and run

- to eat a meal quickly and then leave
  We had to eat and run in order to arrive at the soccer field early.

eat away at (someone)

- to bother someone, to worry someone
  Money problems have been eating away at the man recently.

eat away at (something)

- to rot/destroy something
  The mildew has been eating away at the window frame all year.

eat crow

- to admit that one is mistaken or defeated
  Our boss was forced to eat crow when the figures that he presented at the meeting were wrong.

eat dirt

- to accept another's insults or bad treatment
  The accountant had to eat dirt because of the problems that he had caused.

eat humble pie

- to admit one's error and apologize
  The boy had to eat humble pie when his friends discovered his mistake.

eat like a bird

- to eat very little
  He eats like a bird. That is why he cannot gain enough weight to join the football team.

eat like a horse

- to eat a lot

My friend eats like a horse but he never gains any weight.

edge (someone) out

- to win a competition against someone and get a job or position

  I was able to edge out the other applicants to get the job.

egg (someone) on

- to urge or push someone to do something

  The boy is always egging his friend on to do stupid things.

either feast or famine

- to be/have either too much or not enough of something

  It is either feast or famine for the woman. Sometimes she has lots of money and sometimes she has none.

eke out (a living)

- to earn one's living with difficulty

  My uncle was unable to eke out a living on the farm so he sold it.

elbow grease

- the effort and strength to clean something

  We will have to use a lot of elbow grease to clean the kitchen.

elbow room

- enough space to be comfortable

  The couple moved to the country in order to have more elbow room.

elbow (someone) out of (somewhere)

- to pressure someone out of somewhere

  The woman elbowed the other shoppers out of the way so that she could buy some shoes.

eleventh-hour decision

- a decision that is made at the last possible minute

  The government made an eleventh-hour decision to save the hospital.

an end in itself

- something that one wants for itself alone and not as a way to get/do something else
  For many people travelling is an end in itself and the destination is not important.

end of one's rope

- the last of one's ability or ideas about how to do something
  I am at the end of my rope regarding what to do about my job.

end up (doing something)

- to do something that one had not planned to do
  I ended up studying rather than going to a movie last night.

every minute counts

- time is very important
  Every minute counts when the fire department goes to fight a fire.

every nook and cranny

- every small hiding place where you can put something
  I looked in every nook and cranny of my apartment but I could not find my house keys.

every other

- every second one
  I have to work every other Saturday evening.

every so often

- occasionally
  You should stand up every so often when you are on a long plane trip.

every time one turns around

- frequently
  Every time I turn around my little boy asks me a question.

every Tom, Dick and Harry

- the average person
  The man said that he is not the same as every Tom, Dick and Harry.

every which way

- in all directions
  The small children at the birthday party were running every which way.

everything but the kitchen sink

- almost everything
  We took everything but the kitchen sink on our camping trip.

everything humanly possible

- everything in the range of human powers
  The doctors did everything humanly possible to save the man after the accident.

the exception that proves the rule

- an exception to a rule proves that the rule exists
  The salesman is very quiet and shy and he is the exception that proves the rule in his company. Everybody else is very talkative.

excuse (someone)

- to forgive someone
  We excused the man for his rude comments because he did not know any better.

explain (oneself)

- to give an explanation for something wrong that you may have done
  The director was forced to explain himself after the accounting problems were discovered.

explain (something) away

- to explain something so that it seems less important
  The sales clerk tried to explain away the problem with the sales receipt.

express (one's) anger

- to release one's anger
  The man often loses his temper which is not a good way to express his anger.

extend credit to (someone)

- to permit someone to buy something on credit
  The bank extended credit to the small company so that they could continue to operate.

extend one's sympathy to (someone)

- to express sympathy to someone
  We extended our sympathy to the family of the dead woman.

extenuating circumstances

- the special circumstances that cause something to happen
  We were able to avoid paying the parking ticket because of extenuating circumstances.

eye of the storm

- the centre of a problem
  The politician was in the eye of the storm because of the accounting scandal.

eyeball-to-eyeball

- face to face
  I sat eyeball-to-eyeball with our boss during the meeting.

eyes are bigger than one's stomach

- to take or want more food than you can eat
  The man's eyes are bigger than his stomach. He will never finish all of the food that he took.

eyes in the back of one's head

- the ability to know what is happening behind one's back
  He has eyes in the back of his head and you can never borrow anything without him knowing about it.

eyes pop out

- much surprised
  Her eyes popped out when she saw her name in the newspaper.

face down (someone)

- to confront someone boldly, to defy someone
  We decided to face down our competitors and were able to stay in business.

face the music

- to accept the consequences of something
  The boy must face the music for his actions very soon.

face to face

- in person
  I had a face-to-face meeting with my supervisor to talk about my job performance.

face up to (something)

- to accept something that is not easy to accept
  My friend must face up to the fact that he will never have enough money to buy a car.

face value

- the value or price printed on a stamp/bond/paper money etc.
  I sold the postage stamps for their face value.

face value

- the truth of something on the surface
  The woman is a very nice person but you must take what she says at face value.

facts of life

- the facts about sex/marriage/birth that one should know
  The boy seems to be too young to know about the facts of life.

fair and impartial

- fair and unbiased
  The criminal was given a fair and impartial trial by the court.

fair and square

- completely fair, honestly
  The British team won the game fair and square.

fair game

- someone or something that you feel you can easily attack
  Our company is fair game as a takeover target by other companies.

fair play

- justice, equal and right action
  The boy believes in fair play and is a good person to have on our team.

a fair shake

- honest treatment
  The woman was not given a fair shake at the inquiry into her behaviour.

fair to middling

- a little better than acceptable, so-so
  I said that I was feeling fair to middling when my friend asked me how I was.

fair-weather friend

- a person who is a friend only during good times
  He is a fair-weather friend and you cannot rely on him if you have a problem.

fall apart

- to become to not work properly
  The equipment fell apart soon after I bought it.

fall into a trap

- to become caught in someone's scheme
  The criminals fell into a trap that the police had prepared for them.

fall into line

- to stand properly in a row (like soldiers)
  The soldiers fell into line as they waited for the inspection.

fall into line

- to conform to a certain course of action
  The players fell into line after the coach became more strict during practice.

fall into place

- to fit together, to become organized
  Everything fell into place and we were able to prepare for our trip to Brazil.

fall off

- to decrease
  The number of tourists to the island is falling off.

fall off the wagon

- to return to use alcohol or drugs after stopping for awhile

The man fell off the wagon after he had stopped drinking for three years.

fall on deaf ears

- to ignore something that is intended for you
  My complaints to my boss always fall on deaf ears.

fall on hard times

- to meet many troubles
  The town fell on hard times after the computer company moved to another town.

a far cry from (something)

- something very different from something
  The man's statement is a far cry from what he told me over the telephone.

far from it

- not at all
  "Far from it," I answered when the supervisor asked me if I was finished my work.

far into the night

- late into the night
  I studied far into the night because I had a big test the next day.

far out

- to be strange
  The man's sense of humour was far out and nobody understood him.

farm (something) out

- to have someone else do something, to send something away to have it done
  We farmed out the printing to another company in order to save money.

fast and furious

- very rapidly
  The questions were coming fast and furious during the job interview.

fast buck

- money earned quickly and easily
  The man is always trying to make a fast buck without working very hard.

fast talker

- a con artist, a clever talker who convinces others easily
  The man is a fast talker and you should be careful not to believe everything that he says.

fat chance

- little or no possibility, almost no chance
  Fat chance that my friend will let me borrow his car. He never lets me borrow anything.

fat of the land

- the best of everything (without having to work for it)
  My friend wants to move to the country and live off the fat of the land.

favour (someone) with (something)

- to provide someone with something good
  The queen favored the charity workers with her presence.

favourite son

- a political candidate supported by his home area
  We voted for the candidate because he is the favourite son of our state.

ferret (information or something) out of (someone)

- to get something from someone by being persistent
  I tried hard to ferret out the time of the party from my friend.

few and far between

- not many, rare
  The gas stations were few and far between on the highway through the mountains.

fiddle around

- to tinker with something, to do something in an unplanned way
  I tried fiddling around with the computer printer but it still would not work.

fiddle while Rome burns

- to do nothing while a disaster is happening
  The economy became worse as the government did

nothing. They seemed to fiddle while Rome burned.

field questions

- to answer questions

  The speaker began to field questions as soon as he finished talking.

fifty-fifty

- equally, evenly

  We divided the cost of the trip fifty-fifty.

fill out (something)

- to write down the facts that are asked for (in a report/form etc.)

  We were asked to fill out the forms before we could have an interview for the job.

fill (someone) in

- to tell someone the details about something

  "I will fill you in later about our plans for the weekend."

fill the bill

- to be suitable for what is required

  I think that the new equipment should fill the bill for us.

find one's tongue

- to begin to be able to talk

  I could not find my tongue when I stood in front of the crowd of people.

find one's way

- to discover the route to a place

  We were lost for over an hour but we finally found our way.

find oneself

- to discover what one's talents and preferences are

  The woman went to Europe in order to try and find herself.

find out (something)

- to learn or discover something

  My mother is angry at me because she found out that I had quit my French class.

fine and dandy

- all right, okay
  It is fine and dandy for me that the sale will be held next Saturday.

a fine how-do-you-do

- a predicament
  We were in a fine how-do-you-do when the car stopped working.

fit for a king

- to be totally suitable (especially suitable for a king)
  The food at the wedding was fit for a king.

fit in with (someone or something)

- to be comfortable or in harmony with someone or something
  The new boy fits in with the other children very well.

fit like a glove

- to fit perfectly
  The new pair of jeans that I bought fit like a glove.

fit (someone or something) in

- to make time for someone or something
  I try hard to fit some exercise in everyday.

fit (someone) into a schedule

- to be able to enter someone into a schedule and have time to see him or her
  The doctor was not able to fit me into her schedule.

fit (someone) out with (something)

- to provide someone with something
  The store helped to fit us out with camping equipment for our holiday.

fit (someone) to a T

- to fit a person very well
  My cousin's new job fits her to a T.

fit the mold

- to do what you expect, to do what is considered usual (usually used in the negative - does not fit the mold)
  Our teacher does not fit the mold of someone who volunteers to help homeless people every Saturday.

fit to be tied

- to be very angry or upset
  My boss was fit to be tied when he heard that I was going to take a month off from work this summer.

flea in one's ear

- an annoying hint, an idea or answer that is not welcome
  Our boss has a flea in her ear about changing the way that the business operates.

flea market

- a place where antiques or secondhand goods are sold
  We went to a flea market last Saturday to try and buy some dishes.

one's flesh and blood

- a close relative
  She is my flesh and blood so I felt terrible when she got into trouble.

flesh (something) out

- to make something more detailed or bigger
  We worked hard during the weekend to flesh out our agreement.

a flight of fancy

- an idea that is out of touch with reality or possibility
  It was a flight of fancy for us to think of trying to climb Mt. Everest.

flip one's lid

- to become very excited, to lose one's temper
  My father flipped his lid when I told him about the large telephone bill.

flip out

- to go crazy, to become very angry
  She flipped out when she heard that I had damaged her car.

flirt with the idea of (doing something)

- to think about doing something
  We flirted with the idea of buying a new house but we decided not to.

float a loan

- to initiate or make a loan
  The bank agreed to float a loan for the new business.

flora and fauna

- plants and animals
  We took some books to the cottage so that we could learn about the flora and fauna of the area.

follow one's nose

- to go straight ahead
  We followed our nose until we found the train station.

follow orders

- to do as one has been instructed
  The soldiers said that they were following orders when they attacked the village.

follow (someone's) lead

- to do as someone else does
  Everybody followed my lead and came to work early.

follow suit

- to do as someone else has done, to follow someone's example, to play a card of the same suit that someone else has put down
  I followed suit and left work early on Friday just as my boss had done.

follow the crowd

- to do what everyone else is doing
  Most of the high school students like to follow the crowd.

follow through with (something)

- to continue or finish an action that one has started
  My neighbour said that he would help me paint my house but he has never followed through with his offer.

follow up (something)

- to make (one action) more successful by doing something more

The doctor followed up his phone call in the morning with a visit in the afternoon.

fond of (someone or something)

- to like someone or something

  Our daughter is very fond of her grandfather.

food for thought

- something worth thinking about

  I do not agree with his proposal but at least it is food for thought.

for all I know

- according to the information that I have

  "For all I know, my friend may have already quit his job."

for all intents and purposes

- practically speaking

  For all intents and purposes the meeting was finished and everybody went home.

for all one is worth

- as hard as one can

  "I will try for all I am worth to help you get the job at the supermarket."

for all practical purposes

- for what might be reasonably expected

  For all practical purposes our car was no longer suitable for our large family.

for all the world

- for anything, for any price

  For all the world I do not know what my friend is trying to tell me.

for better or worse

- depending on how one looks at a matter, including both the good or bad effects of something

  For better or worse I have decided to quit my job and move to Brazil.

for certain

- without doubt, certainly, surely

  He will not be playing in the game tonight for certain.

for crying out loud

- used to show that you are surprised or angry
  "For crying out loud please turn your radio down a little."

for days/hours on end

- for many days/hours
  The man is able to go without sleep for days on end.

for sale

- to be available to buy
  There was a sign in front of the house that said it was for sale.

for short

- in a short form
  The man always uses his nickname for short.

for sure

- without doubt, certainly, surely
  I will go to the movie with you for sure next week.

for that matter

- about something, with regard to something
  "I do not want to go shopping with you and for that matter I do not want to go anywhere with you."

for the asking

- by asking, on request
  You can get a free ticket to the concert from the sales manager for the asking.

for the better

- an improvement
  It was for the better that the old hospital was closed down.

for the birds

- something you do not like, something that is not to be taken seriously
  Getting up early every morning is for the birds.

for the duration (of something)

- for the whole time that something continues
  We were forced to use the outside classroom for the duration of the semester.

for the good of (someone or something)

- for the benefit of someone or something
  They added the physical fitness class to the school curriculum for the good of the students.

for the heck/hell of it

- just for fun
  We went down to the river to throw stones just for the heck of it.

for the life of (someone)

- even if one's life were threatened (used with a negative and usually used when trying to remember something)
  For the life of me I could not remember where I had put my house keys.

for the world

- under any conditions
  I would not want to sell my car for the world.

force (someone's) hand

- to make someone do something sooner than planned
  I forced the manager's hand and made him tell me about his plans for our company.

force (someone) to the wall

- to push someone to an extreme position
  We were forced to the wall during the negotiations for the new contract.

force (something) down (someone's) throat

- to force someone to do or agree to something that he or she does not want
  I wish that my friend would not force her ideas down my throat.

a force to be reckoned with

- someone or something that is important and should not be ignored
  The young man is a force to be reckoned with in the boxing world.

foregone conclusion

- a conclusion that is already decided

It was a foregone conclusion that the opposition party would win the election.

forever and a day

- forever, always

  It took forever and a day to get the book that we ordered from the bookstore.

forever and ever

- forever

  The little boy promised that he would be a good boy forever and ever.

fork out money for (something)

- to pay money for something

  I had to fork out much money to have my car fixed.

fork over (something)

- to hand over something, to give something

  The robber told me to fork over my money or he was going to shoot me.

form an opinion

- to make an opinion

  Everybody quickly formed an opinion about the new teacher.

forty winks

- a short nap, a short sleep

  I grabbed forty winks as soon as I got home from work.

foul one's own nest

- to harm one's own interests

  The union fouled their own nest with their dishonest behaviour.

foul up

- to do badly, to mess something up

  There was a problem with our tickets and our plans became fouled up.

one's frame of mind

- one's mental state - either good or bad

  I made sure that my boss was in a good frame of mind before I asked him for a holiday.

fraught with danger

- to be full of something dangerous and unpleasant

Their adventure was fraught with danger when the two boys went to the mountains.

freak out

- to become angry or lose control of oneself
  I freaked out when I discovered that my reservation had not been made.

free and clear

- without owing any money
  The couple finally owned their house free and clear.

free and easy

- informal
  The man's attitude toward his work is free and easy.

free as a bird

- completely free
  We were as free as a bird so we decided to go on a long holiday.

freeze (someone) out

- to prevent someone from getting a share in something by unfriendly or dishonest treatment
  They froze the man out of the profits that they had made on the sale of the land.

fresh out of (something)

- to have used up all of something, to have sold the last of something
  The bakery was fresh out of brown bread so we had to go to the supermarket.

frighten (someone) out of his or her wits

- to frighten someone severely
  The little boy was frightened out of his wits by the big dog.

frighten (someone) to death

- to frighten someone severely
  I almost frightened the woman to death when I met her on the dark stairs.

frighten the living daylights out of (someone)

- to frighten someone very badly
  The horror movie frightened the living daylights out of the young girl.

fritter (something) away

- to waste something little by little
  The man frittered away all of the money that he had won in the contest.

from A to Z

- everything about something
  The man knows about cars from A to Z.

from cradle to grave

- from birth to death
  The government looks after its citizens with good medical care from cradle to grave.

from dawn to dusk

- from the rising of the sun to the setting of the sun
  The farmworkers worked from dawn to dusk everyday in order to pick the lettuce crop.

from the outset

- from the beginning
  I knew from the outset that the recipe would be loved by everybody.

from the top

- from the beginning
  "Let's take it from the top and begin again."

from the word go

- from the beginning
  From the word go we knew that there would be problems with the new contract.

from time to time

- occasionally
  We go to that restaurant from time to time.

from tip to toe

- from the top to the bottom
  We made an effort to clean the statue from tip to toe.

from way back

- since a long time ago, for a long time
  I know my friend from way back. In fact, we went to elementary school together.

fruits of one's labour

- the results of one's work

We decided to enjoy the fruits of our labour so we went on a long holiday to Europe.

full-fledged

- complete, having everything that is needed to be something
  My cousin became a full-fledged nurse before she went to Saudi Arabia to work for a year.

full of beans

- to be in high spirits, to be energetic
  My aunt is full of beans today. She must be excited about something.

full of hot air

- to be full of nonsense, to be talking nonsense
  I knew that the man was full of hot air when he began to tell us how to make lots of money.

full of it

- to be full of nonsense
  I thought that the woman was full of it when she told me that the business was closed.

full of oneself

- to be conceited, to be self-important
  The girl was full of herself and would only talk about things that were important to her.

full steam ahead

- with as much energy and enthusiasm as possible
  It was full steam ahead with the project to build the new stadium.

fun and games

- a very difficult task (often used ironically)
  It was fun and games today when I wrote my two final exams.

funny bone

- the place at the back of the elbow that tingles when hit
  I hit my funny bone today and it still hurts a little.

funny business

- illegal activity
  The truck driver was involved in some funny business that was probably illegal.

funny ha-ha

- amusing, comical
  It was not funny ha-ha but it was still a little bit amusing.

gain ground

- to go forward, to make progress
  The toy company is gaining ground in their effort to sell more products.

game that two can play

- a good or bad strategy that two competing sides can both use
  The insults from my friend are a game that two can play and if she wants to continue then so can I

get a bright idea

- to have a clever thought or idea occur to you (often used as sarcasm)
  My father got the bright idea that he should buy a motorcycle.

get a checkup

- to receive a physical examination by a doctor
  I go to the doctor every year to get a checkup.

get a clean bill of health

- to be pronounced healthy by a doctor
  I got a clean bill of health when I went to see the doctor.

get a dirty look from (someone)

- to receive a frown from someone
  I got a dirty look from the man who was sitting next to my crying child.

get a feel for (something)

- to become accustomed to something and learn how it works, to learn how to do something
  I am beginning to get a feel for my new job.

get a fix on (something)

- to receive a reading of a distant object by electronic means
  We were able to get a fix on the island and took the boat safely to the harbor.

get a foothold (somewhere)

- to find a starting point somewhere
  The new political party is beginning to get a foothold in the big cities.

get a grasp of (something)

- to begin to understand something
  I am beginning to get a grasp of how to operate the new computer system.

get a grip of oneself

- to take control of one's feelings
  The man got a grip of himself and calmed down.

get a head start (on someone or something)

- to start earlier than someone or something, to start earlier than usual
  We tried to get a head start on our holiday.

get a kick out of (someone or something)

- to enjoy someone or something
  My father got a kick out of seeing his old school friend.

get a load of (someone or something)

- to take a good look at someone or something
  "Get a load of that man over there with the four dogs."

get a load off one's feet

- to sit down and relax
  I sat down and tried to get a load off my feet.

get a load off one's mind

- to express what one is thinking or worried about
  I talked with my supervisor and was able to get a load off my mind regarding our recent conflict.

get a lot of mileage out of (something)

- to get much use from something (like a car)
  I hope to get a lot of mileage out of the new sneakers that I bought last week.

get a lump in one's throat

- to feel like there is something in one's throat (like you are going to cry)
  My sister got a lump in her throat when she watched her daughter's graduation.

get a move on

- to hurry up
  "Please get a move on. We are already three hours late."

get a raw deal

- to receive unfair or bad treatment
  The secretary got a raw deal when she was forced to work late everyday.

get along

- to leave
  It's late so I must get along now.

get along in years

- to grow older
  My parents are getting along in years but they are still very healthy.

get along on (something)

- to manage to survive or do well with something
  My friend is able to get along on very little money.
  The young woman gets along on her good looks very well.

get along on a shoestring

- to manage with very little money
  I had to get along on a shoestring during university.

get along (with someone)

- to have a good relationship with someone
  I get along with everybody at my company.

get an earful

- to hear much talk/criticism/complaints about something
  Our boss got an earful when he asked the employees if they had any complaints.

get around

- to go to different places, to move about
  My friend gets around and has been to many different cities.

get around to (do something)

- to finally find time to do something

The apartment manager finally got around to fixing our bath.

get back at (someone)

- to do something bad to someone who has done something bad to you

  The girl is angry at her boyfriend and she is getting back at him by not answering the telephone.

get back to (someone)

- to communicate something to someone at a later time, to contact someone later

  We were very careful that our complaints did not get back to the school principal.

get back to (something)

- to return to something

  I needed a rest before I could get back to my work.

get back together (with someone)

- to resume a relationship or marriage after separating

  The couple got back together after separating for three months.

get better

- to improve one's skill at doing something, to improve one's health

  The little boy is getting better at riding his bicycle.

get by (on something)

- to be able to satisfy your needs with a certain amount of something (usually related to money)

  The man is able to get by on his salary because he does not spend much money.

get carried away

- to be overcome by emotion or enthusiasm, to lose one's control or judgement

  I got carried away yesterday and cleaned all of my apartment.

get close to (someone)

- to become close friends with someone

  The woman tried very hard to get close to her youngest daughter.

get in (someone's) hair

- to bother or irritate someone
  The woman complained that her young child was always getting in her hair.

get in touch with someone

- to contact someone
  I plan to get in touch with my friend when I arrive in New York in August.

get into a jam

- to become involved in trouble or a problem
  I got into a jam when I lost the keys to my apartment.

get into a stew about/over (someone or something)

- to be worried or upset about someone or something
  My mother is getting into a stew about my aunt not phoning.

get into hot water

- to get into trouble or difficulty
  We got into hot water when they found us in the building after it had closed.

get into (something)

- to become interested or involved in something
  I do not want to get into an argument with my friend.
  We will get into the details of the plan tomorrow.

get into (somewhere)

- to enter somewhere
  My friend wants to get into a good university.
  I bumped my head as I was getting into the car.

get into the act

- to try to be part of whatever is happening
  Everybody at the party wanted to get into the act and join the singers.

get into the swing of things

- to adapt to a new environment or situation
  My friend got into the swing of things after the party started.

get into trouble

- to become involved in some kind of trouble

The young boys try not to get into trouble when they are left at home alone.

get mixed up

- to become confused

  "I`m sorry but I got mixed up with the dates. That`s why I came today."

get nowhere fast

- to make no progress

  We are getting nowhere fast in our effort to convince our boss to give us a holiday.

get off

- to escape or avoid punishment

  The criminal got off with a very light sentence from the judge.

get off (a bus/train/plane etc.)

- to leave or exit from a bus or train etc.

  We decided to get off the train at the next station.

get off easy

- to escape a serious punishment

  The criminals got off easy after they robbed the bank.

get off on the wrong foot (with someone or something)

- to make a bad start with someone or something

  I got off on the wrong foot with my boss and our relationship is not good.

get off one's butt

- to get busy, to start working

  My friend should get off his butt and try to find a job.

get off one's high horse

- to become less arrogant

  The manager was forced to get off his high horse and act better toward the employees.

get off (someone's) back

- to leave someone alone and not bother him or her

  I wish that my supervisor would get off my back.

get off the ground

- to make a successful beginning

  My uncle's new business never got off the ground and he must look for a new job.

get off the hook

- to become free from an obligation
  I got off the hook and I did not have to clean the classroom after school.

get one's hands on (someone or something)

- to get someone or something in one's grasp
  "When I get my hands on a hammer I will help you fix the door."

get one's head above water

- to get in control of one's situation (often financial situation)
  When I get my head above water I will be able to spend less time working.

get one's just deserts

- to get what one deserves
  The apartment manager got her just deserts when she was fired for bothering the tenants.

get one's money's worth

- to get value for what you have paid for
  We got our money's worth when we stayed on the golf course for seven hours.

get one's nose out of (someone's) business

- to stop interfering in someone else's business
  The school secretary was told to get her nose out of the teacher's business.

get one's own way

- to be able to do what you want
  The boy always gets his own way with his younger brothers.

get one's rear in gear

- to hurry up, to get going
  "Let's get our rear in gear before it is too late to go to a movie."

get one's say

- to be able to say what one thinks
  The meeting was over very quickly but everyone got their say.

get one's sea legs

- to become accustomed to something (like you would become accustomed to the movement of a ship)
  After we got our sea legs we were able to get up and walk around the boat.

get one's start

- to receive the first major opportunity of one's career
  The newspaper owner got his start by selling papers when he was a child.

get one's walking papers

- to get fired
  The young man got his walking papers for being late too often.

get one's wires crossed

- to get confused about something
  We got our wires crossed and we both went to different places for our meeting.

get out from under (someone or something)

- to escape from a situation that one does not like
  I would like to get out from under my boss who is always watching my work.

get out of a jam

- to get free from a problem or bad situation
  We got out of a jam this morning when enough people came to help finish the job.

get out of bed on the wrong side

- to be in a bad mood
  I think that she got out of bed on the wrong side as she is not talking to anyone today.

get out of hand

- to get out of control
  The party was beginning to get out of hand so we asked everyone to leave.

get out of (somewhere)

- to leave somewhere, to escape
  I want to hurry and get out of my house so I will not be late for work.

get out of the way

- to stop obstructing or interfering with someone or something, to escape from something
  The car was unable to get out of the way of the truck and it was hit.

get over (something)

- to overcome a difficulty, to recover from an illness or shock
  The woman is having trouble getting over her father's death.

get (something) out of the way

- to take care of some business, to do/finish something
  We got our work out of the way and began to plan for the weekend.

get (something) over with

- to finish something (often something that you do not want to do)
  I was very happy to get my exams over with.

get (something) straight

- to understand something clearly
  I could not get what my friend was trying to tell me straight.

get (something) through (someone's) thick skull

- to manage to get someone to understand something
  I could not get it through my friend's thick skull that I would not go on a holiday with him.

get (something) under control

- to be able to control something
  The fire fighters were quickly able to get the fire under control.

get the facts straight

- to get a good understanding of the facts
  I do not believe that our supervisor got the facts straight when she heard about our argument.

get the feel of (something)

- to become used to or learn about something
  After you get the feel of the new computer it is very easy to use.

get the floor

- to receive official permission to address an audience
  When the principal finally got the floor everybody was ready to go home.

get the go-ahead

- to receive a signal to start something
  The construction company got the go-ahead to begin work on the new stadium.

get the goods on (someone)

- to find out true but often negative information about someone
  I think that I have got the goods on the man and will talk to the police soon.

get the hang of (something)

- to learn how to do something
  The boy was asked to help with the sound system after he got the hang of it.

get the jump on (someone)

- to get ahead of someone
  We left home early so we could get the jump on the other travellers.

get the last laugh

- to laugh at someone who has laughed at you
  We got the last laugh when the car that had passed us on the highway got a speeding ticket.

get the lead out

- to hurry
  "Get the lead out," I said to my slow friend.

get the lowdown on (someone or something)

- to receive the full story about someone or something
  I met a friend for coffee to get the lowdown on our friend who is getting married.

get the message

- to clearly understand the meaning of something
  I told my friend to be quiet but I do not think that he got the message.

get the nod

- to be chosen for something

My favourite candidate got the nod to represent us in the election.

get the once-over

- to receive a quick visual examination
  I quickly got the once-over when I arrived for the job interview.

get to do (something)

- to have a chance or to be able to do something
  I did not get to go to the circus last week.

get to first base

- to make a start, to succeed
  I tried to meet the company president but I could not get to first base.

get to one's feet

- to stand up
  The members of the audience got to their feet when the concert finished.

get to the bottom of (something)

- to find out the real cause/answer of something
  The government wants to get to the bottom of the financial problems in the company.

get to the heart of (something)

- to understand the most important thing about something
  We were in the meeting for three hours trying to get to the heart of the problem.

get to the root of a problem

- to get an understanding of the causes of a problem
  The purpose of the meeting was to get to the root of the problem about the money.

get tough with (someone)

- to become firm/strict with someone
  The school plans to get tough with students who are late.

get under (someone's) skin

- to bother or upset someone
  The woman always gets under my skin although I do not really know why.

get under way

- to start
  The festival got under way early this morning.

get up

- to get out of bed, to get to one's feet
  I got up early today so that I could go fishing with my friend.

get what's coming to one

- to receive the good or bad that one deserves
  The criminal got what was coming to him when he was sent to jail for two years.

get wind of (something)

- to hear about something
  I got wind of the changes in our company from my friend.

get wise to (someone or something)

- to learn about something that is a secret
  The man got wise to the fact that someone was stealing his money.

get with it

- to pay attention, to get busy
  I told my friend to get with it or he would have problems with his boss.

get worked up about/over (something)

- to get excited or angry about something
  My friend always gets worked up about his problems at work.

getup

- fancy dress or costume
  "What was that strange getup that your friend was wearing the other day?"

ghost of a chance

- very little chance, the smallest chance
  The boy does not have a ghost of a chance to finish his homework before class.

gift of the gab

- the ability to talk well
  My friend has the gift of the gab and is fun at a party.

give a wide birth to (someone or something)

- to keep away from someone or something, to keep a safe distance from someone or something
  I usually give a wide birth to my boss when he is angry.

give oneself away

- to show guilt, to show that you have done wrong
  The girl gave herself away when she said that she had not been downtown although her boyfriend had seen her there.

give oneself up

- to surrender, to stop hiding or running away
  The robbers gave themselves up when the police surrounded the house.

give oneself up to (something)

- to let oneself enjoy something, to not hold oneself back from something
  The man gave himself up to enjoy the party although he was feeling sick.

give or take (a certain amount of something)

- plus or minus a small amount
  I think that the man is about 45 years old give or take five years.

give out

- to fail, to wear out
  We went hiking last week but my legs gave out so we had to return early.

give out

- to be gone, to finish
  We went camping for a week but our food gave out after only three days.

give (someone) a dirty look

- to frown or make an angry face at someone
  I gave the woman a dirty look when she talked loudly on her cell phone.

give (someone) a fair shake

- to treat someone fairly
  Our company tries to give everyone a fair shake.

give (someone) a free hand (with something)

- to give someone complete control over something
  The city gave the homeowners a free hand to plan the new playground.

give (someone) a hand

- to help someone do something
  "Please give me a hand to move this piano."

give (someone) a hard time

- to tease someone, to make trouble for someone
  The girl gave her boyfriend a hard time about his new haircut.
  The new supervisor is giving me a hard time.

give (someone) a head start

- to allow someone to start earlier than others
  We gave my friend a head start in the treasure hunting contest.

give (someone) a piece of one's mind

- to scold or become angry with someone
  When I met my friend yesterday, I gave her a piece of my mind.

give (someone) a ring/buzz

- to call someone on the telephone
  I plan to give my friend a ring when I get home tonight.

give (someone) a run for their money

- to give someone a challenge
  Our team gave the stronger teams a run for their money during the championship finals.

give (someone) a start

- to startle or surprise someone
  The dog gave me a start when it suddenly appeared.

give (someone) an earful

- to scold someone, to tell someone much information (usually in an angry way)
  I gave my sister an earful when she phoned me.

give (someone) an inch and they will take a mile

- if you give someone a little they will want more, some people are never satisfied

If you give the children an inch they will take a mile so you should be strict sometimes.

give (someone) the low-down (on someone or something)

- to tell someone the full story about someone or something

  I gave my friend the low-down on our plans for the weekend.

give (someone or something) the once-over

- to visually examine someone or something quickly

  We gave the man the once-over when he walked into the restaurant.

give (someone) the red-carpet treatment

- to give someone very special treatment

  The city gave the politician the red-carpet treatment when he came for a visit.

give (someone) the runaround

- to give excuses and delays to someone

  We tried to get a refund for our airplane tickets but the company gave us the runaround.

give (someone) the shirt off one's back

- to be very generous to someone

  My uncle is very kind and he will give you the shirt off his back.

give (someone) the slip

- to escape from someone

  The bank robbers tried to give the police the slip but they were soon caught.

give (someone) the third degree

- to question someone in great detail

  The woman gave her son the third degree when he returned home.

give up the ghost

- to stop working, to die

  My old car finally gave up the ghost so I must buy another one.

give up the ship

- to stop fighting, to stop trying or hoping to do something

"Please don`t give up the ship and quit this company. You still have a useful role to play."

give voice to (one's feelings)

- to express what one feels or thinks
  The man has begun to give voice to his feelings about his new job.

gloss (something) over

- to try to make what is wrong or bad seem unimportant, to hide something
  The accountant tried to gloss over the amount of money that the company lost last year.

glutton for punishment

- a person who likes difficult or unpleasant tasks
  My friend is a glutton for punishment and he will always do the most difficult jobs available.

gnash one's teeth

- to grind one's teeth
  I gnashed my teeth before I went to talk to my boss.

go a long way toward (something)

- to be almost enough, to contribute much to something
  The money from the government will go a long way toward building a new library.

go about one's business

- to be busy or start working on something
  Everybody is going about their business again after the holidays.

go after (someone)

- to try to catch someone
  The police decided to go after the cars that were speeding near the school.

go after (something)

- to attempt to get something, to strive for something
  Our team will go after the championship again this year.

go against the grain

- to go against the natural direction or inclination of something

The man's unfriendly attitude goes against the grain of the usually friendly company.

go away empty-handed

- to depart with nothing

  The boy went away empty-handed after he asked his father for more money.

go back on one's word

- to break one's promise

  My supervisor went back on his word when he refused to give me a day off.

go bad

- to become rotten/bad

  The apples will go bad if they are not eaten soon.

go bananas

- to go crazy or become silly, to become angry

  The father went bananas after he discovered that his son had taken the family car.

go begging

- to be unwanted or unused

  Much food went begging when fewer people than expected came to the dinner.

go broke

- to lose all of one's money

  The company went broke and many people lost their jobs.

go by the book

- to follow the rules exactly

  Most police officers go by the book when they arrest a criminal.

go cold turkey

- to stop doing something (usually a bad habit) suddenly

  I decided to go cold turkey and quit smoking.

go for (something)

- to try to get something, to desire something

  I have decided to go for the new job at the computer centre.

go from bad to worse

- to get worse, to deteriorate

Things are going from bad to worse in our company.

go-getter

- an ambitious person who works hard to become successful
  My friend is a go-getter. He works hard and is very successful.

go in for (something)

- to choose something as one's particular interest, to occupy oneself with something
  My friend is going to university and will go in for medicine.
  Many of the students are going in for water sports recently.

go in one ear and out the other

- to hear something but then quickly forget it
  Everything that the teacher says goes in one ear and out the other for my friend.

go into detail

- to present and discuss the details of something
  The lawyer refused to go into detail about his client's problems.

go into effect

- to become effective (a law or a rule), to start to function
  The new parking regulations will go into effect next week.

go into hiding

- to conceal oneself in a hiding place for a period of time
  The bank robbers went into hiding after the bank robbery.

go into hock

- to go into debt
  I do not want to go into hock in order to buy a new stereo system.

go on a rampage

- to rush around destroying things
  The football fans went on a rampage and destroyed many things.

go on and on

- to continue for a long time
  My friend went on and on with his speech until finally I fell asleep.

go one's own way

- to go or act the way one wants
  My friend plans to go his own way and start his own business next year.

go out for (something)

- to try something (usually a sport)
  My friend is going out for rugby this summer.

go out of fashion/style

- to become unfashionable
  Striped pants have recently gone out of fashion.

go out of one's way

- to make an extra effort
  My aunt went out of her way to help me when I visited her.

go out the window

- to be abandoned, to go out of effect
  The school dress code went out the window when the new principal arrived.

go out (with someone)

- to date someone
  The girl wants to go out with the boy in her history class.

go over like a lead balloon

- to fail, to do badly
  My idea for shorter working hours went over like a lead balloon at the meeting.

go sky-high

- to reach a very high price/level
  The price of gasoline has gone sky-high recently.

go so far as to say (something)

- to put something into words
  The company president went so far as to say that he may be leaving very soon.

go (someone) one better

- to do something better than someone else, to do more than someone
  I decided to go my friend one better and I bought a more expensive present for my girlfriend.

go stag

- to go to an event by oneself (without a date - usually used for men)
  I decided to go stag to the wedding.

go steady with (someone)

- to date the same person all the time (usually used for teenagers)
  My sister has been going steady with her boyfriend for two years.

go stir-crazy

- to become anxious because one is confined to a small space
  After many days of rain I began to go stir-crazy because I could not leave the house.

go straight

- to become an honest person, to lead an honest life
  The man was in prison for two years but now he wants to go straight.

go the distance

- to do the whole amount, to finish something
  I was able to go the distance and finish my project without any help.

go the extra mile

- to do more than one is required to do to reach a goal
  I always try to go the extra mile and help my friends when they need help.

go the limit

- to do as much as possible
  I plan to go the limit and try to get the job.

go through

- to be approved, to pass, to be agreed upon
  The new law will probably go through next week.

go to pieces

- to lose one's self-control
  The woman went to pieces when she learned about her father's death.

go to pot

- to deteriorate
  The business has gone to pot since the new manager came.

go to rack and ruin

- to reach a very bad state of repair
  The building has gone to rack and ruin since the new owners bought it.

go to (someone's) head

- to make someone too proud
  The girl won the beauty contest and now it has gone to her head.

go to the expense (of doing something)

- to pay the cost of doing something
  We had to go to the expense of buying a new tent for camping.

go to the trouble (of doing something)

- to make an extra effort to do something
  My aunt went to the trouble of buying a new sofa bed for her guests.

go to town

- to work fast or hard, to do something with much energy
  We went to town last night and finished painting the bedroom.

go to waste

- to be wasted, to be unused
  I did not want the extra food to go to waste so I invited my friend to visit.

go with (something)

- to choose one thing rather than another
  We decided to go with the small rental car rather than the large one.

go with the flow

- to proceed in an easy manner with what others are doing
  I usually go with the flow and never disagree with my friends.

go without (something)

- to manage to survive or do well without something
  We had to go without water for two days in our apartment.

go without saying

- to be so easy to understand that it does not have to be mentioned
  The man is a hard worker so it goes without saying that his boss is very happy with him.

go wrong

- to fail
  Things began to go wrong as soon as our camping trip began.

goes to show

- something serves to prove a point
  His success goes to show that hard work will lead to success.

(have something) going for you

- to be or have something as an advantage
  The woman should do very well as she has many things going for her.

going rate

- the current rate
  The going rate for carpenters is very high and it will cost much money to build the house.

gold mine of information

- someone or something that is full of information
  The woman is a gold mine of information and she is very valuable to her company.

golden opportunity

- an excellent and rare opportunity
  The hot weather was a golden opportunity for the ice cream seller to make money.

gone but not forgotten

- to be gone/dead but still remembered
  Our grandfather is gone but not forgotten.

grace (someone or something) with one's presence

- to honour someone or something by being present
  The Queen graced the opening of the hospital with her presence.

grain of truth

- the smallest amount of truth
  There was not a grain of truth in what the man said.

grasp at straws

- to try something with little hope of success
  The man is grasping at straws with his weak excuse for his bad behaviour.

grass is always greener on the other side (of the fence)

- a place or situation that is far away or different seems better than one's present situation
  My cousin is always changing jobs because she thinks that the grass is always greener on the other side.

grate on (someone's) nerves

- to annoy/bother someone
  The woman's singing is beginning to grate on my nerves.

gravy train

- a job that gives one much money compared with what you do
  The cleaning contract was a gravy train. We worked for 3 hours but we got paid for 8 hours.

gray area

- something difficult to define or put into a particular category, something that is not clear
  Some of the legal issues were in a gray area.

grease (someone's) palm

- to pay money to someone for some special favour
  We had to grease the border guard's palm in order to enter the country.

greasy spoon

- a small and cheap eating place with basic but not great food
  We went to a greasy spoon for breakfast because the other restaurants were closed.

a great deal of (something)

- much or a lot of something
  There was a great deal of water in our house after the flood.

greatest thing since sliced bread

- the best thing that there ever was
  The new digital camera is the greatest thing since sliced bread.

green

- to be inexperienced or immature
  The new employee is green and does not know his job very well.

a green thumb

- the skill to make plants grow
  The man has a green thumb and has a very beautiful garden.

green with envy

- to be very jealous, to be full of envy
  The little girl was green with envy when she saw her friend's new bicycle.

grin and bear it

- to endure something unpleasant with good humour
  I have to grin and bear it when my supervisor becomes angry with me.

grind to a halt

- to slow down and stop (like a machine when it is turned off)
  The city ground to a halt when the electric power was off for five hours.

grist for the mill

- something that can be used for one's advantage
  The information was grist for the mill of the salesman.

grit one's teeth

- to grind one's teeth together in anger and determination and reluctance
  I grit my teeth and phoned my father to ask if I could borrow some money.

had best (do something)

- should do something, ought to do something
  I had best go home soon as I want to get up early tomorrow morning.

had better (do something)

- should do something, ought to do something
  I had better go now or I will be late for class.

hail from (somewhere)

- originally come from somewhere
  My father hails from a small farming community.

the hair of the dog that bit you

- a drink of alcohol taken when one is recovering from drinking too much
  My friend got up early and had the hair of the dog that bit him to start the day.

(one's) hair stands on end

- become frightened or afraid of something
  My hair stood on end when I saw the scene after the automobile accident.

(to be) hale and hearty

- to be in very good health, to be well and strong
  My uncle is a hale and hearty fellow who never gets sick.

half-baked

- an idea or plan that is not thought about carefully or not studied carefully
  I do not like my supervisor's half-baked idea about the new delivery system.

(to be) half the battle

- to be a large part of the work
  Writing the letters will be half the battle. We can finish the rest of the work next week.

(to be) halfhearted about (someone or something)

- (to be) unenthusiastic about someone or something
  I was halfhearted about joining the group to go hiking.

ham it up

- do something silly or try to exaggerate something in a funny way
  I was hamming it up with my friend in front of the principal's office.

hammer away at (someone or something)

- be persistent in trying to do something
  I worked all weekend to hammer away at my final essay for university.

hammer out (something)

- work something out by discussion and debate
  The union and managers were able to hammer out an agreement before midnight last night.

hammer (something) home

- try hard to make someone understand something
  The speaker tried to hammer home the importance of treating the customers with respect.

hand down a decision

- announce a legal decision
  The judge handed down his decision early in the afternoon.

hand down (something)

- arrange to give something to someone after your death
  My grandmother handed down her silver jewellery to my mother.

hand in (something)

- give something to someone, hand something to someone
  I went to the company early to hand in my job application.

(work) hand in glove with (someone)

- (work) very close to someone
  The supervisor and manager work hand in glove to create a good atmosphere in the company.

be hand in hand

- be holding hands
  I walked to the movie hand in hand with my girlfriend.

to hand it to (someone)

- to give credit or praise to someone
  You have to hand it to our manager for working hard and being successful with his business.

the handwriting is on the wall

- a sign that something bad or significant will happen
  The handwriting is on the wall. Business conditions are bad so nobody will get a pay raise this year.

handy

- can easily fix things
  He is very handy around the house and is always fixing or building something.

hang a left

- turn to the left
  We drove to the end of the block and hung a left there.

hang a right

- turn to the right
  We decided to hang a right when we came to the main street.

hang around

- pass time or stay someplace without any real purpose or aim
  We decided to stay home and hang around rather than go to the game.

hang back

- stay some distance behind or away, hesitate or be unwilling to do something
  He lacks self-confidence and always hangs back when his boss asks for volunteers.

hang on

- wait, continue listening on the telephone
  "Hang on for a minute while I go and get some paper and a pen."

hang on (someone's) every word

- listen with complete attention to everything someone says
  The audience hung on every word of the speaker.

hang on to (something)

- hold tightly, keep firmly
  "Please hang on to your hats or the strong wind will blow them off."

hang one on

- get very drunk
  He hung one on last night after he heard about his promotion.

hang one's hat (somewhere)

- live or take up residence somewhere
  I want to move and hang my hat in a small town somewhere.

hang out one's shingle

- notify the public of the opening of an office - especially an office of a doctor, lawyer or other professional
  He has decided to hang out his shingle now that he has graduated from law school.

hang out (somewhere/with someone)

- spend one's time with no great purpose, spend leisure time with friends
  Recently my friend has been hanging out with a group of people who are not a good influence on him.

hang (someone) in effigy

- hang a dummy of a hated person
  The demonstrators hung the dishonest politician in effigy.

hang tough

- stick to one's position
  I decided to hang tough and stop negotiating with the lawyer.

hang up (something)

- place something on a hook/peg/hangar

Everyone was forced to hang up their jackets before they entered the room.

hang up (the telephone)

- place a telephone receiver back on the telephone and end the call
  After I hung up the telephone I left home to go to work.

a hard sell

- an attitude where you pressure someone to buy something
  The car dealer gave me a hard sell on the new car so I went to another dealer.

be hard up

- be short of money
  I am hard up for money at the moment so I can't go to the movie.

harken back to (something)

- have started out as something
  The new building harkens back to a style that appeared over 100 years ago.

to harp on (something)

- to talk repeatedly and tediously about something
  He has been harping on his lack of money for several weeks now.

hash (something) over

- discuss something in great detail
  We stayed after school to hash over the new contract.

a hassle

- a bothersome thing
  It is a hassle to have to report to my boss two times a day.

a hatchet man

- a politician whose job it is to say negative things about the opposition, a person in a company who must fire extra workers or cut other expenses
  He is acting as a hatchet man for the leader but I don't think that he really believes what he is saying.

hate (someone's) guts

- feel very strong dislike for someone
  I absolutely hate the apartment manager's guts after she caused me so many problems.

have a blowout

- one's car tire bursts
  Our car had a blowout on the road up the mountain.

have a bone to pick with (someone)

- have a disagreement to discuss with someone
  I have a bone to pick with my boss because of his criticism of me.

have a brush with (the law or something)

- have a brief experience with the law or something
  I had a brush with the law when my car was stopped for speeding.

have a case (against someone)

- have much evidence that can be used against someone
  The police have a very good case against the man who is selling the stolen cars.

have a change of heart

- change one's attitude or decision (usually from negative to positive)
  I had a change of heart and will let my friend use my car tomorrow.

have a chip on one's shoulder

- seem to want to start a conflict
  Our neighbour has a chip on his shoulder and is always trying to start a fight.

have a clear conscience

- be free of guilt
  I have a clear conscience and am not worried that I did anything wrong.

have a close call/shave

- almost be involved in an accident or something similar
  I had a close call this morning when I was almost hit by a car.

(not) have a clue (about something)

- (not) know anything about something
  I do not have a clue who took the laptop computer.

have a head for (something)

- have the mental capacity for something
  My father has a head for numbers and is very good at mathematics.

have a (good) head on one's shoulders

- be smart or sensible
  That new salesman really has a head on his shoulders.

have a heart

- be generous and forgiving
  The woman doesn't have a heart and everybody dislikes her.

have a heart of gold

- be generous/sincere/friendly
  The woman has a heart of gold and is always willing to help her friends.

have a heart of stone

- be cold and unfriendly
  The man has a heart of stone and he will never help anybody.

have a heart-to-heart talk (with someone)

- have a sincere and intimate talk with someone
  I had a heart-to-heart talk with my sister about my girlfriend.

have a hold on (someone)

- have a strong and secure influence on someone
  The coach has a very strong hold on the members of the team.

have a/the right to do something

- have the freedom to do something
  The apartment manager does not have the right to tell the tenants when they must leave the building.

have a rough time (of it)

- experience a difficult period
  My friend had a rough time of it when he was forced to leave his job.

have an ax to grind (with someone)

- have something to complain about

  My co-worker has an ax to grind with our boss and is always complaining.

have an ear for (something)

- have the ability to learn music or languages

  My cousin has an ear for music and is a very good musician.

have an itch to do something

- have a desire to do something

  I have an itch to go fishing this summer.

have an out

- have an excuse

  The teacher asked me to do my presentation tomorrow but I have an out and don't have to do it. I will go to the doctor tomorrow

(not) have anything to do with someone

- (not) want to be a friend/work/do business with someone

  My father will not have anything to do with the salesman because he sold him the faulty car.

have arrived

- reach a position of power/authority/prominence

  The manager thought that she had arrived when she was given a beautiful corner office.

have bearing on (something)

- affect or influence something

  The company decision had much bearing on the way that the company was managed.

have been around

- have been to many places and done many things, be experienced

  My brother has been around and has been overseas many times.

idiot box

- television set

  My friend sits in front of the idiot box all day and never gets any work done.

if looks could kill

- used when someone makes an unfriendly look or frowns at someone
  If looks could kill then the horrible way that the woman looked at me would have killed me instantly.

if so

- if that is the case
  The lawyer said that he wants to meet us this afternoon but if so then we will not have any documents ready to discuss.

if the shoe fits, wear it

- if something that is said describes you then it probably is meant for you as well
  He was complaining that many workers at his company were lazy. However, his friend looked at him and said that if the shoe fits, wear it.

if worst comes to worst

- if the worst possible thing happens
  If worst comes to worst we can cancel our holiday and go next year.

ill at ease

- nervous/uncomfortable
  He appeared to be ill at ease during the interview.

ill-disposed to (do something)

- not friendly or favorable to something
  Our company. is ill-disposed to begin working on the project with the other company.

ill-gotten gains

- money or other goods acquired illegally or dishonestly
  The man used his ill-gotten gains from the sale of the stolen car to go on a holiday.

ill will

- hostile feelings or intentions
  There is much ill will between the two departments in our company.

implicate (someone) in (something)

- suggest that someone is involved in something

The man was implicated in the scheme to sell the illegal shares in the company.

in a flash

- quickly

  I was finished with the job interview in a flash.

in a fog (haze)

- confused, not sure what is happening

  He is always in a fog and never seems to know what is going on.

in a fool's paradise

- seem to be happy but in a situation that will not last

  The couple were living in a fool's paradise with their temporary jobs and the high salaries.

in a hole

- in some trouble, in an embarrassing or difficult position

  He is really in a hole now that he has problems both at work and at home.

in a huff

- in an angry or offended manner

  The head of our department left the meeting in a huff.

in a hurry

- moving or acting quickly

  He is very busy and always in a hurry.

in a jam

- in trouble, in a difficult situation

  He is in a jam now that his car is not working properly.

in a jiffy

- very fast, very soon

  I promised that I would be finished with the phone in a jiffy.

in a spot

- in some trouble, in an embarrassing or difficult position

  She is in a spot right now as she was unable to enter university and also has no job.

in a stew (about someone or something)

- upset or bothered about someone or something
  The woman's husband is in a stew because he lost his car keys.

in a stupor

- in a dazed condition
  I was in a stupor after I wrote my last exam.

in a tight spot

- in a difficult situation
  The man was in a tight spot after he lost his job.

in a tizzy

- in an excited and confused condition
  The girl was in a tizzy all morning as she got ready for her friend's wedding.

in a way

- to a certain extent, a little, somewhat
  In a way I want to go to the restaurant but basically I don't care.

in a word

- briefly, to sum up
  In a word, the problem with the car is that it needs a new motor.

in and of itself

- considering one thing alone
  In and of itself there is no problem having a large number of people at the dinner. However, the fire regulations do not allow so many people to be in the building

in and out

- coming in and going out often
  He has been in and out all day but I don't know where he is at the moment.

in any case/event

- no matter what happens, surely, without fail
  I may not be able to meet you next week but in any case I will still give you the books before then.

in arms

- armed, angry and ready to fight

The workers are in arms since they found out about the wage decrease.

in arrears

- overdue (bills or money), late

  I have never been in arrears with my bill payments.

in awe of (someone or something)

- fearful and respectful of someone or something

  All of the children were in awe of the firemen who came to visit the school.

in bad faith

- with bad or dishonest intent

  The man was bargaining in bad faith when he tried to buy the car.

in bad/poor taste

- rude, vulgar

  The jokes that the man told at the dinner were in very bad taste.

in between

- located in the middle of two things/states

  My friend is in between jobs at the moment.

in black and white

- in writing

  I want to get the information in black and white before I go to the meeting.

in bloom/blossom

- a flower/tree at the peak of blooming

  All of the flowers are in bloom in our garden now.

in brief

- briefly

  I explained in brief what the new supervisor was supposed to do while I was on vacation.

in broad daylight

- publicly visible in the daytime

  The robbery of the store took place in broad daylight.

in custody of (someone or something)

- being looked after by someone or something, under guard by someone

The child was placed in custody of the state while her mother got treatment for her substance abuse problem.

in debt

- owing money
  The man has been in debt for most of his life.

in deep

- seriously mixed up in something like debt or trouble
  The man is in deep because of debt and other problems.

in deep water

- in a serious situation, in trouble
  The boy is in deep water because of his problems at school.

a jack-of-all-trades

- a person who can do many things
  We gave the man a job because we needed a jack-of-all-trades to look after the many repairs.

jack up (something)

- raise prices, raise something with a lifting device
  The gas station jacked up their prices during the snow storm.
  We jacked up the car so we could change the tire.

jam on the brakes

- quickly put the brakes on in a car to stop
  He jammed on the brakes and was able to avoid hitting the child.

jam-packed

- crowded, full
  The train that we took this morning was jam-packed with people.

join hands

- hold hands with other people
  Everybody in the group joined hands at the end of the meeting.

Join the club!

- an expression used when the other person is in the same situation (usually bad) as the speaker

"Join the club. None of us have enough money to go on a holiday."

join the fray

- join a fight or argument

  I did not want to join the fray and argue with the other members of the group.

judging by (something)

- considering something

  Judging by the weather, I don't think that we will be able to go to the festival today.

jump all over (someone)

- criticize/scold/blame someone

  As soon as I began to talk about my plans for the summer my boss jumped all over me.

jump at (something)

- seize the opportunity to do something

  He jumped at the chance to go to France on company business.

jump bail

- run away and fail to come to trial and therefore give up the money that you have already paid to the court

  The man jumped bail and went to live in a foreign country.

kangaroo court

- an illegal court formed by a group of people to settle a dispute among themselves

  The men were convicted by a kangaroo court in the town and nobody agreed with the decision.

Katie bar the door

- get ready for trouble, a desperate situation is at hand

  The gang arrived at the hotel and were ready to come in and fight. "Katie bar the door."

keel over

- fall over and faint

  Three of the members of the band keeled over because of the heat.

keel over

- turn upside down, tip over
  The boat keeled over in the middle of the lake but everybody was safe.

keen on (someone or something)

- be enthusiastic about someone or something
  My girlfriend is keen on going to a movie this weekend.

keep a civil tongue

- speak decently and politely
  The angry customer was asked to keep a civil tongue when talking with the sales clerk.

keep a close watch on (someone or something)

- monitor or observe someone or something
  The woman always keeps a close watch on her child when she is at the shopping centre.

keep a close watch over (someone or something)

- guard or care for someone or something
  I kept a close watch over the soup as it was cooking.

keep a secret

- to not tell a secret to others
  I have been trying to keep a secret about my friend's boyfriend for a long time now.

keep a stiff upper lip

- be brave, face trouble bravely
  The storm victims tried hard to keep a stiff upper lip in spite of the hardships of their situation.

keep body and soul together

- keep alive, survive
  It was very cold during the winter but somehow she was able to keep body and soul together and survived.

keep books

- keep records of money gained and spent, do the work of a bookkeeper
  My first job was to keep books for a small company in my hometown.

keep harping on (something)

- continue to talk or complain about something
  The boy's father keeps harping on the fact that his son never does his homework.

keep house

- look after a house or a household
  She has been keeping house for her father while he is sick.

keep on (doing something)

- continue
  She is careless and keeps on making the same mistakes over and over.

keep on an even keel

- remain cool and calm
  I was very busy with my job and school but I tried very hard to keep on an even keel and get everything done.

keep on one's toes

- stay alert and watchful
  I try to keep on my toes during a class where the teacher may ask me a question.

keep one's chin up

- be brave, be determined
  "Try and keep your chin up. Things will get better in the future."

keep one's cool

- to stay/remain calm
  I tried to keep my cool during the argument with my neighbour.

a labour of love

- something done for personal pleasure and not for money
  The man's book is a labour of love and he doesn't expect to make any money from it.

lace into (someone)

- attack or scold someone
  The mother laced into her child when he came home late from the movie.

lace into (something)

- devour/eat food

  We laced into our dinner as soon as we entered the house.

lady killer

- a man who some women find very charming and attractive

  The man in the movie was a lady killer who broke the hearts of many women.

lady's man

- a man who is popular with women

  He is a lady's man and always seems to have a woman interested in him.

laid-back

- relaxed, not worried by things

  Our teacher has a very laid-back attitude about how long we should spend preparing for our class.

be laid up

- be confined to bed or unfit for work

  He has been laid up for a few days because of a cold.

a lame duck

- a public official who has a short time left to serve in office and therefore has less power than before

  He was a lame-duck leader so it was difficult for him to accomplish some things.

land of Nod

- sleep

  I entered the land of Nod as soon as my head hit the pillow.

land on one's feet/both feet

- come out of a bad situation successfully

  My friend always manages to land on his feet no matter how difficult the situation is.

lash out (at someone)

- attack someone with words

  They were walking along the beach when the girl suddenly lashed out in anger at her boyfriend.

lash out (at someone)

- suddenly try to hit someone
  The boy suddenly lashed out and hit the man who was sitting beside him.

last but not least

- in the last place but not the least important
  Last but not least the boy came up to the front of the class to receive his report card.

a last-ditch effort

- a final effort
  The government made a last-ditch effort to prevent a strike by the teachers.

the last person

- the most unlikely person to do something or to be seen somewhere
  My friend is the last person that you would expect to see in a clothing store buying clothes.

the last straw

- the last insult or mistake that one can endure and which then causes some reaction
  The fourth time that the girl came to work late was the last straw and we finally fired her.

last will and testament

- one's will (especially its latest version)
  After my grandfather's funeral my uncle read out his last will and testament.

the last word

- the last remark in an argument, the final say in deciding something
  She always expects to have the last word when she and her husband go shopping together.

late in life

- when one is older
  Some very great painters never started painting until rather late in life.

lay down the law

- tell someone what to do by using your power or influence

The new manager plans to lay down the law to the workers regarding long lunch breaks.

lay eyes on (someone or something)

- see someone or something

  I have never laid eyes on a more beautiful dog in my life.

lay hold of (something)

- get possession of something

  If I can lay hold of some tools I will help you fix your toilet.

lay in (something)

- store up a supply of something, get and store something for future use

  They are trying to lay in as much food as possible before winter comes.

mad as a hatter

- crazy

  My neighbour is mad as a hatter and we never know what she will do next.

mad as a hornet

- very angry

  Our boss was mad as a hornet when we saw him at the meeting yesterday.

made for each other

- two people are very well suited romantically

  The young couple are made for each other and seem to be very happy.

made to measure

- made especially to fit the measurements of someone

  When I was working in Hong Kong I purchased several suits that were made to measure.

made to order

- put together on request

  My father decided to buy a new computer desk that was made to order.

maiden voyage

- the first voyage of a ship or boat

The maiden voyage of the new cruise ship was popular with many people.

the main drag

- the most important street in a town
  We spent Saturday evening driving up and down the main drag of the town.

make a bed

- arrange the sheets and blankets of a bed neatly
  My mother always told me to make my bed when I was a child.

make a beeline for (someone or something)

- hurry directly toward someone or something
  When I enter the cafeteria I always make a beeline for the dessert section.

make a big deal about (something)

- exaggerate the seriousness of something
  I wish that my friend would not make a big deal about every small problem.

make a break for (something/somewhere)

- move or run quickly to something or somewhere
  The audience made a break for the doors as soon as the concert was over.

make a bundle/pile

- make a lot of money
  My father made a bundle on the stock market several years ago.

make a check out (to someone)

- write a check to give to someone with their name on it
  I made a check out to the animal hospital after they cared for our dog.

make a clean breast of (something)

- confess something bad that you have done in order not to feel guilty/bad
  The woman made a clean breast of things and worked hard to start over.

make a long story short

- bring a story to an end by omitting some details

I had to make a long story short in order to finish my story and leave to catch my train home.

make a meal of (something)

- eat one main dish/food as an entire meal

  We were able to make a meal of the chicken that my mother gave us last night.

make a mistake

- make an error

  I made a mistake on the math test.

make a mountain out of a molehill

- make a big problem out of a small problem

  He is making a mountain out of a molehill by worrying about his son's problem.

make a name for oneself

- become well-known or famous

  He has made a name for himself in the field of computers.

make a night/evening of (doing something)

- do something for the entire night/evening

  We decided to stay home and make a night of playing cards.

make a note of (something)

- to write something on a piece of paper

  I made a note of the people that I was going to phone on the weekend.

naked eye

- the human eye (with no binoculars etc.)

  It was difficult to see the bird with the naked eye.

one's name is mud

- a person's reputation is bad

  His name is mud now that he has been charged by the police with stealing money from his company.

the name of the game

- the main part of a matter

  The name of the game is selling cars and not worrying about other things.

name (someone) after (someone or something)

- to give someone the name of another person/place/thing
  My cousin was named after his mother's grandfather.

a narrow escape

- an escape with little chance of error
  He had a narrow escape when he almost fell from his bicycle.

near at hand

- to be close or handy (to someone)
  I looked for a pair of scissors that were near at hand.

neck and neck

- to be equal or nearly equal in a race or contest
  The two teams were neck and neck in the race to win the national championship.

neck of the woods

- an area or part of the country
  He has never been to my neck of the woods since he was a child.

need (something) like (one needs) a hole in the head

- to not need something at all
  My friend needs a new computer like he needs a hole in the head.

need (something) yesterday

- to need something in a very big hurry
  I need a new computer yesterday.

a needle in a haystack

- something that is very hard to find
  Looking for the lost receipt among the thousands of other receipts was like looking for a needle in a haystack.

neither fish nor fowl

- something that does not belong to a definite group
  The man's opinions were neither fish nor fowl and nobody could put them into an identifiable category.

occur to (someone)

- to come into someone's mind (an idea or thought)
  It occurred to me that I will not be able to meet my friend on Saturday because I have to go to the airport to meet someone else.

ocean(s) of (something)

- a very large amount of something
  There was oceans of food at the party.

odd man out

- an unusual person or thing
  I always feel that I am the odd man out when I go with my coworkers to a restaurant.

(the) odd (something)

- an extra or spare something, one or two of something
  We saw the odd interesting bird on our hike through the mountains.

an oddball

- a person who does not act like other people
  The man is an oddball and nobody at his company likes to work with him.

odds and ends

- a variety of small items (sometimes remnants of something)
  We made games for the children from odds and ends that we found around the house.

an odor of sanctity

- an atmosphere of excessive holiness or piety
  There was an odor of sanctity surrounding the chambers of the judge at the courthouse.

of age

- to be old enough to be allowed to do something (vote,drink etc.)
  When my cousin came of age we had a big party for him to celebrate.

of age

- to be fully developed, to be mature

Rapid transportation came of age when the first jets were built.

of all the nerve

- How shocking!
  Of all the nerve for my friend to ask me for more money when she never repaid me what she had already borrowed.

of all things

- Imagine that!
  "Of all things," the woman said when the post office worker told her that her package was too large for delivery.

of benefit to (someone)

- to be good for someone, to be a benefit to someone
  Another meeting to solve the problem would be of no benefit to myself so I decided not to attend.

of course

- certainly, definitely, naturally
  "Of course you can use my car if you want to."

of interest (to someone)

- to be interesting to someone
  The man who works at the gas station is of interest to the police in their investigation of the murder.

of late

- lately
  Of late there has been almost no rain in our city.

of no avail

- with no effect, unsuccessful
  My complaints to the company were of no avail and nothing was done.

of one's own accord/free will

- by one's own choice
  The supervisor decided to leave her job of her own free will and was not fired.

of the old school

- to have attitudes from the past which are no longer popular

Our teacher's attitudes are of the old school and are not often found these days.

off and on

- occasionally

  My friend has been seeing a woman off and on but I do not think that their relationship is very serious.

off and running

- to be started up and already going

  The candidates are off and running in the race to become mayor of the city.

off balance

- to be not prepared for something, to be unable to meet the unexpected

  I was off balance when my boss asked me to deliver the speech instead of him.

off base

- to be inaccurate/wrong

  He was off base with his estimate of next year's budget.

off campus

- to be not on the grounds of a college or university

  The used bookstore was off campus but it was very popular with the university students.

off-centre

- to be not exactly in the centre or middle of something

  The picture was off-centre and did not look good on the wall.

the off chance

- a slight possibility

  I went to the department store on the off chance that I would find a new jacket that I liked.

off-colour

- to be in bad taste, to be not polite, to be not the exact colour

  He likes to tell off-colour jokes which most people do not like.

  We painted the walls an off-colour of white.

off duty

- to be not working
  The police officer was off duty when he saw the bank robbery.

off guard

- to be not alert to the unexpected
  It caught me off guard when my friend suddenly asked me to lend her some money.

off like a shot

- to go away quickly
  The children were off like a shot when the school bell rang.

off limits

- to be forbidden
  The factory was off limits to everybody except the workers who worked there.

off one's back

- to be not bothering someone
  I wish my father would get off my back and stop asking me when I am going to look for a job.

off one's chest

- to talk about a problem to someone so that it does not bother you anymore
  I talked to my friend and I was able to get some of my problems off my chest.

off one's hands

- to no longer be in one's care or possession
  I sold my old computer and got it off my hands.

off one's high horse

- to be not acting proud and scornful, to be not acting like you are better than others
  We got our boss off his high horse when he admitted that he had made many mistakes with the new product launch.

off one's rocker

- to be crazy
  He must be off his rocker if he thinks that he can spend much money and not have financial problems.

pack a punch/wallop

- to provide a burst of energy/power/excitement
  The storm packed a wallop and did much damage to the coast.

a pack of lies

- a series of lies
  Everything that the man said was a pack of lies and nobody believed him.

pack them in

- to attract a lot of people
  The new restaurant is able to pack them in with its new and exciting menu.

packed in like sardines

- to be packed very tightly
  The commuters on the train were packed in like sardines during the morning rush hour.

pad the bill

- to add false expenses to a bill
  The salesman always pads the bill when he goes on a business trip.

paddle one's own canoe

- to do something by oneself
  I was forced to paddle my own canoe when the rest of the staff went away for a seminar.

a pain in the neck/ass

- an annoying/bothersome thing or person
  Dealing with my neighbour is always a pain in the neck.

paint oneself into a corner

- to get into a bad situation that is difficult or impossible to get out of
  My friend has painted himself into a corner now that he has begun to fight with his supervisor.

paint the town red

- to go out and party and have a good time
  We decided to go out and paint the town red after we passed our exams.

pal around (with someone)

- to be friends with someone
  I have begun to pal around with a friend from my evening language class.

pale around the gills

- to look sick
  My colleague was looking a little pale around the gills when he came to work today.

palm (something) off on (someone)

- to deceive someone by a trick or a lie, to sell or give something by tricking
  The man palmed off his old television set as one that was new and reliable.

pan out

- to end or finish favorably, to work out well
  "I hope that your plans to go back to school pan out."

paper over the cracks (in/of something)

- to try to hide faults or difficulties
  Our boss is trying to paper over the cracks in the office and will not deal with the problems of the staff.

par for the course

- to be just what was expected, to be nothing unusual
  That was par for the course. He always comes late when there is a lot of work to do.

paradise (on earth)

- a place on earth that is as lovely as paradise
  The resort in the mountains was paradise on earth.

part and parcel of (something)

- a necessary or important part of something
  The house that we bought is part and parcel of a much larger piece of property.

part company (with someone)

- to leave someone, to depart from someone
  The two business partners decided to part company and begin their own businesses.

partake of (something)

- to eat or drink something

I decided not to partake of the large dinner before the golf tournament.

partial to (someone or something)

- favoring or preferring someone or something
  Our boss is partial to the new person who recently began to work in our company.

the particulars of (something)

- the specific details about something
  I have no knowledge of the particulars of my father's business dealings.

parting of the ways

- a point at which people separate and go their own ways
  I had a parting of the ways with my closest friend from high school.

party line

- the official ideas of a group (usually political) that must be followed by all members
  The members of the political party were forced to follow the party line on most issues.

the party's over

- a happy or good time has come to an end
  The party's over and I must now begin to work after my long holiday.

pass away

- to die
  His father passed away when he was 96 years old.

pass for/as (someone or something)

- to succeed in being accepted as someone or something
  The young woman was trying to pass for a reporter when she went to the concert.

pass muster

- to pass a test or checkup, to measure up to a certain standard
  The player was not able to pass muster and was not included on the team.

pass off (something) as (something else)

- to sell or give something by false claims, to offer something as genuine when it is not

The man passed off the watch as a diamond watch and received more money than it was worth.

pass on

- to die

  My grandmother passed on when she was 92 years old.

pass on (something)

- to give away something that you don't use anymore

  The girl always passes on her old clothes to her younger sister.

pass oneself off as (someone or something) else

- to claim to be someone one is not, to pretend to be someone else

  My friend passed himself off as a reporter and was able to get into the concert free.

pass out

- to faint

  Three teenage girls passed out at the rock concert.

pass the buck

- to shift responsibility to someone else

  Our supervisor always tries to pass the buck if someone tries to criticize his work.

pass the hat

- to attempt to collect money for some project

  We passed the hat in order to raise money for the movie projector.

pass the time

- to fill up time by doing something

  My grandfather usually passes the time reading and working in his garden.

quake in one's boots

- to be afraid, to shake from fear

  I was quaking in my boots when my boss told me to come to his office.

queer as a three-dollar bill

- to be very strange

  The woman is the strangest person that I have ever seen and she is as queer as a three-dollar bill.

quick and dirty

- fast and cheap, fast and careless
  The method that the company chose to cut expenses was quick and dirty.

quick as a flash

- very quickly
  I was able to get out of the house as quick as a flash and go to work.

quick as a wink

- very quickly
  The woman turned around and quick as a wink her purse was stolen.

quick as geased lightning

- very quickly, very fast
  The cat climbed up the tree as quick as greased lightning.

quick on the draw

- to be quick to respond to something, to be quick to draw a gun and shoot
  The man is quick on the draw and can answer most questions immediately.

quick on the trigger

- to be quick to respond to something, to be quick to draw a gun and shoot
  The man was too quick on the trigger and should have thought more carefully about what he was going to say.

quick on the uptake

- to be quick to understand something
  The student is quick on the uptake and understands most scientific theories very quickly.

quiet as a mouse

- very quiet, shy and silent
  The little boy was quiet as a mouse as he moved around the kitchen.

quite a bit

- much or many
  I had quite a bit of time so I decided to go to the library.

quite a few

- many

  The boy has quite a few DVDs at home.

quite a lot

- much or many

  There are quite a lot of chairs in the meeting hall.

quite a number

- much or many

  Quite a number of the teachers agreed to use the new textbooks.

quite a (something)

- definitely something

  The girl is quite a pianist and everybody loves her.

quote a price

- to state in advance the charge for doing or supplying something

  I asked the moving company to quote a price to move our furniture.

a race against time

- a rush to beat a deadline

  It was a race against time to rescue the miners who were trapped in the mine.

rack one's brains

- to try hard to think or remember something

  I have been racking my brains all day trying to remember the man's name.

racked with pain

- to be suffering from severe pain

  The man was racked with pain after he fell from the ladder.

rail at (someone) about (something)

- to complain loudly to someone about something

  The customer was railing at the clerk about the bad service.

rain cats and dogs

- to rain very hard

  It has been raining cats and dogs all morning.

a rain check

- a free ticket to an event that replaces a ticket that was cancelled because of rain or for some other reason
  We received a rain check for the concert that was suddenly cancelled.

a rain check

- a promise to repeat an invitation at a later date
  I did not have time to go to the restaurant with my friend so I decided to take a rain check.

rain on (someone's) parade

- to spoil someone's plans
  I tried not to let my friend's bad mood rain on my parade during the concert.

rain or shine

- no matter whether it rains or the sun shines
  We plan to go to the beach tomorrow rain or shine.

rain (something) out

- to spoil something by raining
  The music festival was rained out yesterday evening.

raise a fuss

- to make trouble, to cause a disturbance
  The woman at the restaurant raised a fuss when her meal arrived late.

raise a hand against (someone or something)

- to hit or threaten to hit someone or something
  If the man raises a hand against his supervisor the police will be called.

raise a stink about (something)

- to make a major issue out of something
  The small business owners began to raise a stink about the new parking tax.

raise an objection to (someone or something)

- to object to someone or something
  My friend raised an objection about including my parents in our travel plans.

raise Cain

- to create a disturbance, to cause trouble

The boys began to raise Cain at the dance and were asked to leave.

raise eyebrows

- to cause surprise or disapproval
  It raised eyebrows when the actress appeared at the party with no invitation.

raise havoc with (someone or something)

- to create confusion or disruption for or against someone or something
  The bad weather raised havoc with our plans to clean up the area around our house.

raise hell with (someone or something)

- to make trouble, to behave wildly
  The woman began to raise hell with her supervisor after she heard about the new policy.

raise one's sights

- to set higher goals for oneself
  Our team is doing very well this year and we are now raising our sights on the city championship.

raise one's voice to (someone)

- to speak loudly or shout at someone in anger
  The teacher asked the child not to raise his voice.

to be raised in a barn

- to behave crudely like a barnyard animal
  When the boy did not shut the door his mother asked him if he had been raised in a barn.

rake in the money

- to make a lot of money
  My cousin's new pizza franchise has been raking in the money since it opened.

rake (someone) over the coals

- to scold/reprimand someone
  My boss raked me over the coals when he heard about the lost sales report.

rake (something) off

- to take money from something illegally
  The sales clerk was accused of raking money off of the daily cash sales.

rally around (someone or something)

- to come together to support someone or something
  Everybody in the small town began to rally around the mayor when he was accused of wrongdoing.

ram (something) down (someone's) throat

- to force someone to do or agree to something that is not wanted
  Our teacher always tries to ram her ideas down our throats which makes us angry.

ramble on about (someone or something)

- to talk aimlessly and endlessly about someone or something
  My friend spent the entire evening rambling on about his problems at work.

rank and file

- the members of a group and not the leaders, regular soldiers and not the officers
  The rank and file of the large union were happy with their new contract.

sack out

- to go to bed, to go to sleep
  I sacked out as soon as I arrived home last evening.

a sacred cow

- something that is never criticized or laughed at even if it sometimes deserves to be
  The medical insurance system is a sacred cow of the government and is never criticized by anyone.

sadder but wiser

- unhappy about something but having learned something from the experience
  The man was sadder but wiser after he learned that his wallet had been stolen.

saddle (someone) with (something)

- to give someone something undesirable or difficult to deal with
  I try not to saddle my friend with the problems that I am having at work.

safe and sound

- to be safe/whole/healthy
  We arrived at our destination safe and sound after a long journey.

to be on the safe side

- to take no chances
  It may rain so to be on the safe side I think that I will bring my umbrella.

safety in numbers

- to feel safe by being surrounded by a large number of people
  There was safety in numbers when the students went to complain to the principal about their new teacher.

sage advice

- very good and wise advice
  I waited for my friend to ask me for my sage advice regarding his problems.

sail into (someone)

- to scold or criticize someone very hard, to attack someone
  When I entered the office my supervisor sailed into me for being late.

sail right through (something)

- to finish something quickly and easily
  I was able to sail right through the material for my final exam.

sail under false colors

- to pretend to be something that one is not
  The politician was sailing under false colors when he appealed to the citizens for votes.

salt away money

- to save money
  My friend has salted away much money from her new job.

salt of the earth

- basic and fundamentally good people
  The members of our club are all the salt of the earth and are fun to spend time with.

same as (someone or something)

- to be identical to someone or something
  My sister is exactly the same as the girl who lives down the block.

Same here!

- Me too! I agree!
  "Same here," I replied when someone said that they were having problems with their Internet provider.

same old story

- something that occurs or has occurred in the same way before
  It is always the same old story with my friend. He borrows money but he never wants to pay it back.

same to you

- the same comment applies to you
  "The same to you," the boy said when his friend said that he was stupid.

sands of time

- the accumulated tiny amounts of time (like the sand in an hourglass)
  The sands of time have done much to change the woman's attitude toward her sister.

save face

- to preserve one's good reputation or dignity when something has happened to hurt it
  Our boss was very embarrassed when our company lost a lot of money. However, he was able to save face when he showed that the problems were outside of his control.

save one's breath

- to remain silent because talking will do no good
  You may as well save your breath and not talk to her as she will not believe you anyway.

save one's neck/skin

- to save oneself from danger or trouble
  The man left the scene of the fire as soon as possible in order to save his neck.

save (something) for a rainy day

- to reserve something/money for the future
  I always try to save some money for a rainy day when I get paid.

save the day

- to bring about victory or success (when defeat is likely)
  The player saved the day for his team when he played his best game of the season.

save up for (something)

- to save money in order to buy something
  My friend's brother is saving up for a new digital camera.

saved by the bell

- to be rescued from a difficult situation just in time by something that brings the situation to a sudden end
  I was saved by the bell and do not have to give my presentation until tomorrow.

saving grace

- something that saves someone or something that would otherwise be a total disaster
  The man's saving grace was his mathematical ability. His other personality traits were very strange.

say a mouthful

- to say something of great importance/meaning/length
  "You certainly said a mouthful," I said when my friend began to tell me about his complaint.

say grace

- to say a prayer of thanks before or after a meal
  The bride's father was asked to say grace before the wedding banquet.

say one's piece

- to say openly what one thinks
  I said my piece at the meeting and then left quietly by the back door.

say (something) in a roundabout way

- to say something indirectly
  I had to say what I wanted to say in a roundabout way in order to make my point.

say (something) to (someone's) face

- to say something (often unpleasant) directly to someone
  My supervisor always complains about me but she is afraid to say anything to my face.

say (something) under one's breath

- to say something so softly that almost nobody can hear it
  The woman said something under her breath but I could not understand it.

say the word

- to give a sign, to show a wish
  "Just say the word and I will come and meet you at the airport."

say uncle

- to surrender, to give in
  The little boy was forced to say uncle and agree to do what the older boy wanted.

scale (something) down

- to make something smaller by a certain amount or proportion
  The government decided to scale down their plans for the sports stadium.

scare (someone) out of his or her wits

- to frighten someone very much
  The dog scared the little boy out of his wits.

table a motion

- to postpone the discussion of something during a meeting
  We tabled a motion to discuss the safety issue at another time.

tag along with (someone)

- to go with someone, to follow along with someone
  The little boy tagged along with his older brother when they went to the beach.

tail between one's legs

- feeling ashamed or beaten
  The salesman resigned from his company with his tail between his legs after he told a lie about his expense account.

tail wagging the dog

- a situation where a small part controls the whole thing
  It is like the tail wagging the dog when the receptionist is able to control everything in the office.

take a backseat to (someone or something)

- to accept a poorer or lower position than someone, to be second to someone or something
  I had to take a backseat to my boss when we went on the business trip.

take a bath (on something)

- to come to financial ruin, to lose much money on something
  My aunt took a bath on the stock market last year and she is afraid to buy stocks now.

take a beating

- to lose money
  My father took a beating when he sold his car.

take a bow

- to bow and receive credit for a good performance
  The violinist stopped to take a bow before she went backstage with the orchestra.

take a break

- to have a short rest period in one's work
  I stopped to take a break after working all morning.

take a chance/risk

- to try something where failure or bad fortune is likely
  I plan to take a chance and visit my friend without phoning first.

take a course in (something)

- to enroll in a class to study/learn something
  I am planning to take a course in photography next year.

take a crack at (something)

- to try/attempt to do something
  "Have you decided to take a crack at writing the entrance examination?"

take a dig at (someone)

- to criticize someone, to say something that will irritate someone
  The man is always taking a dig at his wife.

take a dim view of (something)

- to be against something, to disapprove of something
  Our company takes a dim view of people who do not wear a suit and tie.

take a fancy/liking to (someone or something)

- to develop a fondness or a preference for someone or something
  The woman took a fancy to the new person who she was working with.

take a gander at (someone or something)

- to examine someone or something
  I asked the car mechanic to take a gander at the steering system on my car.

take a hand in (something)

- to help plan or do something
  The man is always ready to take a hand in any work that needs to be done.

take a hard line (with someone)

- to be firm with someone, to have a firm policy for dealing with someone
  The company takes a hard line with people who come to work late.

take a hint

- to understand what is hinted at and behave accordingly
  The man is unable to take a hint and does not notice when people are angry at him.

take a leaf out of (someone's) book

- to behave or do something in the way that someone else would

We plan to take a leaf out of our competitor's book and advertise our product on the Internet.

take a leak

- to urinate
  The man stopped at the side of the road to take a leak when he was walking home last night.

take a look at (someone or something)

- to examine (usually briefly) someone or something
  I will take a look at the problem with the computer tomorrow.

take a look for (someone or something)

- to look for someone or something
  Tomorrow I will take a look for the pen which I lost.

ugly duckling

- an ugly or plain child who grows up to be attractive
  She was an ugly duckling when she was a child but now she is very beautiful.

unaccustomed to (someone or something)

- not used to someone or something
  The man was unaccustomed to waking up early in the morning.

under a cloud

- depressed, sad
  She has been under a cloud of depression since her cat died.

under a cloud (of suspicion)

- not trusted, suspected of doing something wrong
  The politician has been under a cloud of suspicion over the possibility of taking bribes.

under arrest

- arrested by the police before being charged with a crime
  The three men were under arrest for robbing a bank.

under certain circumstances/conditions

- depending on or influenced by something
  Under certain circumstances the children were permitted to use the indoor stadium for practice.

under (close) scrutiny

- being watched or examined closely
  The business owner was under close scrutiny after the accounting scandal.

under construction

- being built or repaired
  The hotel was still under construction, two years after it began.

under control

- not out of control, manageable
  The fire was under control after the fire department arrived.

under cover

- hidden, concealed
  The police officer went under cover to look for the drug dealers.

under fire

- being shot at or attacked, under (verbal) attack
  The owner of the company is under fire for not paying his employees a fair salary.

under oath

- having taken an oath (solemn promise)
  The man was under oath when he spoke before the judge.

under one's belt

- in one's experience, memory or possession
  When he has more experience as a cook under his belt he will begin to look for a job.

under one's belt

- in one's stomach
  After he had a big breakfast under his belt he was ready for work.

under one's breath

- in a whisper, with a low voice
  He was talking under his breath in the movie theater and somebody complained.

under one's nose

- within sight of someone, easily seen or found

He found his driver's license right under his nose where he had left it.

under one's own steam

- by one's own efforts, without help
  He was able to go home under his own steam even though he was feeling very sick.

vanish into thin air

- disappear without leaving a trace
  The university student vanished into thin air and was never seen again.

variety is the spice of life

- life is made more interesting by doing new or different things
  My grandmother believed that variety is the spice of life and is always starting new projects.

vent one's spleen

- get rid of one's angry feelings
  I was able to vent my spleen at the manager of our apartment for the problems that she was causing.

verge on (something)

- come close or approach something
  The accident verged on becoming a major disaster but luckily it was not.

very last

- the end of something
  We were able to buy the very last tickets to the concert.

very thing

- the exact thing that is required
  The new sofa was the very thing that we needed to make our house comfortable.

very well

- agreed, all right
  "Very well, if you want me to go I will go with you."

vicious circle

- unbroken sequence of cause and effect with bad results

He had fallen into a vicious circle of drinking too much and then losing his job and then drinking even more.

vim and vigour

- energy and enthusiasm
  Our great aunt is always full of vim and vigour when we see her.

vote down

- defeat in a vote
  The proposal to extend the opening hours of nightclubs was voted down in the election.

vote of confidence

- a vote to see if a person or political party still has the majority's support
  The government received a vote of confidence when everyone supported their new proposal.

wade into

- attack, join in
  The football player waded into the fight to help his teammate.

wait-and-see attitude

- an uncertain attitude where you wait and see what will happen
  We decided to take a wait-and-see attitude regarding what our new boss was going to do.

wait on (someone) hand and foot

- serve someone in every possible way, do everything for someone
  He always waits on his wife hand and foot.

wait tables

- serve food (in a restaurant etc.)
  He spent the summer waiting tables at the resort.

wait up (for someone)

- not go to bed until someone arrives or something happens
  The woman always waits up for her daughter to come home.

wait with bated breath

- feel excited or anxious while waiting

I waited with bated breath for the results of my exams.

waiting in the wings

- ready to do something such as take over someone's job

  The vice-president was waiting in the wings to help the president.

wake the dead

- be very loud and able to wake even those who have died

  Our neighbors told us that our stereo was so loud that it would wake the dead.

walk a tightrope

- be in a situation where you must be very cautious

  The Prime Minister is walking a tightrope regarding the international trade deal.

walk all over (an opponent)

- win a game easily

  They walked all over the other team at the soccer tournament.

walk all over (someone)

- treat someone badly

  He tried to walk all over me when I began working but after I became used to the job he stopped.

walk away/off with (something)

- take and go away with something, steal

  Somebody walked away with the computer from the library last night.

walk of life

- social rank, occupation

  People from every walk of life came to the concert in the park.

walk on air

- feel happy and excited

  She has been walking on air since she heard that she passed her exams.

walk out

- go on strike

More than half of the workers at the factory decided to walk out on strike this morning.

walk out of (something)

- leave suddenly

  Three people walked out of the meeting yesterday.

walk the floor

- walk back and forth across the floor

  He spent the night walking the hospital floor while waiting for his wife to have a baby.

walk the plank

- be forced to resign from a job

  The vice-president was forced to walk the plank when the new president joined the company.

walk the plank

- be forced by pirates to walk a long plank from the ship out over the water to your death

  The pirates captured the small ship and forced the captain to walk the plank.

Chapter 4

English Usage: Misused Words

CONFUSED WORDS

Accept and **except**. While they both sound the same, *except* is a preposition that means "apart from", while *accept* is a verb that means "agree with", "take in" or "receive". Except is also rarely used as a verb, meaning to leave out.

Accept is a verb that means to "receive or take" or "to give a positive answer to a proposition or offer."

"Do you accept travelers' checks?" (receive, take)

Susan accepted his offer of a job. (gave a positive answer)

The club accepted three new members. (received)

Except as a preposition, meaning "with the exception of." (Commonly used)

"Everybody except John went to the party." (John didn't go)

Except as a verb means, "to exclude," "to keep out." (Rarely used)

The boys excepted Frank from their club.

(They did not accept him)

Expect is a verb that means, "waiting for sth to happen" or "believed to be the state of sth"

She expected her husband home from work at any minute.

"I expect you are hungry after such a long trip?"

accidently, slip, mistake

Accidently means to happen by chance: I ***accidently*** dropped the cup. ***Slip*** means to reveal something unintentionally; as in a ***slip*** of the tongue. ***Mistake*** means to err in identifying; misjudge; misevaluate; an error in opinion, judgement, or perception due to inadequate knowledge, carelessness or the like; an act done unintentionally. This text may contain ***mistakes***.

all right/alright

Although *alright* is widely used, it is considered nonstandard English. As the *American Heritage Dictionary* notes, it's not "all right to use alright."

all together/altogether

All together is applied to people or things that are being treated as a group. "We put the pots and pans all together on the shelf." *All together* is the form that must be used if the sentence can be reworded so that *all* and *together* are separated by other words: "We put all the pots and pans together on the shelf." *Altogether* is used to mean entirely: "I am altogether pleased to be receiving this award."

allusion/illusion

Allusion is a noun that means an indirect reference: "The speech made allusions to the final report." *Illusion* is a noun that means a misconception: "The policy is designed to give an illusion of reform."

alternately/alternatively

Alternately is an adverb that means in turn; one after the other: "We alternately spun the wheel in the game." *Alternatively* is an adverb that means on the other hand; one or the other: "You can choose a large bookcase or, alternatively, you can buy two small ones."

Acute and **chronic**. Acute means "sharp", as an acute illness is one that rapidly worsens and reaches a crisis. A chronic illness may also be a severe one, but it is long-lasting or lingering.

Affect and **effect**. The verb *affect* means "to influence something", and the noun *effect* (noun) means "the result of". *Effect* can also be a somewhat formal verb that means "to cause to be".

Advice/Advise (note spelling differences between British English and American English)

Advise is a verb.

The doctor advised her to quit smoking.

Advice is a noun.

She gave me some good advice.

adapt, adopt

Adapt means suited to the purpose, therefore, ***adapt*** means to make suitable: The movie, Gone With The Wind, was ***adapted*** from the novel by Margaret Mitchell. ***Adopt*** means to choose or to make one's own selection: Will the NFL ***adopt*** Canadian Football rules?

adverse, averse

Adverse means opposing: The ***adverse*** weather made driving hazardous. ***Averse*** means disinclined, not wanting to: She was ***averse*** to my suggestion.

advert, avert

Advert means refer: The teacher ***adverted*** to an earlier examination. ***Avert*** means to ward off: The Bank of Canada narrowly ***averted*** a run on the dollar.

aggravate, irritate

Aggravate means to make a bad situation worse: He***aggravated*** the situation by slamming the door. ***Irritate*** means to annoy: He ***irritated***the rash by rubbing it.

aid, aide

Aid means to assist and can be a verb: John will ***aid*** Bill with the newsletter.***Aid*** can also be a noun: The rich should give ***aid*** to the poor. ***Aide*** is always a noun and means an assistant: The Prime Minister's ***aide*** refused to answer any more questions.

aloud, allowed

Aloud means to vocalize: He read the poem ***aloud***. ***Allowed*** means to permit: He was ***allowed*** to go to the library.

all ready/already

All ready is an adjective phrase meaning "completely ready."'

We were all ready to leave at eight o'clock.

Already is an adverb of time meaning "by or before a specific time."

They had already left by three o'clock.

He had already eaten when I arrived. (before I arrived)

allusion, illusion, delusion

An ***allusion*** is an indirect reference to a statement by another (written or verbal): The reporter ***alluded*** to the mayor's speech. An ***illusion*** is something that appears to be real, but isn't: A magician's art is nothing more than***illusion*** because it is based on misdirection. A ***delusion*** is a false perception of self or others based on false beliefs: Jason though he was attractive to women, but it was only a ***delusion***.

altogether/all Together

Altogether is an adverb meaning "completely."

"I am altogether upset with you."

All together is an adjective phrase meaning "in a group."

The children sang a song all together.

Among/Between: Use among when referring to three or more people/things, but only use between when you are referring to two people/things.

- *The conversation was **between** Shane and Lisa.*
- *The manager will divide the work **among** the four employees.*

ambiguous, ambivalent

Ambiguous is a statement that can be misinterpreted because it is not clear: The politician was so ***ambiguous*** that no one new what he was promising to do. ***Ambivalent*** means to have mixed feelings about a person or an idea: Jayne's ***ambivalence*** over choosing what to order for lunch was annoying.

amend, emend

Amend means to alter for the better: The minutes were ***amended*** to show the correct number of members present. ***Emend*** means to remove errors from text: Philip spent hours ***emending*** the grammatical errors in his essay.

amiable, amicable

Amiable is used to describe people who are kind, friendly and gentle: The amiable, old man wrapped the sobbing child in his embrace. Amicable is used to describe peaceful settlements or arrangements between two parties: Management and strikers came to an amicable agreement over the contract.

among, between

Among is used in connection with more than two: His will divided his assets equally ***among*** all of his children. ***Between*** is used with two people or things: The candy was divided ***between*** Alice and Mary. **EXCEPTIONS**: If more than two are united in a situation, ***between*** is used: They ran fifty miles in one hour ***between*** the ten of them. If a comparison or opposition is involved, ***between*** is used: He could not choose ***between*** the grey suit or the black one. There are vast cultural differences ***between*** the ten Canadian provinces.

assure/ensure:

Assure means **to eliminate uncertainty, fear or something troubling a person.** Ensure should be used express a guarantee of an outcome.

- *The doctor **assured** the patient that nothing was wrong with her.*
- *A college degree does not **ensure** a job good after graduation, but it helps a lot.*

averse/adverse:

Averse means **opposed to.** Adverse means **bad or unfavorable,** such as the weather conditions.

- *I am **averse** to the death penalty.*
- *Classes were cancelled because of **adverse** weather conditions.*

admission/admittance

I went to the U.S. Consulate but was refused admittance.

No admission will be charged at the school concert.

There is no admittance into that country without a visa.

air/airs

There was air pollution near the factories.

I don't like people who put on airs.

There was an air of excitement when the match began.

allude/elude

To ***"allude"*** to something is to make an indirect reference to it. ***"Elude"*** means "to avoid" or "to escape."

The police report **alluded** to Jim's unusually strong sense of smell.

Harry **eluded** Snape, thanks to his invisibility cloak.

Daniel **alluded** to the Tollan's advanced technology.

Merry and Pippin **eluded** the Orcs for a while.

all right/alright

Traditionally, ***"all right"*** has been properly written as two words, and many people still think that that's the only correct way. "All right" is usually an adjective, and the two-word form fits with the adjectives "all ready" and "all together," as opposed to the adverbs "already" and "altogether." However, "alright" is used fairly frequently, and many dictionaries say that it's correct. Just be aware that if you use "alright," some of your readers will be grinding their teeth, correct or not.

Alone/Lonely

"Leave me alone", shouted John.

John felt lonely when he remained alone in the house.

alter/altar

An ***"altar"*** is a place or a table that's involved in religious rites. Any usage besides that should be ***"alter."***

Daniel was intrigued by the hieroglyphs at the base of the **altar**.

Qui-Gon needed to have his robes **altered**.

almost/most/mostly

She is the most intelligent student in the class.

The people in Hong-Kong are mostly Chinese.

Most of the students wish to have a rest after long hours of work.

anal/annals

"Anal" is an adjective that means "referring to the anus." Colloquially, it can also be shorthand for "anal-retentive" and mean "parsimonious, meticulous; stick-in-the-mud." ***"Annals"*** is a plural noun that means "a record of events arranged in a yearly sequence; chronicles." Annals is always plural.

Boromir had never had **anal** sex before.

The War of The Ring was recorded in the **annals** of Gondorian history.

Han thought Threepio was rather **anal**.

ante-/anti-

"Ante-" is a prefix meaning "before" or "front." ***"Anti-"*** is a prefix meaning "against" or "opposite."

Antebellum: before the war (esp. the U.S. Civil War)
Anteroom: a small room that leads into a larger room
Antediluvian: antiquated or old-fashioned
Antibiotic: a medicine that destroys micro-organisms
Antisocial: antagonistic or hostile to others
Antiquate: to make obsolete

as a whole/on the whole

Let us take the whole incident into consideration as a whole.

Jack is on the whole an industrious student.

assure/ensure/insure

The manager assures us that the recorder would be repaired properly.

The owner of the goldsmith wants to insure against robbery.

You must check your work carefully to ensure that you do not make any mistakes.

amount, number

Amount refers to quantity: A large ***amount*** of money is wasted by the government. ***Number*** refers to things which are thought of a individual units: She bought a large ***number*** of oranges, pears, grapes and apples. Words following ***amount*** are usually singular, those following ***number*** are usually plural.

and/or

And/or is a legal term that is quickly becoming common in current English. It is a fad best to be avoided. The word ***or*** carries the same meaning (in most cases) and does not draw attention to itself.

ante-, anti-

These prefixes, though similar, are very different in meaning: ***Ante*** means before, as in: ***ante***chamber (a small room that comes before a larger one) ***Anti*** means against or opposed to, as in: ***Anti*** Christ, ***anti***toxin.

appraise, apprise

Appraise means to give value to: The goldsmith ***appraised*** the necklace at over one thousand dollars. ***Apprise*** means to tell or inform: Joan went in to shock when ***apprised*** of the necklace's value.

apt, likely, liable

Apt refers to a habit: Because of his big feet, he was ***apt*** to trip over the stairs. ***Liable*** infers the probability of something unfortunate: The President is***liable*** to lose the next election. ***Likely*** means possible: It is ***likely*** to rain tomorrow.

as, like

When used as a preposition, ***like*** should never begin a clause: **NOT** *like* I said. When introducing a clause, ***as*** is used: *As* he said yesterday,...

ascent, assent

Ascent is a noun referring to climbing or upward movement:The***ascent*** to the peak was delayed by the weather. ***Assent*** is a noun or verb having to do with agreement: The senate gave their ***assent*** to the President's budget.

averse/adverse

"Averse" means "having an active feeling of repugnance or distaste."

Harry was **averse** to Potions.

Snape is **averse** to washing his hair.

"Adverse" means "acting against or in a contrary direction" or "opposed to one's interests."

Harry hated playing Quidditch in **adverse** weather.

Jim's testimony was **adverse** to the DA's position.

besides/beside

The preposition **besides** means "except."

Everyone besides Jane went to the party.

The preposition **beside** means "next to."

Jane was standing beside me." (NOT: besides me)

Beside is a preposition that means next to: "Stand here beside me." *Besides* is an adverb that means also: "Besides, I need to tell you about the new products my company offers."

bimonthly/semimonthly

Bimonthly is an adjective that means every two months: "I brought the cake for the bimonthly office party." *Bimonthly* is also a noun that means a publication issued every two months: "The company publishes several popular bimonthlies." *Semimonthly* is an adjective that means happening twice a month: "We have semimonthly meetings on the 1st and the 15th."

Bad/Badly: Bad should be used as an adjective, and badly should be used as an adverb. More specifically, you can not feel badly about something, unless you are referring specifically to your sense of feeling, say in your fingertips.

Bare/Bear: Bare means **uncovered, naked or without supplies**. Bear is of course an animal, but it also means **to carry, to put up with or to undertake a burden.**

blond/blonde

"Blond" and "blonde" both refer to people with light-colored hair. Traditionally, blond has been used for men, blonde for women. However, it's becoming more common to use "blond" to refer to someone of either gender, and you can safely use "blond" to refer to hair, regardless of the gender of its owner.

Lucius Malfoy is **blond**.

Cassie Wells is **blonde**.

Cassie Wells has **blond** hair.

boarder/border

A ***"boarder"*** is someone who pays for lodging that includes meals. That's it. Otherwise, use ***"border."***

Martha had to take in **boarders** after Jonathan died.

Harry stopped at the **border** of the Forbidden Forest.

Daniel's love of coffee **borders** on a fixation.

borne/born

"Borne" and ***"born"*** are both past participle forms of ***"bear."*** According to dictionary, "Traditionally, born is used only in passive constructions referring to birth: *I was born in Chicago*. For all other uses, including active constructions referring to birth, borne is the standard form: *She has borne both her children at home. I have borne his insolence with the patience of a saint.*"

Lucius Malfoy was a **born** leader.

Harry was **borne** up by his broom.

The petals were **borne** on the wind.

Blair was **born** in 1969.

Jim didn't want Brackett to release the air-**borne** virus.

Bring/Take: Put simply: use bring when you mean carrying/leading something toward something/someone and use **take** when you mean carrying/leading something away from something/someone.

- *Are you going to **bring** me dinner after work?*
- *Are you going to **take** this paper to her office?*

breach/breech

"Breeches" are, in the US, anyway, pants that come down to the knees. In addition, a baby can be "breeched," that is, coming out legs first. That's it for "breech."

A ***"breach"*** is a break of some sort. "Breach" can also be a verb, meaning "to form a breach."

The whale **breached** the water.

The Asgard **breached** their agreement with the SGC.

Draco's behaviour was a **breach** of Quidditch protocol.

Once more unto the **breach**, dear friends.

breath/breathe

"Breath" is a noun and is pronounced with a soft th (like with). Most of the time it means the air one takes into and pushes out of one's lungs. It can also mean "spirit" or "suggestion," as in "the faintest breath of scandal." ***"Breathe"***is a verb and is pronounced with a hard th (like father). It means, mostly, "to respire" or "to pause and rest before continuing."

Harry used Gillyweed to **breathe** underwater during the Tri-Wizard Tournament.

Obi-Wan watched as Qui-Gon drew his last **breath**.

broach/brooch

A ***"brooch"*** is "an ornament that is held by a pin or clasp and is worn at or near the neck." ***"Broach"*** is usually adverb; it can mean "to pierce," "to open up" or "to make known for the first time." If you "broach" a subject, there's a definite connotation of its being a difficult discussion. "Broach" has other, less common meanings as well, but it's never a piece of jewelry.

This is another case where British English is more strict than U.S. English—in the U.S. you can get away with using "broach" for "brooch," but anyone speaking British English would say that's incorrect.

Hermione pinned the **brooch** to her collar.

Obi-Wan was afraid to **broach** the subject of Anakin.

Sam **broached** the cask of beer.

Burglary/Robbery: Burglary is a crime that involves breaking and entering to steal something, but without the confrontation between the criminal and the victim. Conversely, robbery is a crime where force or a threat is used to steal something from someone. The difference is whether or not confrontation was involved.

- *There was a **burglary** last night on Maple Street while the residents were on vacation.*
- *There was a **robbery** last night in which three people were shot.*

capital/capitol

The city or town that is the seat of government is called the *capital;* the building in which the legislative assembly meets is the *capitol.* The term *capital* can also refer to an accumulation of wealth or to a capital letter.

cite/site

Cite is a verb that means to quote as an authority or example: "I cited several eminent scholars in my study of water resources." It also means to recognize formally: "The public official was cited for service to the city." It can also mean to summon before a court of law: "Last year the company was cited for pollution violations." *Site* is a noun meaning location: "They chose a new site for the factory just outside town."

complement/compliment

Complement is a noun or verb that means something that completes or makes up a whole: "The red sweater is a perfect complement to the outfit." *Compliment* is a noun or verb that means an expression of praise or admiration: "I received compliments about my new outfit."

comprise/compose

According to the traditional rule, the whole comprises the parts, and the parts compose the whole. Thus, the board comprises five members, whereas five members compose (or make up) the board. It is also correct to say that the board is composed (not comprised) of five members.

cannon/canon

A ***"cannon"*** is a very large gun. ***"Canon"***, in fandom, is usually used to mean the characterizations and events that are taken directly from the source. In the dictionary, "canon" means "an accepted principle or rule." (It can also refer to the accepted list of books of the Bible, or to a song like "Row, Row, Row Your Boat.") In fandom, you almost always want to use "canon," even though it seems like no one else does. They're all wrong.

concurrent/consecutive

Concurrent is an adjective that means simultaneous or happening at the same time as something else: "The concurrent strikes of several unions crippled the economy. "*Consecutive* means successive or following one after the other: "The union called three consecutive strikes in one year."

choose/chose/chosen

"Choose" - present tense "Chose" - past tense "Chosen" - past participle

I **choose** not to go on the roller coaster. **(present)**

Qui-Gon **chose** Obi-Wan as his padawan. **(past)**

Jim was **chosen** Detective of the Year. **(past participle)**

connote/denote

Connote is a verb that means to imply or suggest: "The word 'espionage' connotes mystery and intrigue." *Denote* is a verb that means to indicate or refer to specifically: "The symbol for 'pi' denotes the number 3.14159."

convince/persuade

Strictly speaking, one convinces a person that something is true but persuades a person to do something. "Pointing out that I was overworked, my friends persuaded [not convinced] me to take a vacation. Now that I'm relaxing on the beach with my book, I am convinced [not persuaded] that they were right." Following this rule, *convince* should not be used with an infinitive.

council/councilor/counsel/counselor

A *councilor* is a member of a *council,* which is an assembly called together for discussion or deliberation. A *counselor* is one who gives *counsel,* which is advice or guidance. More specifically, a *counselor* can be an attorney or a supervisor at camp.

compliment/complement

A *"compliment"* is when someone says something nice to you. Plural, it means best wishes, as in "**compliments** of the season." As a verb, "compliment" means "to pay a compliment to." Everything else is *"complement"*. It usually has to do with something that makes a thing complete, or the number required to make something complete.

Jack **complimented** Daniel on his translating skills.

"Was that a **compliment** I just got from Jack?" Daniel wondered.

Harry's dress robes **complemented** his eyes.

The ship's entire complement disembarked for shore leave.

congratulations/congradulations

It's spelled *congratulations*. With a "t". This is one that drives me absolutely up the wall.

conscious/conscience/conscientious/unconscionable

"Conscious" is an adjective with several meanings, mostly relating to being awake and aware.

"Conscientious" is also an adjective, but it means "governed by or conforming to the dictates of conscience," or scrupulous, meticulous or careful.

"Unconscionable" is another adjective. It means "not guided or controlled by conscience: unscrupulous."

Finally, *"conscience"* is a noun that means, well, Jiminy Cricket. It's that little voice that tells you whether you're behaving.

It's tough keeping all these words straight, because they're all related, but it's important. People who know the difference will be very jarred if you get them wrong.

Harry's **conscience** nagged him after he snuck into Hogsmeade without permission.

couldn't care less/could care less

The phrase *"couldn't care less"* means that one has the lowest possible level of interest in something. Taken literally, "could care less" means just the opposite—that one does have some sort of interest. However, people do say they *could* care less when they really mean they *couldn't*, and some American sources say this is accepted usage. In writing, using "could" instead of "couldn't" tends to lead to confusion. "Could care less" is much more informal; some characters might use it in dialogue, but, in general, it's safer to stick with "couldn't care less," which can't be misunderstood.

cloth/clothes

Cloth is a noun (usually as a non-count noun) that means "material or fabric."

She bought some cloth to make a new dress.

Clothes is a plural count noun meaning "garments used to cover the body."

She bought a lot of clothes in Paris.

I feel nice when I wear new clothes.

Can/May: Can is used when meaning ability and may is used when meaning permission.

- ***May** I please leave class early?*
- ***Can** you do 15 pushups?*

Cant and **can't**. There are several meanings for the word *cant* (without an apostrophe); however, none of them is "unable to". One meaning of *cant* is "a kind of slang or jargon spoken by a particular group of people". *Can't* is a contraction of *cannot*.

- *Standard*: I can't understand the dialogue in this book because it's written in cant.
- *Non-standard*: I cant swim; I've never taken lessons.

Compose/Comprise: The rule is that parts compose the whole, while the whole is composed of the parts.

- *Peanut butter, jelly and bread* ***compose*** *a peanut butter and jelly sandwich.*
- *A peanut butter and jelly sandwich is* ***comprised*** *of peanut butter, jelly and bread.*

complimentary/complementary

Complimentary is an adjective which means "given freely, or giving praise"

The teacher was very **complimentary** about my work.

Complementary is an adjective, which means, "supplying needs"

The **complementary** relationship of the bee and the flower is quite remarkable.

cause/reason

What are the causes of their quarrel?

What is your reason for studying in this school?

charge/cost/price/value/worth

These books cost a lot of money.

These books are worth a lot of money.

The price of the books has been raised recently.

An antique has no value if it is broken.

We did not need to pay any service charge after using the hall.

censure, criticize

To *censure* always expresses disapproval. To *criticize* may be neutral, expressing approval of some parts and disapproval of others.

cents, scents, sense

Cents refers to money, usually small coins I have a few *cents*in my pocket.. *Scents* refers to smell, or odors: The *scents* of roses and wood smoke dominated the evening breeze.*Sense* refers to one of the five senses; to feel something: I *sensed* his approach even though I could not see him

chose, choose

Chose in legal terms means an incorporeal right enforceable by legal action, as in a franchise. *Chose* is also used to indicate someone has made a choice: He chose the red truck. The *Choose* means to select from a number, or in preference to another or others. Choose one of the following: Red, Blue, Green, or Yellow.

cite, site, sight

To *cite* is to make a reference to a specific original source. The noun*site* refers to a specific piece of ground where a building is or will be erected: The*site* of the new playground. *Sight* refers to: vision, a field of vision, something worth seeing, a shocking or spectacular event, an observation from surveying instruments or sextants, the guides on a firearm.

claim, assert

Claim refers to a legal or justified demand: He *claimed* the first piece of cake. *Assert* means to come forward and assume one's rights: The President*asserted* that he was innocent of all charges.

compare to, compare with

Compare to is used to indicate a definite resemblance: Compared *to* last year, this year's sales are better. *Compare with* is used to indicate an examination of similarities and dissimilarities: He compared Bill Gates *with* Socrates.

complement, compliment

Complement is something that fills up or completes: Black Forest Cake is a decadent *complement* to any meal! A*compliment* is an expression of praise: He *complimented* her new hair style.

comprehensible, comprehensive

Comprehensible means able to be understood: Although the manual contained technical language, it was *comprehensible*. *Comprehensive* means to include all, or covering a wide range:The *comprehensive* study of the art of writing does not necessarily lead to a best selling novel.

compulsion, compunction

Compulsion means forced to comply or a strong, irresistible impulse to carry out an act: She was *compelled* to eat the cherries.*Compunction* (noun) means to feel shame, unhappiness, guilt, or regret for one's actions: He filled with *compunction* at the thought of cheating on his wife.

confidant, confident

A *confidant* (*confidante,* if female) is a trusted friend.*Confident* means you are certain: You were *confident* that your story would sell.

congenital, congenial

Congenital means existing in an individual from birth.*Congenial* refers to a person who is agreeable, pleasing, compatible, or sympathetic.

connotation, denotation

Denotation refers to the exact meaning of a word as found in a dictionary. *Connotation* refers to what the word suggests beyond it's dictionary meaning: Damsel *denotes* a young woman, but *connotes* a a beautiful maiden from the centre ages who is usually in distress.

consensus

Consensus means a general agreement or majority of opinion. Many of today's respected newspapers misspell the word as concensus. Note: The phrase: *Concensus of opinion* is redundant and should NOT be used.

contemptible, contemptuous

Contemptible means worthy of contempt; deserving scorn or disdain; mean; vile: When Jason punched his wife, his actions were*contemptible*. *Contemptuous* means to express contempt or disdain; scornful: He stared at the politician with a *contemptuous* frown.

continual, continuous

A *continual* action is one that occurs over a long period of time, with pauses or intermissions: He *continually* called attention to her poor posture. A *continuous* action occurs without the the pauses: The tap leaked in a*continuous* stream. **council, counsel** To *counsel* is to give advice: He*counselled* her to wait for the bylaw to be passed. As a noun, *counsel* means advice: I sought legal *counsel* after the car accident. *Council* is a group of people who act in an advisory capacity, or meet for discussions or decision making: They submitted their proposal to the mayor's *council*

credible, credulous

Credible means capable of being believed: He gave a*credible* rendition of Elvis' love song, Love Me Tender. *Credulous* means willing to believe without sufficient evidence, easily deceived, gullible: a con man's *credulous*victim

councilor, counselor

A *councilor* is a member of a council. A *counselor* is one who gives advice.

clash/crash

What a pity that the two meetings clash.

He saw a bus crash into the lamp post.

Ann and Mary often quarrel because their ideas often clash.

cloth/clothing/clothes

John cleaned the table with a cloth.

He laid a cloth on the ground and put down some clothes.

Her clothes got wet after the rain.

I don't like wearing thick clothing in winter.

compose/comprise/consist

The class club committee comprises eight members.

The class club committee consists of eight members.

The committee is composed of teachers and students.

compare to/compare with

You may compare your work with David's and see which is better.

Your work is nothing compared with David's.

Many poets like to compare life to morning dew.

concern/concerning/concern

All the classmates are concerned about his health.

The topic is concerned with careless driving.

They are discussing something concerning the youth problem.

continual/continuous

The continual rain made us feel bored.

They enjoyed a continuous performance till midnight.

copy/imitate

You should not copy your neighbor's answers.

The teacher advised his students not to imitate him.

credible/credulous/incredible

That is really an incredible story. I don't think it's real one.

He is such a credulous man that he often believes what you say.

Did the committee find his statement credible?

cue/queue

A ***"queue"*** is a line of people or things. To "queue," or "queue up," means to get in line, or to form a line. (A queue can, incidentally, also be a braid, but it's not used that way very often—unless you're in an Age of Sail fandom.)

As a verb, ***"cue"*** means "to prompt" or "to position in readiness for playing" or "to insert into a continuous performance." A "cue" is a signal or a hint, or the stick you use to play pool with.

damage/injure/hurt/wound

He hurt his leg after jumping down from a tree.

Many huts are damaged by the fire.

A tall man hurt him with an axe.

Many fire victims were injured and taken to hospital.

defuse/diffuse

"Defuse" means "to remove the fuse from," or "to make less harmful, potent, or tense." ***"Diffuse,"*** as a verb, refers to spreading out or thinning.

When Harry and Draco pulled out their wands, Dumbledore stepped in to **defuse** the situation.

The nerve gas **diffused** throughout the room.

desert/dessert

A ***"dessert"*** is a sweet course or a fruit course served at the end of a meal. So far so good.

"Desert" can be a verb, in which case the accent is on the second syllable, and it means "to leave in the lurch" or "to abandon," especially in the military. As a noun, "desert" is usually pronounced with the accent on the first syllable, and it means "an arid land with sparse vegetation," or "a desolate or forbidding area."

However, "desert" has another meaning that most people aren't aware of. As a noun, it can be pronounced with the accent on the second syllable, like "dessert," and in that case it means "a deserved reward or punishment." So it's actually "just deserts," *not* "just desserts."

When Malfoy ended up in the infirmary, Hermione thought he had got his just **deserts**.

Jack was tired of having pie for **dessert**.

Most of "Lawrence of Arabia" takes place in the **desert**.

The soldier was court-martialed for **deserting** his unit.

deduce, deduct

Deduce means to draw a conclusion from something known or assumed: That may be ***deduced*** from the statistics. ***Deduct*** means to subtract, or infer: ***Deduct*** my contribution from my pay check.

deprecate, depreciate

Deprecate means to plead or argue against; express strong disapproval: His ***deprecatory*** speech had the audience in an uproar. ***Depreciate*** means to bring down the price or value of: The accountant ***depreciated*** the value of the truck.

desert, dessert

This is usually a spelling error. ***Desert*** means a region of rock or sand that receives very little or no precipitation. ***Dessert*** means something (usually sweet) that is served after the main course.

detract, distract

Detract means to take away a part or lessen: Her gaudy clothes***detract*** from her beauty. ***Distract*** means to divert, confound, or harass; to provide a diversion: Her attention was ***distracted*** by the birds in the feeder.

different from

Different from is the correct idiom, NOT ***different than.***

differ from, differ with

Differ from applies to differences between one person or things and others: My stove ***differs from*** hers because it is self-cleaning. ***Differ with*** means to have a difference in opinion: His views on politics ***differed with*** mine.

discover, invent

To ***discover*** is to find or uncover something already in existence, but unknown: Franklin ***discovered*** electricity. To ***invent*** is to create something new: Edison ***invented*** the light bulb.

discreet, discrete

Discreet means prudent in conduct; cautious; heedful; guarded: He was ***discreet*** with his money. ***Discrete*** means separate or distinct from others: Each grain of rice was ***discrete,*** not clinging to the rest in a sticky pile.

disinterested, uninterested

Disinterested means impartial; unconcerned: He was ***disinterested*** with the weather report. ***Uninterested*** means not interested; indifferent; not personally concerned: He sat like a lump, ***uninterested*** in the world around him.

dual, duel

Dual always refers to two things. ***Duel*** refers to a formal contest with guns or pistols.

due to *Due to* replaces the phrases **attributable to** and **because of**: The flood was **attributable to** (***due to***) the heavy rain. **Because of** the accident, (***Due to***) he was late for work.

disinterested/uninterested

A disinterested judge is said to make a fair judgment.

He is uninterested in dancing.

discreet/discrete

Discreet is an adjective that means prudent, circumspect, or modest: "Her discreet handling of the touchy situation put him at ease."

Discrete is an adjective that means separate or individually distinct: "Each company in the conglomerate operates as a discrete entity."

disinterested/uninterested

Disinterested is an adjective that means unbiased or impartial: "We appealed to the disinterested mediator to facilitate the negotiations." *Uninterested* is an adjective that means not interested or indifferent: "They seemed uninterested in our offer."

divide/share

John shared the books among themselves.

The teacher divided the students into four groups.

desert/dessert

A **desert** is "a dry area with little vegetation and rainfall."

The Sahara desert in Africa is the largest in the world.

A **dessert** is "sweet food usually eaten after a meal."

We had chocolate cake and ice cream for dessert.

different from/different than

Different from is a preposition, which precedes a noun phrase

He is **different from** your average shop owner.

Different than is a preposition which precedes a noun clause

London is**different than** we had imagined.

differ from/differ with

To **differ from** is "to be dissimilar."

Men differ from women physically.

To **differ with** is "to disagree with."

I differ with you on this issue. (I disagree with you)

elicit/illicit

Elicit is a verb that means to draw out. *Illicit* is an adjective meaning unlawful. "No matter how hard I tried to elicit a few scandalous stories from her, she kept all knowledge of illicit goings-on discreetly to herself. "

emigrant/immigrant

Emigrant is a noun that means one who leaves one's native country to settle in another: "The emigrants spent four weeks aboard ship before landing in Los Angeles." *Immigrant*is a noun that means one who enters and settles in a new country: "Most of the immigrants easily found jobs." One emigrates *from* a place; one immigrates *to* another.

enough

Enough is an adverb, which precedes a noun and follows an adjective

He knows **enough** English to study in England.

She is fast**enough** to win the race.

every so often/ever so often

Every so often is an adverb meaning "occasionally"

They come **every so often**. I wish they could come more frequently.

Ever so often is an adverb meaning "frequently"

They come **ever so often**. I wish they would stay home.

emigrate/immigrate

To **emigrate** means, "to leave one country to live in another."

My grandfather emigrated from Europe to the USA in 1864.

To **immigrate** means, "to move to a new country."

Many immigrants living in Greece work on farms and in construction.

It's probably **easiest** to remember that to emigrate means to leave a country while immigrate means to enter to live.

economic/economical/economics/economy

Mrs. Young is said to be an economical housekeeper.

He is going to study economics in the university.

Tourism plays an important part in the economy of Greece.

The economic indicators say we are headed towards a depression.

eligible/legible

She is eligible for promotion due to her hard work and dedication.

Mr. Kontogeorgakis' handwriting is almost not legible.

elicit, illicit

Elicit means to bring out or draw forth: His comments ***elicited*** groans from the audience. ***Illicit*** means unlawful: His ***illicit*** affair broke up their marriage.

eminent, imminent

Eminent means famous or prominent as in: His ***Eminence,*** The Pope. ***Imminent*** means soon to take place: The Christmas concert is ***imminent.***

enormity, enormousness

Enormousness refers to something of extraordinarily large size. ***Enormity,*** used to describe something monstrously evil should never be confused with ***enormousness.***

eminent/imminent

Dr. Chevereney is an eminent surgeon in our city.

Most people were in a hurry to go home as a typhoon was imminent.

equal/identical/similar

The tow applicants are of equal ability.

Your book is similar to the one that I lost last week.

They are surprised to find that their shirts are identical.

error/mistake

I took his book by mistake.

An error of judgment can be disastrous.

There are so many errors in this letter I don't understand it.

exciting/excited/excitement

The boys became excited when they watched such an exciting basketball match.

When they heard that he had passed the examination, he jumped up and down out of excitement.

exacerbate/exasperate

"Exacerbate" means "to make more violent, brutal or severe."

"Exasperate" means "to excite the anger of," or "to cause irritation or annoyance to." In general, people are exasperated; situations are exacerbated. Make sure you're using the right one.

Jim was **exasperated** by Blair's sloppiness.

Closing the factory will **exacerbate** unemployment problems.

everyday/every day

What do you do every day?

John seems to be very busy with everyday work.

She writes ten letters every day.

fare/fee

A student has to pay the fare when he takes a bus.

The fare is more by taxi than by minibus.

When will the students pay the school fee?

farther/further

Farther means "towards a more distant point in space." (actual distance)

The beach is a few miles farther away.

Further means "towards a more distant point in time, degree, or quantity." (figurative distance)

Let us consider this problem a bit further. (time)

We should do further research on this matter. (quantity)

Be careful not to excite the children any further. (degree)

farther, further

Farther means more remote; more distant: He threw the ball *farther* than anyone else. *Further* means at or to a more advanced point in time; to forward, as a work: He was *further* along with the count than expected.

fewer, less

Fewer pertains to a smaller number: *fewer* oranges, *fewer* girls, *fewer*cars. *Less* means a smaller amount or quantity: *less* money, *less* coal, *less* weight.

flotsam, jetsam

Flotsam means wreckage found afloat. ***Jetsam*** means objects thrown overboard and then washed ashore.

Flout and **flaunt**. One *flouts* a rule or law by flagrantly ignoring it. One *flaunts* something by showing it off.

- *Standard*: If you've got it, flaunt it.
- *Standard*: He continually flouted the speed limit.
- *Non-standard*: If you've got it, flout it.
- *Non-standard*: He continually flaunted the speed limit.

fiancé/fiancée

A ***"fiancé"*** is a male person who's engaged to be married. If the person is female, it's ***"fiancée"***. In English, both these words tend to be used without the acute accents fairly often, just because accents are hard to type on an English keyboard. Technically, though, the words are borrowed from French, and the accent is correct.

Before they were married, Carolyn was Jim's **fiancée**, and Jim was Carolyn's **fiancé**.

flaunt/flout

"Flaunt" means "to display or obtrude oneself to public notice" or "to display ostentatiously or impudently." It generally has to do with showiness and attention-getting. ***"Flout"*** means "to treat with contemptuous disregard" or "to indulge in scornful behaviour." In the U.S., it's not uncommon to see "flaunt" used in place of "flout," and not all dictionaries say this is non-standard, but if you use "flaunt" in this way, many readers will think it's wrong.

Harry was known for **flouting** Professor Snape's rules.

Amidala tried not to **flaunt** her expensive clothes.

Hermione sometimes **flaunts** her knowledge.

formally/formerly

Formally means "in a formal way."

He was formally charged with the crime.

Formerly means "previously," or "at an earlier time."

She was formerly a dancer in a club.

fallow/follow

"Fallow" has several uses, mostly relating to farming. If a farmer decides not to plant in a particular field one season, he's letting that field lie fallow. It's much more likely that you want to use *"follow"*, which means, generally, to come after something, or to obey something.

Farmer McDonald decided to let twenty acres lie **fallow** this year.

Don't forget to **follow** the directions.

forceful, forcible

Forceful means powerful; vigorous; effective: His *forceful*personality dominated the interview. ***Forcible*** means exercising force or by force or violence: He made a ***forcible*** entry into the hose by kicking down the door.

former, latter

Former and *latter* are used to designate one of two persons or things: When given a choice between chocolate and ice cream, I prefer the ***former*** to the ***latter***.If more than two things or people are involved: He had the choice of coffee, tea, juice or milk. He preferred the ***first*** and ***last*** to the others.

fortuitous, fortunate

Fortuitous means an event which happens by accident that may or may not be favorable. ***Fortunate*** means lucky or receiving good from an uncertain or unexpected source.

founder, flounder

Founder is a nautical term referring to the collapsing or sinking of a boat. ***Flounder*** means to move clumsily or to struggle to gain footing: The horse ***floundered*** in the deep snow.

fulsome

Fulsome means excessive and insincere. NEVER use it to mean plentiful. The critic gave ***fulsome*** praise to the sculpture, which angered the. artist.

first/former

First as an adjective refers to three or more items

The **first** five skiers fell.

Former as an adjective refers to two or fewer items

The **former** Secretary of State for the U.S., Colin Powel, was the first black to hold that position.

from/since/for

From is a preposition followed by a noun or noun phrase. As a time marker, it requires **to** or another preposition.

From now on I will lead the way.

From Monday **to** Friday, I work like a slave.

Since is a subordinate conjunction followed by a clause. It expresses "the time something began" or "the beginning of time"

Since Wednesday, I have walked 6 miles a day.

For is a preposition followed by a noun or noun phrase. It expresses "the length of time (**duration**) something has lasted."

For two weeks I have walked to work every day.

farther/further

Farther is an adjective and adverb that means to or at a more distant point: "We drove 50 miles today; tomorrow, we will travel 100 miles farther." *Further* is an adjective and adverb that means to or at a greater extent or degree: "We won't be able to suggest a solution until we are further along in our evaluation of the problem." It can also mean in addition or moreover: "They stated further that they would not change the policy."

few/less

Few is an adjective that means small in number. It is used with countable objects: "This department has few employees." *Less* is an adjective that means small in amount or degree. It is used with objects of indivisible mass: "Which jar holds less water?"

figuratively/literally

Figuratively is an adverb that means metaphorically or symbolically: "Happening upon the shadowy figure, they figuratively jumped out of their shoes." *Literally* is an adverb that means actually: "I'm not exaggerating when I say I literally fell off my chair." It also means according to the exact meaning of the words: "I translated the Latin passage literally."

flammable/inflammable

These two words are actually synonyms, both meaning easily set on fire. The highly flammable (inflammable) fuel was stored safely in a specially built tank. Use nonflammable to mean *not* flammable.

flaunt/flout

To *flaunt* means to show off shamelessly: "Eager to flaunt her knowledge of a wide range of topics, Helene dreamed of appearing on a TV trivia show." To *flout* means to show scorn or contempt for: "Lewis disliked boarding school and took every opportunity to flout the house rules."

foreword/forward

Foreword is a noun that means an introductory note or preface: "In my foreword I explained my reasons for writing the book." *Forward* is an adjective or adverb that means toward the front: "I sat in the forward section of the bus." "Please step forward when your name is called." *Forward* is also a verb that means to send on: "Forward the letter to the customer's new address."

founder/flounder

In its primary sense *founder* means to sink below the surface of the water: "The ship foundered after colliding with an iceberg." By extension, *founder* means to fail utterly.*Flounder* means to move about clumsily, or to act with confusion. A good synonym for*flounder* is blunder: "After floundering through the first half of the course, Amy finally passed with the help of a tutor."

hanged/hung

Hanged is the past tense and past participle of hang when the meaning is to execute by suspending by the neck: "They hanged the prisoner for treason." "The convicted killer was hanged at dawn." *Hung* is the past tense and participle of hang when the meaning is to suspend from above with no support from below: "I hung the painting on the wall." "The painting was hung at a crooked angle."

healthful/healthy

Healthful means "good for ones health."

Vegetables and fruits are healthful foods.

Healthy means "in a good condition of health."

Due to their outdoor lifestyle, all of his children are healthy.

hang/hanged/hung

Last night the criminal was hanged to death.

John hung a picture on the wall a few minutes ago.

handed/hand

He took her by the hand to cross the street.

John was handed an award for being on time all semester long.

hard/hardly

Hardly had he finished his work when the bell rang.

He could hardly see in darkness.

He tried hard to improve himself.

hire/let/rent

This house is not to let.

The young couple rented a flat in the building.

They hired a truck to take the furniture to their new flat.

Hear, hear!/Here, here!

"Hear, hear!" is an expression used to indicate approval, e.g. during a speech. It's absolutely *not* "Here, here!" – which makes no sense at all. **historic/historical**

In general usage, *historic* refers to what is important in history, while *historical* applies more broadly to whatever existed in the past whether it was important or not: "a historic summit meeting between the prime ministers;" "historical buildings torn down in the redevelopment."

hope/expect/wish

I don't expect to see him at the airport next Monday.

What do you expect him to do?

I wish I could help you to solve the problem.

She hopes she will be admitted to the university.

hoard/horde

"Horde" is a noun, meaning "a teeming crowd or throng."

Genghis Khan led the Mongolian **hordes.**

Anakin was amazed by the **horde** of people on Coruscant.

The noun ***"hoard"*** means "a supply or fund stored up and often hidden away." Hoard can also be used as a verb, meaning "to lay up a hoard of."

Harry needed to access his **hoard** of Galleons.

Squirrels **hoard** acorns for the winter.

Hermione **hoarded** her thoughts.

illusion/allusion

An **illusion** is "a false idea" or "unreal image."

The magician's illusion convinced the crowd that he was flying.

An **allusion** is "an indirect reference."

The professor made an allusion to modern art.

imply/infer

To **imply** is "to suggest without saying directly." A speaker or writer can imply.

Susan implied that she was not happy with her studies.

To **infer** is to "to make a conclusion based on evidence not stated."

Only a listener or reader can infer.

I inferred from the report that our taxes would be raised again.

It's and **its**. *It's* is a contraction that replaces *it is* or *it has* (see apostrophe). *Its* is the possessive pronoun corresponding to *it*, in the same way that *his* corresponds to *he*. In standard written English, possessive **nouns** take an apostrophe, but possessive **pronouns** do not.

Its is the singular possessive pronoun for things.

The car had its tires stolen last night.

It's is the contraction for "it is."

It's a nice day today. (It is a nice day today.)

Imaginary/Imagination/Imaginative

This story was about an imaginary situation.

Why does John have so much imagination?

He's got an imaginative mind.

Interesting/Interested/Interest

These story books do not seem to interest the students.

He is very interested in taking photographs.

You can never find this book interesting if you don't read it.

i.e./e.g.

The abbreviation *e.g.* means for example (from Latin *exempli gratia*): "Her talents were legion and varied (e.g., deep sea diving, speed reading, bridge, and tango dancing)." The abbreviation *i.e.* means that is or in other words (from

Latin *id est)*: "The joy of my existence (i.e., my stamp collection) imbues my life with meaning."

insist/persist

John insisted on going for a walk despite the heavy rain outside.

The boy persisted in his plan though it was not very practical.

intense/intensive

Most of the onlookers felt hot because of the intense heat.

Last year I took an intensive course in Japanese.

in spite of, despite

In spite of means in opposition to all efforts of; notwithstanding: We held the picnic *in spite of* the rain. *Despite* means the same, but is written or spoken as: *Despite* the rain, we held the picnic. *Despite* also means extreme malice; contemptuous hate; and act of spite or contempt: His voice full of*despite,* he said, "You will pay for that!"

imply, infer

Imply means to indicate more than the words plainly say; to hint: The politician's smile *implied* he could be trusted to keep his promises. *Infer* means to draw a conclusion; as by reasoning; to deduce; to indicate as a conclusion: The reporter *inferred* from his manner that the politician was sincere.

impracticable, impractical

Impracticable means unfeasible; unmanageable; not useful for an intended purpose. *Impractical* means not taking a common sense view; not workable: He was *impractical,* always wasting his allowance on candy.

intense, intensive

Intense means stretched out or tight; existing or occurring in a high or or extreme degree: She blushed, unable to endure the *intense* passion in his gaze. *Intensive* means increasing in intensity or degree, more laborious. expensive or concentrated methods of cultivation: As in *Intensive* Care Unit of a hospital.

invaluable, priceless

Invaluable means having a value so great that its worth

cannot be evaluated. ***Priceless*** means having a value beyond all price; or in slang, very amusing or absurd.

its, it's

Its (no apostrophe) is the possessive case of ***it***: ***Its*** tail was too long. ***It's*** is the contraction of ***it is***: ***It's*** too soon to tell.

journey/voyage/tour/trip

We shall take a trip to Vienna on Sunday.

Mr. Chan had a tour in Europe during the summer vacation.

How long does a journey from Chicago to New York take?

One of the tourists caught a cold on the voyage.

kind of, sort of, type of, variety of

Never use ***a*** or ***an*** after these expressions: ***Variety of an apple*** is confusing because ***an*** is used for one particular member of a class. ***Variety of apple*** is preferable because apple by itself correctly refers to the general idea of apple.

Lay (*lay, laid, laid, laying*) and **lie** (*lie, lay, lain, lying*) are often confused. *Lay* is a transitive verb, meaning that it takes an object. "To lay something" means to place something. *Lie,* on the other hand, is intransitive and means to recline (and also to tell untruths, but in this case the verb is regular and causes no confusion).

The distinction between these related verbs is further confused by the fact that past tesne of *lie* is *lay*. A quick test is to see if the word in question could be replaced with *recline*; if it can you should use *lie*.

Loathe: Often incorrectly used for 'loth' or 'loath' in phrases such as "She was loathe to accept." 'Loathe' is only properly used as a verb.

leave/let

To **leave** means, "to go away from."

He leaves work at five o'clock every day.

To **let** means, "to permit."

Jane let me borrow her bike.

lead/led

Let's start with the most common verb form of ***"lead"***: It's pronounced *leed*, with a long e, and it means, more or less, "to guide," "to direct," or "to be first." So far so good. Its past tense is ***"led,"*** pronounced with a short e. So, "lead"=present, "led"=past. Sounds easy, right?

The reason this gets confusing is that "lead" can also be a noun. With a long e it means "the person in front" or "leash" or "the first card played" or "the distance a base runner is from the base," as well as some others. But it can also be pronounced with a short e, in which case it's the metal that's in a pencil. (Or was, before lead poisoning, but anyway.) So because "lead" can properly be pronounced with a short e, it's easy to think that that's how the past tense of the verb is spelled—but it's not.

Harry **leads** his year in detentions

Jack has **led** SG-1 into some interesting situations.

The **lead** in my pencil needs sharpening.

Why isn't your dog on a **lead**?

You can **lead** a horse to water, but you can't make him drink.

Jim **led** Blair to the temple.

leech/leach

"Leech" is a noun, meaning an aquatic bloodsucking worm. As a verb, it means to apply leeches to someone, as a method of bloodletting. Ninety-five per cent of the time, this is the only meaning 'leech' should have. (The other five per cent: if you write Age of Sail fic, "leech" can mean "the vertical edge of a square sail;" if you write LotR or medieval fic, "leech" is an archaic word for "physician," and can also can mean "to heal.") ***"Leach"*** is a verb. It means "to percolate a liquid through some material"; its subject may be the liquid or the person causing the action; its object may be the material the liquid goes through, or the substance it dissolves and carries away.

"Leach" may also be used figuratively, if you want to talk about some intangible quality (e.g., courage) being taken away.

As a rule of thumb, if it's a verb, you probably want "leach"; if it's a noun, you probably want "leech."

Leeches lived in the mud by the lakeshore and would attack any student who went wading.

Théoden to Gríma: "Your **leechcraft** ere long would have had me crawling on all fours like a beast."

Snape **leached** the phoenix ashes of their magical components.

Rain has **leached** nutrients from the topsoil.

The dementors closed in on the house, **leaching** warmth and courage from everyone inside.

loose/lose

The adjective **loose** means "not tight."

This shirt is too loose. I need a smaller size.

To **lose** is a verb meaning "to leave (forget) behind by accident"

I often lose my house keys.

lie/lay

Everyone's favourite. Basically, ***"lie"*** is ***intransitive,*** meaning it doesn't have an object. ***"Lay"***is ***transitive,*** which means it does have an object. (Yes, lay does have some intransitive usages, too, but they're not the ones that get confused with lie.) So, you lay something on a table. You lay down your cards. You lay the baby in the crib. But when you go to bed, you lie down. You lie in wait. You lay a book on the desk, and then the book lies on the desk.

This is made more complicated by the various forms of these verbs.

Lie: past tense, lay; past participle, lain

Present: *I lie down.*

Past: *I lay down.*

Past participle: *I have lain down.*

Lay: past tense, laid; past participle, laid

Present: *I lay the book on the table.*

Past: *I laid the book on the table.*

Past participle: *I have laid the book on the table.*

Then there's the other meaning of "lie": "to make an untrue statement." Its forms are different from those of the other "lie":

Past tense, lied; past participle, lied

Present: *She lies habitually – she never tells the truth.*

Past: *She lied to her teacher.*

Past participle: *She has lied to everyone.*

Both forms of "lie," however, have the same present participle: "lying."

Lie means **to recline,** and unlike lay it does not have an object. The past tense is lay, the past participle is lain and the present participle is lying.

Lie also means **to tell an untruth**, it also does not have an object. The past tense and past participle are lied and the present participle is lying.

Less/Fewer: The rule is that if you can separate items into a countable number then use fewer. If the items cannot be separated use less.

- *Ted didn't get the job because he has* **less** *skill in writing than the other applicant.*
- *That store has* ***fewer*** *DVDs than Best Buy.*

Like/As: As or as if should be used as a conjunction to introduce a clause, and such as should be used to mean **exactly or similar to**. Like should be used as a preposition for comparisons.

Lie is an intransitive verb meaning "to recline"

He **lies** down for a nap after his lunch.

Lay is a transitive verb which means "to put or place"

He **lay** the book on the desk and left the room.

late/lately/later/latter/latest/last

I haven't seen Mary lately.

Both John and Jack are hardworking students, but the latter was more active at school.

Mary is always fascinated by the latest fashion.

Read the last line of the third paragraph carefully.

Jane is always late for school.

laid/lain/lay

Laid is the past tense and the past participle of the verb lay and not the past tense of lie.*Lay* is the past tense of the verb lie and *lain* is the past participle: "He laid his books down and lay down on the couch, where he has lain for an hour."

lend/loan

Although some people feel *loan* should only be used as a noun, *lend* and *loan* are both acceptable as verbs in standard

English: "Can you lend (loan) me a dollar?" However, only *lend* should be used in figurative senses: "Will you lend me a hand?"

lightening/lightning

Lightening is a verb that means to illuminate; *lightning* is a noun referring to the electrical charges the cause flashes of light during storms: "The lightning struck, lightening the sky."

loud/loudly/aloud

Would you mind not talking so loud?

You have to speak aloud; otherwise your classmates can't hear what you say.

It's impolite to speak in a loud voice.

A woman shouted loudly that her handbag was stolen.

loath/loathe

"Loath," usually pronounced with a soft th, means unwilling or reluctant. (It's sometimes spelled "loth" in Britain.)***"Loathe,"*** pronounced with a hard th, means to dislike greatly or to detest.

Harry and Ron **loathe** Draco Malfoy

Blair was **loath** to tell Jim that his fly was undone.

Me, myself and **I**. In a traditional prescriptive grammar, *I* is used only as a subject, *me* is used only as an object, and *myself* is used only as a reflexive object, that is to say when the subject is I and the object would otherwise be *me*.

Myself is often used in way that makes usage writers bristle, particularly when someone is trying to be "extra correct". Like the other reflexive pronouns, in prescriptive usage, *myself* should be used only when both the subject and object of the verb are the speaker, or as an intensifier.

loose/lose

"Loose" is usually used as an adjective, meaning "not tight." It can also be a verb, but only if it means "to release" or "to make less tight." ***"Lose"*** is a verb that means "to not win," or "to misplace," or "to get rid of."

If Neville were to **lose** weight, his pants would be **loose**.

Did you **lose** your way?

"Obi-Wan, how in the world did you **lose** your tunic?"

most/almost

The adjective **most** is the superlative of many or much; meaning " largest number/amount."

Most coffee comes from Brazil.

Almost is an adverb meaning "not quite," or "very nearly" or "nearly all"

Almost all the students are here.

He is almost ready to leave.

He almost won the race.

maybe/may be

May be he is unable to solve the problem himself.

David may be doing his work now.

memorize/memory/memorial/memorable/remember

I shall never forget taking part in such a memorable occasion.

I remembered seeing him read a newspaper a few minutes ago.

I do not take history because there are too many facts to memorize.

My uncle has bad memory for dates.

A memorial school is built for the chairman of the association.

movable/portable

The large cupboard in the kitchen is not movable.

You may bring along your portable cassette recorder when you go for the picnic.

neglect/negligent/negligible

Good parents never neglect their children.

It was said that John was rather negligent in his work.

He was dismissed because he was negligent of his duties.

The manager did not report the burglary to the police because the amount of money stolen was negligible.

minuet/minute

A ***"minuet"*** is "a slow graceful dance in 3/4 time characterized by forward balancing, bowing, and toe pointing." If you're looking for the unit of time, or for notes taken during a meeting, you want ***"minute"***. "Minute" can also be an adjective meaning "very small."

Obi-Wan had to learn to dance the **minuet** for a diplomatic mission.

Just a **minute**!

mean, median

Mean is the centre point between two extremes: ie. The arithmetic*mean* of 1, 2, 3 is 2. *Median* refers to the centre value in a distribution: The *median*salary of local politicians is ridiculously high. The *median* divided the four lane highway.

meantime, meanwhile

Meantime refers to action taking place while waiting for another action or event to take place: *In the meantime,* let's watch television.*Meanwhile* has the same meaning: *Meanwhile,* we watched television.

militate, mitigate

Militate means to oppose; to fight or act for or against; to manifest weight or influence; usually followed by **against**: His anger *militated against* a reconciliation. *Mitigate* means to lessen; to diminish in severity; to become milder: The heating pad on my back *mitigated* my suffering.

myself

Myself, like **yourself, himself, herself, itself, themselves** is an intensive and reflexive pronoun. It should never be used in a sentence without its corresponding noun or pronoun: I hurt *myself*. They sent for Susan and I. (NOT *myself*)

mysterious, mystic

Mysterious means not revealed or explained; unintelligible; beyond human comprehension: The *mysterious* light appeared in the sky and disappeared without explanation. *Mystic* means hidden from human knowledge or comprehension; involving some secret meaning, often religious: The appearance of the angel was a *mystical* experience.

moot/mute

In its most common American usage, *"moot"* can mean "open to question" or "deprived of practical significance: made abstract or purely academic." Law schools often have moot courts. In British English, naturally, "moot" has a rather different ***meaning***: "tending to be discussed or argued about and having no definite answer." As an adjective,***"mute"*** means "unable to speak" or "silent."

Jim said, "It's a **moot** point whether the suspect was home that night."

The question is **moot**.

Merry and Pippin attended the **Entmoot**.

nonplussed

Meaning perplexed or bewildered, *nonplussed* is very often thought to mean just the opposite—calm, unruffled, cool-as-a-cucumber. A common mistake is to think the word means not "plussed," but no such word exists. *Nonplussed* originates from the Latin *non*(no) and *plus* (more, further), and means a state in which no more can be done—one is so perplexed that further action is impossible. "The lexicographer grew increasingly agitated and nonplussed by the frequency with which she noted the misuse of*nonplussed*."

noise/sound

Don't make any noise; otherwise you'll be punished.

Some strange sounds were made by the wild bird.

Of and **have**. In spoken English, *of* and the contracted form of *have, 've,* sound the same. However, in standard written English, they aren't interchangeable.

- *Standard*: Susan would have stopped to eat, but she was running late.
- *Standard*: You could've warned me!
- *Non-standard*: I should of known that the store would be closed. (Should be "I should've known")

navel/naval

A ***"Naval"*** refers to the navy or to warships. Sounds simple, but mixing them up can lead to some very strange images.

Ewan McGregor's **navel** is no stranger to the big screen.

Horatio Hornblower learned a great deal about **naval** warfare.

Over/More than: Very simply, more than (also less than) refers to a number or an amount, whereas over (and under) refers to spatial locations.

- *Saturday's picnic is expected to attract a crowd of* ***more than*** *100 people.*
- *Put your hands* ***over*** *your head.*

passed/past

Passed is a transitive verb and past participle of the verb pass

She barely **passed the exam.**

Past is a preposition or adjective meaning "by"

We will keep school open **past** June.

She walked **past** without saying hello.

"Passed" is the past tense of "pass."

Harry **passed** Potions with an O.

Jim **passed** the basketball to Blair.

Obi-Wan's speeder **passed** Qui-Gon's.

Also, if someone dies, he or she has **passed** away.

"Past" is not a verb, but it can be an adjective, adverb, preposition or noun.

Obi-Wan was Anakin's master in the **past**.

We drove **past** his house.

Harry has been working hard for the **past** few months.

pacific, specific

This is a mispronunciation. ***Pacific*** means making peace; conciliatory. ***Specific*** means explicit or definite.

precede, proceed

Precede means to go ahead of: The introduction will ***precede*** the reading. ***Proceed*** means to go ahead with an action: ***Proceed*** with the reading.

presently, at present

Presently means soon or will happen shortly: We are waiting for our test results, which will be posted ***presently***. ***At present*** means now, happening currently: At ***present***, he is in the office.

pedal/peddle/petal

A ***"pedal"*** is the thing your foot uses on a bicycle. When you ride a bike, you "pedal." ***"Peddle"*** means to sell. A" petal is the colorful leafy thing on a flower.

Blair **pedaled** his bicycle.

Harry and Ron wanted to see what kinds of gags Fred and

peek/peak/pique

We're talking verbs here: ***"Peek"*** means "to look furtively" or "to glance." ***"Peak"*** means "to reach a maximum" or "to come to a peak."

The inscriptions **piqued** Daniel's curiosity.

Harry **peeked** around the corner.

The temperature **peaked** at 95F.

"Pique" can also be a noun, meaning "a transient feeling of wounded vanity." I'll assume you can figure out "peek" and "peak."

Pansy stormed out of the room in a fit of **pique**.

per se/per say

"Per se" is a Latin phrase meaning "as such" or "intrinsically." "Per say" is totally incorrect. In general, you shouldn't use a foreign word or phrase unless you're very sure of its usage. If you're not sure, there are usually ways to get the point across in English.

It was a good enough film **per se**, but as an adaptation of the book it was based on, it left a lot to be desired. (Thanks, Fox!)

Partisanship **per se** does not preclude political action.

perfect/prefect

This one's mostly for HP writers. A ***"prefect"*** is a kind of official—in particular, it's a student monitor in a private school. Notice that the "r" comes before the "e" in this case. ***"Perfect"***, of course, means "without flaw."

Ron was stunned to find he'd been chosen as **prefect**.

Percy always thought he was the **perfect prefect**.

phase/faze

"Faze" means "to disturb the composure of."

Daniel wasn't **fazed** by Jack's sarcastic remarks.

"Phase" means "to adjust so as to be in a synchronized condition," or "to conduct or carry out by planned phases," or "to introduce in stages."

plane/plain

The noun **plane** usually means "airplane."

His plane arrives in New York at 9:00am.

The adjective **plain** means "simple," "not fancy."

Her dress was very plain.

principal/principle

The **adjective** principal means "chief" or "very important."

The **noun** principal means "chief official."

The principal reason for his failure was lack of support.

I am the principal of this school.

The noun **principle** means "fundamental truth."

He is studying the principles of accounting.

passed/past

Passed is the past tense and past participle of *pass*. *Past* refers to time gone by; it is also a preposition meaning beyond. "In the past decade, I passed over countless opportunities; I was determined not to let them get past me again."

penultimate

Meaning "next to last," *penultimate* is often mistakenly used to mean "the very last," or the ultimate: "The perfectionist was crestfallen when he was awarded the penultimate prize; the grand prize went to another."

precede/proceed

The verb *precede* means to come before. *Proceed* means to move forward. "He preceded me into the room; once I caught up with him I proceeded to tell him off."

principal/principle

Principal is a noun that means a person who holds a high position or plays an important role: "The school principal has 20 years of teaching experience." *Principal* is also an adjective that means chief or leading:

"The necessity of moving to another city was the principal reason I turned down the job offer." *Principle* is a noun that means a rule or standard: "They refused to compromise their principles."

Pretense/Pretext: Pretense means a false appearance or action intended to deceive, and pretext is **a false or fabricated reason developed to hide the truth**.

- *The CEO later realized that the applicant's claim that he had a bachelor's degree was only a* ***pretense.*** (The claim of the degree was false and it was intended to deceive the person hiring him.)

- *The woman called in sick, but it was only a* ***pretext*** *to hide the fact that she going on a vacation.*

personal/personnel

It is only my personal opinion. What's yours?

The personnel manager of the firm interviewed all the candidates for the job.

presently/recently

A new metro will be built in Thessaloniki presently.

John has made much improvement recently.

pore/pour

"Pore" means "to read studiously or attentively."

Harry **pored** over the Divinations text.

Jim **pored** over the report.

prescribe/proscribe

"Prescribe" means "to lay down a rule" or "to designate or order the use of as a remedy." ***"Proscribe"*** means "to condemn or forbid as harmful or unlawful." Completely different meanings, but it's easy to get them confused.

The doctor **prescribed** antibiotics for Blair's strep throat.

The doctor **proscribed** drinking as long as Blair was taking the antibiotics.

Dumbledore **proscribed** entering the Forbidden Forest.

prostate/prostrate

The ***"prostate"*** is the gland that is mentioned so often in slash and in which men occasionally get cancer.

All men over 40 should have a **prostate** exam.

"Prostrate" can be an adjective that means "lying on the ground," or a verb that means "to throw on the ground," or "to put in a humble and submissive posture or state."

Lucius **prostrated** himself before Voldemort.

Luke was **prostrate** from the cold on Hoth.

quiet/quite

Quietis an adjective meaning "not noisy."

It was a very quite party."

Quite is an adverb meaning "completely" or "to a degree."

He is quite upset today.

He is quite short.

rain/rein/reign

"Rain" is the water that falls from the sky, and that's pretty much all it refers to. It can also be used figuratively, as in "raining cats and dogs" or "it's raining men."

"Rein" is the piece of leather that keeps a horse under control. It's used figuratively rather often—you keep someone on a tight rein, or give them free rein.

"Reign" has to do with monarchy—as a noun, it's the period of time during which a monarch rules; as a verb, it's the act of ruling.

Harry hated playing Quidditch in the **rain** because his glasses fogged up.

Hermione kept a tight **rein** on her thoughts.

Professor Dumbledore tended to give Harry free **rein**.

Professor Snape never allowed chaos to **reign** in his classroom.

Silence **reigned** for several minutes.

rare, scarce

Rare means coming or occurring far apart in time; seldom seen; unusual; uncommon: The ***rare*** works of Van Gogh are worth millions. ***Scarce*** means small in quantity in proportion to the demand; not plentiful or abundant; deficient; **rare**, uncommon: The supply of fresh vegetables is ***scarce*** during the winter.

ravish/ravage

To ***"ravage"*** is to "wreak havoc on" or to "commit destructive actions." ***"Ravish"*** means "to seize and take away by violence," "to overcome with beauty," or "to rape." If it's being done to a person, it's probably "ravishing. "***Bartleby.com*** has a good ***note*** on this. (Incidentally, ***"ravishing"*** can also mean "unusually attractive, pleasing, or striking"—like **ravishing** beauty.)

The Death Eaters **ravaged** the house.

The Death Eaters **ravished** Hermione.

A hurricane **ravaged** the coast.

Redundant does not mean useless or unable to perform

its function. It means that there is an excess of something, or that something is "surplus to requirements" and no longer needed.

Reluctant/Reticent: If you are reluctant, you are unwilling or against something. If you are reticent, you are unwilling to speak.

reason is because

The words ***reason is (was, etc)*** should always be followed by a statement of the reason: The ***reason*** for his error ***was*** lack of knowledge. The words ***reason*** and ***because*** convey the same meaning. To use them together is redundant: ***Because*** he lacked the knowledge he made an error.

regardless, *irregardless

Irregardless is a nonstandard word, probably patterned after irrespective. ***Regardless,*** which means without regard or to despite is the correct form: ***Regardless*** of the weather, the picnic will proceed.

respectable, respectful

Respectable means worthy of respect; having a good reputation: He has a ***respectable*** command of computer languages. ***Respectful*** means showing respect for something or someone else: He treated the cliff he was climbing with ***respectful*** caution.

respectively, respectfully

Respectively means individually, in their respective (listed or given) order: He mentioned taxes, education, and health care ***respectively,*** as the most serious issues. ***Respectfully*** means showing respect, courtesy, regard for something or someone else: He answered the judges questions ***respectfully.***(Note: ***respectfully*** is always used to define an action and must refer to the verb preceding it.

respectfully/respectively

Respectfully means "with respect."

The audience rose respectfully when the President entered.

Respectively means "in the order given."

The Suttons lived in Chicago, Los Angeles and New York respectively.

raise/rise

Raise is a transitive verb meaning to move to a higher place.

Tom **raised** his hand to answer a question.

Rise is an intransitive verb meaning to go up or ascend.

The sun**rises** in the morning.

respectable/respectful/respective/respectively

The candidates went to their respective classrooms when the bell rang.

He belongs to the respectable upper classes.

The crowd stood at a respectful distance from the governor.

Our principal is a respectable man.

The students went back to their classrooms respectively after the assembly.

raise/rise/arouse/arise

Many problems arise after the government announced the new taxation policy.

refuse/reject/decline

He refused to help us organize the annual carnival.

He was disappointed to hear that this application was rejected again.

He was so busy that he declined his friend's invitation to dinner.

The committee had considered carefully before rejecting his proposal.

Mr. Wright refused to discuss his plan with his colleagues.

roll/role

"Role" is a noun that can mean "a socially expected behaviour pattern usually determined by an individual's status in a particular society," or "a part played by an actor or singer," or "a function or part performed especially in a particular operation or process." For any other meanings, or a verb, use ***"roll."***

Harry must figure out his **role** in the wizarding world.

What **role** did Alec Guinness play?

It depends on the **roll** of the dice.

Jack was on a **roll**.

Hermione gave the teacher the **roll** of paper.

rightfully, rightly

Rightful or *rightfully* means having a right or just claim, as to some possession or position: He was the *rightful* owner of the vehicle. *Rightly* means properly or correctly, without the legal claim: She *rightly* refused to sign the petition.

say/tell

Say is a transitive verb meaning to express in words

I **said** that she should stay home tonight.

Tell is an intransitive verb also meaning to express in words

I**told** him to stay home but he didn't listen.

(Never, **never, NEVER** told **to** him)

same

Same is not a pronoun and should NOT be used as one: I have your request for the instructions and I will fax **them**. (NOT will fax **same**)

sit/set

Sit is an intransitive verb meaning to rest on something.

Sit on the bench and not on the grass.

Set is a transitive verb meaning to place something.

She **set** the soup and spoons on the table.

sheer/shear

As a verb, ***"shear"*** means to cut the hair or wool off, or "to subject to a shear force," or "to become divided under the action of a shear." As a noun, it's the scissor-like implement used for shearing, or "internal force tangential to the section on which it acts." ***"Sheer"*** is usually an adjective that means transparent or diaphanous—it can also mean unqualified, like **sheer** ignorance. "Sheer" can also be a verb or noun having to do with changing direction.

"There's no way I'm wearing leggings made of such a **sheer** fabric!" complained Obi-Wan.

Jim wondered where Blair had put the kitchen **shears**.

It's time to **shear** the sheep so we can sell the wool.

should of/should have

would of/would have

could of/could have

In all these cases, it's "have." "Of" is wrong.

Ron **should have** finished his Transfigurations homework.

Jim **would have** kissed Blair, but he missed his chance.

In speech, you can contract it to *'ve*. "Of" is still wrong.

"I **could've** gone to Hogsmeade," Harry said.

stationary/stationery

Stationary is an adjective that means fixed or unmoving: "They maneuvered around the stationary barrier in the road." *Stationery* is a noun that means writing materials: "We printed the letters on company stationery."

Sight and **site**. A site is a place, a sight is something seen. The internet may be dazzling to some, but it is not a web-sight!

- *Standard*: You're a sight for sore eyes.
- *Standard*: I literally found lots of sights on the internet—I was looking at a tourist site for Rome.
- *Non-standard*: I found lots of sights on the internet.

speak/speech

Speak is a verb meaning "to say out loud"

"**Speak** louder. I can't hear you!"

Speech is a noun meaning "what is said aloud"

Politicians give the same boring **speech** over and over again when running for political office.

so/so that

So is a conjunction joining a clause of result to a main clause.

It rained a lot last year, so there were lots of wildflowers to enjoy.

(result)

So that joins a clause of purpose to a main clause.

We wore raincoats so that we would not get our clothes wet.

(purpose)

stationary/stationery

Stationary means "in a fixed position."

The car was stationary parked in the driveway.

Stationeryrefers to writing supplies.

That stationery store sells writing paper, envelopes and office supplies.

stanch/staunch

"Stanch" means "to check or stop the flowing of" or "to stop or check in its course." ***"Staunch"*** means "steadfast in loyalty or principle" or "watertight." "Stanch" is a verb; "staunch" is an adjective. In the U.S., the two words are sometimes used interchangeably, but it's generally best to stick with their strict definitions.

Harry was glad to have a **staunch** friend like Ron.

Horatio thought the Indefatigable was the **staunchest** ship in the British Navy.

Blair tried to **stanch** the flow of blood from Jim's wound.

Obi-Wan managed to **stanch** his tears after Anakin threw his teddy bear out the window.

The police are working hard to **stanch** the crime wave.

scene/scenery

They were fascinated by the scenery of the countryside.

That soldier never forgets the scene of a great battle.

The drama consists of five scenes.

sometime/sometimes/some time

He will leave for Scotland sometime next year.

Sometimes I watch television till midnight.

We haven't seen Amy for some time.

successive/succession/success/successful

They were busy with their work in five successive days.

They did not give up in spite of a succession of defeats.

It is said that John will be in succession to his father's property.

Congratulations! Your plan is really a treat success.

supine/prone

"Supine" means lying on one's back. ***"Prone"*** means lying on one's front.

Snape lay **prone** before Voldemort.

Blair lay **supine**, staring up at the ceiling.

That/Which: Which should be used to introduce essential clauses, and that should be used to introduce nonessential clauses. An essential clause is needed in order for the sentence to convey its message; however, a nonessential clause is simply extra information added to the sentence for description or other purposes.

than/then

Than is a conjunction used in comparisons

She is taller **than** her sister.

Then as an adjective or adverbial conjunction relates to time

First we will work; **then** we will go out for lunch.

There, their and **they're**. While they all sound the same, in standard written English they all have separate, definite meanings, and are not interchangeable. *There* refers to the location of something.*Their* means "belonging to them". *They're* is a contraction of "They are".

Their is the third-person plural possessive pronoun.

They sold **their** car last week.

There is an adverb of place or an expletive that tells of existence.

"Your package is there on the counter."

"There are fifty states in United States."

There're is the contraction of "they are".

"They're ready to see you now."

tenet/tenant

"Tenants" are people who rent property. ***"Tenets"*** are principles or doctrines.

I have to follow the **tenets** of my religion.

to/too/two

To is (1) part of the infinitive form or (2) a preposition.

"I like to walk in the snow."

"I walked to the park on Saturday."

Too is an adverb indicating an excess.

"It is too cold to go swimming."

Two is a number (2).

"I have two cats; one named kitty and one called whiskers."

than/then

"Than" is used in comparisons.

Hermione is older **than** Harry.

Jim is taller **than** Blair.

Harry would rather eat dirt **than** study Potions.

Otherwise, you want *"then"*, which usually involves some sort of sequences, but not necessarily.

They ate dinner, **then** they had pudding.

If you want to learn to drive, **then** you must take lessons.

Your mind is made up, **then**?

Killing Voldemort will require all Harry's determination and **then** some.

Blair lost the election, but **then** he didn't expect to win.

Since **then**, Obi-Wan has been practicing.

Teal'c misses his family now and **then**.

Than is a conjunction used in comparisons

She is taller **than** her sister.

Then as an adjective or adverbial conjunction relates to time

First we will work; **then** we will go out for lunch.

their/they're/there

"Their" is the possessive form of "they." See below for more on this.

"They're" is a contraction of "they are."

Everything else is *"there."*

Jim and Blair bought **their** tickets for the Jaguars game.

Jack yelled, "**They're** coming to take me away!"

The landspeeder is over **there**.

thorough/through

The police carried out thorough investigation into the murder case.

That window is too narrow to get through.

I wondered how he got through his examination.

tired/tiresome

He felt tired after Working for a long time.

The tiresome students made the teacher very angry.

that/which/who

"That," "which" and *"who"* are all ***relative pronouns***, but there are some differences in how they're used.

First, though, let's talk about restrictive vs. non-restrictive clauses. A restrictive clause is information that's necessary to figure out what's being talked about. For instance, let's say I'm standing on a sidewalk in front of two blue houses. I could say, "I live in the blue house that has the red door." In this case, "that has the red door" is necessary because, without it, you wouldn't know which blue house I'm referring to. This is a restrictive clause.

threw/through

"Threw" is the past tense of "throw." ***"Through"*** isn't a verb, although it can be a lot of other things. Make sure you're using the right one.

Oliver Wood **threw** the quaffle to Katie Bell.

The path goes **through** the Forbidden Forest.

throe/throw

A ***"throe"*** is a pang or spasm, or a hard, painful struggle. A ***"throw"*** is the act of tossing something, or it can be a light cover or wrap.

The injured dog was in its death **throes**.

France was in the **throes** of revolution.

Qui-Gon bet Watto on the **throw** of the die.

trooper/trouper

A ***"trooper"*** is a soldier or a policeman. A ***"trouper"*** is a member of an acting troupe, or "a person who deals with and persists through difficulty or hardship without complaint." If you want to say someone is a real trouper, it's the word with the "u."

The four-year-old was a **trouper** for not complaining while he was in the hospital.

venal/venial

Venal is an adjective that means corruptible; *venial* is an adjective that means a slight flaw or offense: "In the Catholic church, a venial sin is one that is minor and pardonable, whereas a mortal sin is a serious transgression involving more venal or depraved behaviour."

valuable/invaluable/priceless/worthless

I would like to thank Sergeant Alexander for his invaluable service to us.

This is really a very valuable gift.

She was given a priceless diamond ring for her wedding anniversary.

Nobody will take care of a worthless old car.

tortuous, torturous

Tortuous means full of twists, turns or bends: *tortuous* road. *Torturous* means full of, involving, or causing torture: *Tortuous* devices, such as the rack, were use during the Spanish Inquisition.

unique

Unique means without a like or equal; unmatched; unequaled; single in its kind; uncommon or rare. It cannot logically be used in a comparative or superlative for. Something may be more or less rare but NOT more or less *unique*.

vial/vile

A *"vial"* is "a small closed or closable vessel especially for liquids." *"Vile"* means despicable, repulsive, abhorrent, or "disgustingly or utterly bad."

Snape put the potion in the **vial**.

Snape is known for his **vile** temper.

What **vile** weather we're having!

vicious/viscous

"Vicious" means depraved, impure, spiteful, damaged or malicious. *"Viscous"* means "having a glutinous consistency." Make sure you're choosing the right one and spelling it correctly.

Harry, Ron and Hermione thought Fluffy looked **vicious**.

wake/awake/awaken/waken

Mary got up late this morning because her mother forgot to wake her up.

It is difficult to make him awake to the problem.

The accident awakens him to the danger of careless driving.

Is the patient awake or asleep?

He woke up at half past six yesterday.

waist/waste

The *"waist"* is the part of a body where you'd wear a belt. All the other meanings are *"waste"*.

Jim wrapped the belt around his **waist**.

If you don't eat, you'll **waste** away to nothing.

Television has been referred to as a vast **wasteland**.

Don't **waste** food; there are children starving in China.

A mind is a terrible thing to **waste**.

A **waist** is a terrible thing to mind.

weather/whether

"Weather", in general, is what's going on outside—rain, snow, wind, sun, etc. It can also be a verb meaning "to subject to the elements" or "to bear up against and come safely through." ***"Whether"***, on the other hand, is either a pronoun or a ***conjunction*** having to do with choosing one of two alternatives.

Blair **weathered** the storm of the dissertation fiasco.

What's the **weather** like today?

I can't decide **whether** to watch the first or second Harry Potter movie.

Weather is a noun meaning "atmospheric conditions."

"The weather was not nice enough to go out."

Whether is a conjunction meaning "if."

"I don't know whether he will stay at home or not."

Won't and **wont** (rhymes with *font*). Won't is a contraction for "will not", and wont is a rarely-used archaism: as a noun it means *habit;* as a verb it is an auxiliary with the same function as *used*.

who's/whose

Who's is the contraction for who is.

"I don't know who's coming tonight."

Whose is (1) a question word or (2) a possessive relative pronoun.

"Whose pen is this?"

"I met the man whose child scored the winning goal."

Who's is the contraction of *who is*. *Whose* is the possessive form of *who*. "Who's going to figure out whose job it is to clean the stables?"

who/whom

"Who" is the subject form; ***"whom"*** is the object form. If you're trying to figure out which to use, try replacing it with "he" or "him." If "he" is correct, then use "who." If "him" is correct, use "whom."

Ask not for **whom** the bell tolls. (The bell tolls for him.)

Who was at the door? (He was at the door.)

Whom did you speak to? (You did speak to him.)

The prize is for the student **who** has the highest score. (He has the highest score.)

You're, your, yore and **ewer**. While they sound the same in many dialects, in standard written English they all have separate meanings. *You're* is a contraction for "you are", and *your* is a possessive pronoun meaning "belonging to you". When in doubt, just see whether you can logically expand it to "you are". The third homonym, *yore,* is an archaism meaning in the distant past, and is almost always used in the phrase "in days of yore". The fourth is the name of a once common piece of household equipment made obsolete by indoor plumbing: the large jug holding washing water.

wrack/rack

This one gets really complicated; use it at your own risk. The ***"wrack,"*** as a noun, can mean "wreckage," "ruin," "destruction" or "marine vegetation (like kelp)." As a verb it means "to utterly ruin." American dictionaries say the phrase "wrack and ruin" is proper usage. ***"Rack"*** has a lot of meanings, but the ones that tend to get confused with "wrack" generally have to do with pain. It can mean "to torture on a rack," or "to stretch or strain violently," or "to cause anguish." A "rack" is a torture instrument on which a person is stretched—it can also be "a cause of anguish and pain" or "the action of straining or wrenching."

In British English, "wrack" definitely has the "marine vegetation" and "shipwreck" meanings, but after that, things get a little confusing. Its usage tends to vary by geography; in some areas, "wrack and ruin" would be correct, but other areas would use "rack and ruin."

Unit 5

English Usage: Words and Phrases

A whole	:	Used when a man of substance is belittled e.g See how mobile police trash the guy, a whole managing director for dat matter
Abeg	:	Please.
Abi?	:	Is it not?.
Abi na wetin!	:	What is it?
ABU	:	Amadu Bello University.
Acada	:	1. Intellectual 2. University student 3. Book worm.
Adire	:	Dyed cloth.
Adonkia	:	contraction for I don't care attitude
Afang	:	Efik soup made from Afang leaves, beef, dried fish, crayfish, palm oil, and periwinkle.
Afraid catch me	:	I was scared.
Afta	:	After
Agaracha	:	Woman of easy virtue.
Agbada	:	Large traditional garment usually worn by men over a shirt.
Agip	:	Any Government In Power. Derisory term for person who changes alliances as goverments come and go.
Agument	:	Argument.
Ah-ah	:	For goodness sake.
Aircon	:	Abbreviation for air conditioner.
Ajasco	:	Dancing with fanciful footwork. Also called Ajasco Toronto.

Ajebota	:	One used to butter; rich spoilt kid. See Ajepako.
Ajepako	:	Literally means -one used to eating wood i.e. uses a wooden chewing stick as toothbrush.
Akamu	:	Pap made from corn. See Ogi.
Akara	:	Bean cake made from fried ground black-eyed beans.
Akara school	:	Nursery school.
Alan Pozza	:	Poser.
Alau	:	Allow.
Alau him	:	Give him a break.
All na	:	It is all a .e.g All na wayo.
All night	:	Night vigil.
All Weda	:	Shoes worn all the time, come rain come sunshine.
Along!	:	Shouted when hailing taxi cabs in some states in Nigeria.
Am	:	Used in place of 'him' or 'her' in sentence e.g. 'Warn am O!'
Amala	:	Dough like meal made from yam flour and hot water. Usually served with Ewedu soup.
Amebo	:	1. Gossip 2. Name of a character in a Nigerian soap opera (The village headmaster), with a penchant for gossiping.
Amerika	:	America.
Any attempt!	:	Don't even think about it!
Anyhow	:	1. Shoddy 2. Inappropriate
Akpere	:	1. Basket 2. Bad goalkeeper in soccer match.
Apoti	:	Yoruba word for small stool
Appear	:	1. Arrive unexpected usually to something good such as a meal. Host will then say 'you waka well o'. 2. Arrive uninvited.
Arrange yua sef	:	1. Make your own arrangements 2. Everyman to himself.

Arrangee	:	1.Soiree. 2. Exclusive 3.Preplanned set up.
Area boys	:	Unemployed street-wise youth loitering in the neighbourhood. Also called 'Alaye boys' in Lagos.
Area girls	:	Female Anopheles mosquitoes.
Ariya	:	Good time.
Aro	:	1.Abbreviation for large psychiatric hospital in western Nigeria. 2. Lunatic.
Aromental	:	1. Lunatic 2. Eccentric personality. (See Mentalo).
As	:	How it e.g. 'Tell am as e take happun'.
As for	:	That's the way it is.
Ashewo	:	Prostitute. See Agharacha.
Aunty	:	Any older female. Used when first name terms not appropriate.
Awa	:	Our.
Awoko	:	Burning the midnight oil.
Awoof	:	Freebie. Without charge. See FOC.
Away	:	Foreign especially Europe and America.
Away Baffs	:	Imported clothes from Europe and America; especially designer labels. See Sputs, kack and Sputeez.
Baba	:	Father (Yoruba)
Baba Jiga	:	Derisory name for a person suffering from Jiga infestation. Also Baba sore.
Babawilly	:	Internet pen name of the author of this dictionary.
Babar	:	Verb. Hair cut
Babariga	:	Large traditional robe worn by man. See Agbada.
Babo!	:	WOW! Also Ibabo!
Babi	:	1.Baby 2. Pretty girl.
Babi pancake	:	Girl fond of make-up.
Back	:	Carry a baby tied to the back with lappa
Backyard	:	Bottom. See Yarnsh.
Bale	:	Eat greedily.
Baler	:	One who eats greedily. See Long throat.
Bam	:	In good condition. See Kampke.

Banga	:	Palm tree fruit.
Banga soup	:	Soup made from Palm tree fruit.
Barawo	:	Thief
Basia	:	Large aluminium metal basin.
Bata	:	Shoe.
Battalion	:	Large family. See Papa Battalion.
Baze	:	Woo a girl. See Spin.
Beat am die	:	Beat to the point of death.
Been to	:	Well travelled.
Belle-turn me	:	1. Diarrhoea 2. Abdominal colic. 3. Nausea.
Bi as e get	:	See Get as e bi.
Biam Bia	:	Beard .Also- Byah-byah.
Bico	:	Please.
Bicos	:	Because
Bicos why?	:	The reason is
Black soap	:	Traditional soap made from Palm oil. Also called Ose Dudu in Yoruba.
Bleach	:	Use of skin lightening creams. Also Bleaching.
Blokkus	:	Scrotum.
Blow	:	1 Punch 2 Speak with arrogance e.g. sofri-sofri blow Oyinbo.
Bodi dey inside cloth	:	I am surviving.
Bodi do me	:	Premonition.
Bodi no bi firewood	:	The body has its limitations.
Boi	:	Boy.
Bole kaja	:	Yoruba for come down and let's fight and used for over crowded commuter bus in Lagos. See Molue.
Bold face	:	To bluff one's way through a situation.
Boli	:	Roast plantain.
Bom-boy	:	Baby boy.
Boma boi	:	Thug. Derived from Burma boy. Term probably originates from Nigerians who served under the British in Burma during WW2.
Bosaut	:	1. Burst out 2. Come out 3. Explode.
Bottom Box	:	Treasured attire worn only on important

		occasions. e.g Dat yua dress na real bottom box o!
Bottom-pot	:	Dregs at the bottom of the pot.
Boyi-boy	:	Houseboy.
Branch	:	Detour during pre arranged trip.
Bread	:	Naira (money)
Break Kola	:	Ritual breaking of the Kola nut at the beginning of a ceremony.
Brekoyan	:	Yoruba slang for Brassiere.
Broda	:	Brother.
Broda-broda	:	Nepotism. See Fren-fren and Who know man.
Broke	:	1. Break e.g Na you broke di plate.2. Speak with big English words e.g Abeg sofri broke the grammar now.
Brokun	:	1. Broken English 2. Pidgin English.
Brokun plate	:	Breakable plates especially China.
Brush	:	Hit someone hard.
Buba	:	Traditional blouse.
Bubble	:	1 Dance 2 Party.
Burukutu	:	Illicit homemade gin. See Apketeshi.
Bush man	:	Unsophisticated man. (derisive usage)
Bush meat	:	Game.
Bust	:	1 Write off 2 Ignore. See Fashie.
Butta my bread	:	Answered prayer. E.g God don butta my bread.
Butter	:	Another name for Ajebota. Also Omobota
Buredi	:	Bread.
Call	:	To be beckoned by unseen forces. Juju is usually implied e.g. dem dey call you?
Cantab	:	Run full circle and over take fellow athlete in long distance race.
Carry dey do	:	Behave badly.
Carry go	:	Used playfully to mean -Get away or Get out of here.
Carry woman	:	verb 1. Womaniser e.g. you too carry woman.
Cease light	:	Power failure. See Nepa.

Chai!	:	Good grief
Characteristics of Tombo	:	Sang to the tune of Michael Jackson's You wanna be starting something. (See Tombo)
Chance	:	1 Take advantage of. 2 Intimidate 3 Cheat e.g. abeg no chance me jo!
Changer	:	Hifi
Charge	:	Loose one's temper.
Chassis	:	Brand new car
Chei!	:	Goodness! See Chai.
Chickito	:	Young pretty girl.
Chin	:	1. Frowning 2. Angry. Also - Chinning.
Chop-remain	:	Leftovers of meal.
Coke and Fanta	:	Derisory term used to describe the mottled complexion one who uses skin bleaching products.
Comot for road	:	1. Make way 2. Get away!
Compin	:	Company.
Compound	:	Fenced off house, bungalow or groups of huts.
Condemn	:	Spoilt beyond repair e.g. see how she juss condemn the moto.
Confido	:	1 Confidence 2 Self confidence.
Confra	:	University Campus Fraternity. See Cult Guy.
Congo-meat	:	Cooked snail
Coolee	:	1 Relaxed 2 Cool 3 Chill.
Coolu-down	:	Simmer down.
Coolu temper	:	1. Control your temper! 2. Title of song by Nigerian saxophonist Lagbaja.
Corner-corner	:	Illegal.
Corofo	:	Army recruit.
Coror	:	1. Dark corner 2. Crevice.
Correct	:	Very good. e.g Di bobo na correct guy.
Correct Correct	:	Extremely good.
Cortex	:	Nail varnish.
Count	:	Afford e.g You fit count Twenty thousand as you stand so?

Crape	:	Defraud completely e.g. e crape all my money or E don crape my head pata-pata. 2 Finish (food) completely. See Level.
Crash helmet	:	Prominent forehead. Also Opun.
Craw-craw	:	Skin ailment especially rashes.
Craze	:	Crazy.
Cross leg	:	Idleness. e.g see as e cross leg dey wait awoof.
Cruise	:	Use excessively.
Cry blood	:	Threat. E.g. you go cry blood today today.
Cry-cry	:	Cry baby.
Cry dey call you	:	Threat to a child before a smacking. See Trouble dey call you.
Cut	:	Share of the loot. Usually involves a bribe.
Cut and sew	:	Bespoke tailor. See Mobile tailor.
Dabaru	:	Spoil.
Dada	:	Dread locks. Also called Bob Marley.
Danfo	:	VW Combi bus.
Dash	:	1. Gift 2. Bribe.
Dat	:	That.
Dat na question?	:	Rebuff to a silly question.
Dey there now	:	1 Keep on in self deceit 2 It is there at present.
Deshine	:	Public humiliation.
Die for	:	In love with.
Di	:	The.
Different different	:	Assorted e.g Na different different kain fish dey inside dat soup.
Dig am out	:	Fight e.g We two go dig am out.
Diopka	:	Elderly wise one.
Dis	:	This.
Dishi	:	Embarrass. See Deshine.
Do	:	Participate e.g. I no do again. 2. Afflicting one's health e.g. Wetin dey do am?
Do anyhow	:	Unruly.
Do betta	:	Show us the colour of your money. See Shake bodi.
Do quick	:	Hurry up!.

Doing laik dis	:	Acting this way e.g. Why are you doing laik dis now?
Don	:	1. Has e.g. e don come. 2. Has it? E.g. e don come? 3. Have e.g. I don tell am (present tense) 4. Have e.g. I don been tell am (Past tense).
Don run	:	Has ran away.
Donatus	:	(Derisory) One in habit of giving their services to others for free. Derived from-donate.
Done	:	Cooked e.g. yua own done?
Dormot	:	1 Door mat 2 Area in front of main door to house.
Dorti-dorti	:	Garbage.
Dorti slap	:	dirty slap Hard slap across the face.
Doz bin	:	Garbage can.
Draw	:	Slimy e.g Di Okra soup draw well well.
Draw bodi take	:	1. Withdraw 2. Make hasty exit. 3. Avoiding getting drawn into a dicey situation.
Draw my throat	:	1 Stimulate my appetite 2 Entice me.
Draw rain	:	Make an empty boast. Also Rake and Shakara.
Draw soup	:	Slimy soup usually containing Okra.
Dress	:	1. Any kind of clothing. 2. Move your butt.
Drink garri	:	1.In trouble e.g. you go drink garri today.2. Meal of garri and water. See Soak garri.
Drop	:	1. A taxi journey e.g Oga, na fifty Naira per drop. 2. To alight from a bus. 3. Pay up 4. Monetary bribe.
Dros	:	Voluminous underwear.
Dry	:	1 Slim person.
Dub	:	1. Make extra copy of music tape 2. Copy neighbour's work during examination.
Dudu	:	Dark skinned person.
Dundi	:	Fool.
E Dey hard	:	It is a rarity e.g E dey hard make Saturday night meet am for house.

E don do	:	It is enough.
Eagles	:	See Super Eagles.
Eba	:	Meal made with garri and hot water. Usually eaten with soup with bare fingers of right hand. See Garri.
Econs	:	(Abbreviation of economy) Stingy. See Tight hand.
Effa	:	Ever.
Efritin	:	Everything.
Egbe	:	Fool.
Ego	:	Money.
Egunje	:	1. Bribe or 2. Kick back..
Eh?	:	1. What? 2. What!
Eh-eh	:	1. No 2. Not at all.
Eh-yah	:	1. Sorry 2. What a pity 3. How touching
Ehen?	:	So what?
Ehen	:	Is that so.
Enta	:	Enter.
Enta road	:	1. Get out of control. 2. Drive car into the streets.
Enta market	:	1 Go crazy.
Enta trouble	:	Get into trouble.
Everywhere tinted	:	Wearing really dark sun glasses. See Bones and Shaded up.
Ewa	:	Beans.
Ewa Agoyin	:	1. A kind of beans 2. Street hawkers who sell cooked beans.
Expo	:	1. Leaked examination question paper. 2. Contraction of exposed
Eye glass	:	Spectacles.
Eye go come down	:	Come back to reality.
Fabu	:	1. Unlikely tale. 2. Tall Tale
Fa fa fa foul!	:	1. That is totally objectionable.
Face to face	:	Rooms rented to families which all open onto a long corridor. Also Room and parlour.
Face yua front	:	Face forward.
Fada	:	Father.

Fain	:	See Fine.
Fain-fain	:	Completely.
Fain for face	:	Pretty face.
Faif	:	Five.
Fait	:	Fight.
Falcons	:	Nigerian national female football team.
Fap	:	Steal. Also Tap or Tapping.
Fashie	:	1. Ignore 2. Forget.
Fawul	:	Fowl.
Faya	:	Fire.
Feferity	:	1. Showing off 2. Pretending to be classy.
Felele	:	1. Light plastic football. 2. Neighborhood in Ibadan
Fence	:	Exclude.
Fiam	:	At lightening speed e.g See as the car overtake us fiam.
Fillage	:	Village.
Fine fine	:	Extremely well.
Find my mouth	:	To extract a comment.
Find my trouble	:	Get on one's nerves.
Fine	:	1. Beautiful person or object 2. Alright.
Fine boy connection	:	Handsome lad.
Fi si	:	See Jara.
Fly	:	1. Jump across a fence e.g the tief fly di fence fiam. 2. Jump across open drainage gutter.
Fly your polo	:	Wear shirt with collar turned up. Also- Fly your shirt.
FOC	:	Free of charge.
Forbid	:	Have an aversion to certain foods e.g. I dey forbid goat meat on Sundays. Usually related to Juju.
For life	:	No chance in a million! See lai-lai
For where?	:	Impossible See Whosai
Form fool	:	Fool around.
Foto	:	Photograph.
Four-o-four	:	1. Peugeot 404 2. Cooked dog meat i.e. the dogcatcher needs to be fast to make the kill

Fren-fren	:	Favouritism.
Front	:	Presence e.g Who born am to talk dat nonsense for mai front
Frovlem	:	Problem.
Fufu	:	Dough like meal made from hot water and either cassava or plaintain flour. Usually served with soup
Fun won ton	:	Meaning - Give dem finish. 1. To make a memorable entrance. 2. Dress very well.
Full ground remain	:	Excess e.g. See how food full ground remain for the party. Shoo!
Gaining calories	:	Couple in tight embrace. Also-Gaining electrons.
Garium Sulphate	:	Garri. [pseudo chemical composition of Gari]
Garri	:	Dried cassava flour.
Gauge	:	Bellyful.
Gbagam	:	Loud clapper of bells.
Gbagbati	:	Excessive display.
Gbagbe!	:	Dismissive. Means Forget that one!.
Gbaladun	:	Enjoyment.
Gbana	:	Marijuana. See Igbo.
Gba summer	:	Enjoy.
Gba winter	:	1. Suffer 2. Loneliness
Gbanjo	:	Cheap market sale.
Gbedu	:	1. Rhythmic Afro beat sound 2. Loud sound system.
Gen-gen	:	1. Exciting 2. On the edge.
Gerrout	:	Get out of here.
Geisha	:	Brand of sardines in tomato sauce.
Get	:	1. To have or own e.g. I get shirt like dat. 2. To understand e.g. I don get wetin you dey yarn.
Get as e bi	:	There's something odd about it.
Get belle	:	Get pregnant. See Pregnapoline.
Get bodi	:	Overweight.
Get gist	:	Important information to tell e.g. I get gist for you.

Get head	:	1. Sensible 2. Genuine e.g that deal no get head at all
Get mouth	:	1 Talkative 2 Acid tongue. 3 Gift of the garb.
Get road	:	1. Right of way while driving e.g. Na mi get road but e come shunt me. 2. Delusions of grandeur e.g. See poor man dey waka as if na im get road.
Get sense	:	Intelligence e.g. So you think say na you get sense pass?
Gettaway you	:	Get out.
Giddying	:	Kissing.
Gidi	:	Lagos. Also Las Gidi.
Gif	:	Give.
Gi mi	:	Give it to me.
Giraffe	:	Examination malpractice were the neck is stretched to spy neighbour's work.
Girls follow me	:	Hair cut with horizontal parting on back of head.
Gism	:	GSM phone.
Gist	:	1. conversation 2. Idle chat
Give chance	:	1. Excuse me! 2. Get lost!
Give dem finish	:	Big entrance.
Give raps	:	See Spin.
Go	:	1. Will 2. Indicating intent. (In present tense) e.g. I go beat you O!
God forbid	:	God will not allow that to happen.
God forbid bad thing	:	God will not allow that to happen. Also God forbid.
Gorimapka	:	Derived from name of soap character with clean- head. Clean shaven head. See Moro-moro.
Got gist	:	Hear through the grapevine. Also Gotten gist and Them say.
Grab	:	Muscular.
Grabeez	:	Big muscles.
Gra-gra	:	1. Commotion 2. Hustle 3. Overactive 4. Aggressive

Gree-gree	:	See Gra-gra.
Gree	:	Agree.
Gree yua own	:	1. Takes a fancy to you e.g. di bobo gree yua own o! 2. Agree with you.
Ground no level	:	I don't have enough money.
Gulder	:	Brand of Nigerian beer.
Guud	:	Good.
Guguru	:	Pop corn.
Guy	:	Man about town.
Guy name	:	Trendy nickname.
Guy way	:	Acting cool.
Gwaince	:	To eat.
Haba!	:	Good grief!
Hail	:	Cheer someone.
Hala	:	1. Raise ones voice 2. Scream.
Hear di smell	:	Smell the aroma.
Hear word	:	Obey instruction. e.g. you no dey hear word
Heart cut	:	Frightened e.g. My heart juss cut.
Heavy men	:	Tough guy.
Helele	:	Exceptional.
Highway manager	:	Public cleaner of major roads in Lagos.
Hiss	:	sound emitted while sucking ones teeth. Duration is proportional to emotional state ay the time
Hold belle	:	Prevent hunger e.g Abeg take dis chin-chin hold belle till the yam cook.
Hold this one for hand	:	1.Take 2.Take this monetary gift.
Hold-up	:	Traffic jam.
Home delivery	:	Girl sent off to meet husband for first time following arranged marriage.
Home training	:	Well brought up. E.g. e no get home training meaning she wasn't brought up well.
Home trouble	:	A personal disaster blamed on a family member using Juju to cause problems.
Hor!	:	See Shoo!

Hot drink	:	Alcoholic beverages.
House	:	1. Room 2. Anywhere inside a house.
How bodi?	:	How are you?
How dey go dey go?	:	1. How are things with you? 2. How are things going?
How e bi?	:	How is it?
How far?	:	See How bodi?
How for do?	:	How are we going to do it?
How I go come do?	:	What am I supposed to do?
How manage?	:	How did it happen?
How now?	:	See How bodi?
How pepper ?	:	How are you financially?
I never see!	:	Oh, I never!
I no get yua time	:	I have no time for you
I think?	:	Is it not so?
Iacon	:	Air conditioner.
Iapot	:	Air port.
Ibeji	:	Twins.
Ikebe	:	Bottom. See Yarnsh.
Ikpekere	:	Fried unripe plantain chips. See Dodo.
Ja	:	Run away.
Jab	:	1. Profession 2.Place of work.
Jack	:	Read seriously especially for examination.
Jaga-jaga	:	Haphazard
Jaki	:	1. Very hard worker 2. Worker being taken advantage of.
Jaku-jaku	:	Carelessly put together.
Jagbajantis	:	Nonsense
Jaguda	:	Crook.
Jam	:	1. Collision, especially cars. 2. Meet up see also Block.
Jam bodi	:	Rough bodily contact.
Jamb	:	Joint Admission and Matriculation Board. Body in charge of University entrance in Nigeria who organise a yearly entrance examination.
Jambite	:	Freshman in Nigerian university.
Jambito	:	See Jambite.

Jambress	:	Female freshman in Nigerian universities.
Jandon	:	London.
Jankara	:	1. Market in Lagos 2. Fake products.
Janglova	:	1.Merry-go-round. 2. Playground swing
Jara	:	Extra helping. Also Fi si.
Jare	:	See Ojare.
Jazz	:	Nonsense. e.g Ol' boy why you dey talk Jazz laik dat?
Jedi Jedi	:	Piles.
Jeje	:	1.Gentle. 2. Polite. 3. Up standing individual.
Jejeli	:	Adverb of Jeje meaning Gently.
Jibiti	:	Fraudster. See 419.
Jiga	:	Parasitic worm infestation on legs or foot such as Guinea worm. See Baba Jiga.
Joke na joke	:	This is no longer funny! Also - If na joke stop am!
Jollof	:	Paella like dish of rice made with tomatoes, peppers and spices. A Nigerian party dish.
Joint	:	1. Watering hole where food and drinks are sold.
Judge	:	Say ones side of the story in a dispute.
Jugunu	:	Rough neck.
Juju	:	Black magic.
Jump up pee	:	See Koko ise trousa
June 12	:	1. Date election result was annulled in Nigeria. 2. Fraud 3. Election malpractice.
Jungle city	:	Ajejunle. A rough part of Lagos.
Juss	:	Just.
Juss dey patch am	:	Just surviving
K-leg	:	1. Knock-knees 2. Unexpected Complications in a situation 3. Unexpected problems e.g. K-leg don enta di matter.
Kabu-kabu	:	See carbu-carbu.
Kack	:	Dress well. See Sput, Spoot, Baffs and Give dem finis.
Kai-kai	:	Home made gin. See Apketeshi.
Kain	:	Kind of.

Kampke	:	1.Complete 2. Completely at ease.
Kanda	:	1. Peelings 2. Hide 3. Skin.
Kari	:	Carry.
Kashi	:	Gambling especially with cards.
Kata-kata	:	Commotion.
Kaun	:	Potash.
Keep Lagos clean	:	Large bell bottomed trousers that drags on the floor. See Labu
Kekere	:	Small; Yoruba word.
Khaki bois	:	The army.
Kick moto	:	Turn car engine on.
Ki lo de	:	What is wrong? Yoruba phrase.
Ki lon' haps	:	Whazuuppp??
Kobo	:	Nigerian coin. 100 kobo= 1 Naira.
Kobo-leg	:	Bow leg.
Ko ko e se	:	Trouser that barely reaches ankle. Also Jump up pee.
Kol	:	Call.
Kondishon	:	Condition.
Korodoome	:	Large vessel for storing water.
Kudi	:	Money.
Kuk	:	1. Cook. 2. To be given protective charms by witch doctor e.g Babalawo don kuk am well well.
Kuku	:	Word placed in sentence for emphasis e.g. I no Kuku sabi am, meaning I really don't know him. Also Kukuma.
Kulikuli	:	Small fried balls of peanut paste.
Kunu	:	Refreshing Nigerian drink made from Sorghum or Millet. Drunk in Northern Nigeria.
Labu	:	Bell bottomed trousers.
Lahila Hilalau!	:	Oh gosh!
Lai	:	Lie.
Lai lai	:	Not in a million years. Also Lai lai to lai lai.
Lait	:	1. Light 2. Electricity e.g. NEPA don commot lait again.

Lakuli!	:	Oh my word!
Lama	:	Cow.
Land	:	Arrive e.g. e don land
Land you slap	:	Threat meaning I will slap you face e.g I go land you slap o! Also Wipe and Tear you slap.
Lanko	:	Guinness stout drink. Also called Odeku.
Lap	:	Carry someone on your laps during ride in a car or bus.
Las Gidi	:	Lagos.
Lasu	:	Lagos State University.
Last year tori	:	Old news.
Launch	:	Use newly brought item for first time.
Learn work	:	Do apprentice.
Lef	:	Leave.
Leg no dey comot	:	Someone who seems to always be present e.g. dat bobo leg no dey comot church.
Leg no dey house	:	One who goes out too much. Also Waka about and Waka waka
Leg no dey stay one place	:	1. Restless 2. Constantly moving about.
Leke leke	:	Type of bird. Cattle Egret
Lepa Shandy	:	Slim (skinny) girl
Let my people go	:	Result that is barely above the pass mark in examination.
Level	:	Eat and finish a substantial amount of food. E.g. See as e level di eba.
Like play like play	:	Before you knew it. Also - No do no do.
Light	:	Electricity power supply.
Listen well well	:	Pay good attention.
Load	:	Eat too much E.g. E juss load poundi finis come dey ask for eba.
LOC	:	Local organising committee. Usually formed to run a major sporting event.
Local champion	:	A provincial super star.
Lokito	:	Uninformed and not travelled.
Lookery	:	Looking at things one's eyes are not supposed to see.

Long leg	:	Well connected. e.g. na long leg e use enta dat school
Long throat	:	Greed. Also Lagga throat.
Love in Tokyo	:	Excessive public show of affection by couple.
Machine	:	Motor cycle. See Okada
Mach	:	Trample upon. Also Mash.
Magani	:	Native aphrodisiac.
Maggi	:	Maggi cubes. Brand of seasoning cubes for cooking containing herbs and spices.
Mago-mago	:	Ilegal deal.
Magun	:	Spell put on woman said to kill her partner if involved in adulterous relationship.
Mai	:	My. e.g Commot mai front
Make	:	1. Made e.g. Wetin make am sick. 2. Should I? E.g. Wetin make I do? 3. Let me e.g. Make I warn you o! 4. Parade one's self e.g. E juss dey make up and down.
Make eye	:	Wink.
Make mouth	:	Boast.
Make yeye	:	1. Make fun 2. Crack jokes 3. Misbehave.
Mek	:	Make.
Make I hear word	:	Shut up.
Make I see road	:	Get out of my face.
Malu	:	Cow. Also Lama.
Mama dash	:	Hand me down clothes from a lady.
Mammy wagon	:	Wooden construction on the chassis of a lorry for carry passengers.
Mammy water	:	Mermaid.
Man	:	1 Myself.
Man picken	:	1. Me.
Man no die, man no rotten	:	1. I am barely surviving.
Manage	:	Make do with second best.
Many leg	:	Complications e.g. Dat business don get Many leg.
Markit	:	1. Merchandise
Mash	:	Trample upon. See Mach

Mate	:	1. Age group. 2. Same social class. e.g. which day we become mate?
Matric	:	Matriculation into university.
Matric gown	:	Matriculation gown.
Mayguard	:	Night watch man.
Meanwilli	:	Mean while.
Mede-mede	:	1. Salads 2. Foreign cuisine.
Medicine	:	1. Juju 2. Tablets. Also called Melesin and medi.
Megida	:	Big man. Also Oga.
Mentalo	:	See Aromental.
Me shio nu	:	Shut up; Igbo word.
Mescaform	:	Mess up e.g Ol'boy, why you kon dey mescaform now?
Mesej	:	Message.
Mess	:	Fart. See Pollute.
Micro stuff	:	Small print information.
Miliki	:	Enjoyment.
Minerals	:	Soft drinks
Mind tell me	:	Intuition.
Mister man	:	Hey you!
Moin moin	:	Steamed cake of ground black eyed beans containing pepper, bits of fish or corned beef. Also spelt Moyin moyin.
babon dey chop	:	The workers don't partake of the harvest despite their hard work.
Molue	:	Rickety bright yellow bus used for transportation in Lagos.
Moro-moro	:	Clean-shaven head. Also Gorimapka.
Morning food	:	Breakfast.
Morocco	:	Indian hemp. See Igbo.
Mono mono	:	Lightening.
More-more	:	In addition.
Moto	:	Car.
Mouth organ	:	Cob of roasted or boiled corn.
Move	:	Brisk trade.
Move stuff	:	Show off one's academic prowess. Also Vibrate

Mugun	:	Fool.
Mumu	:	See Mugun.
Murd	:	1. Die e.g. Di Baba don murd o! 2. Murder e.g. Wo, if you touch mi I go murd you o!
My own don betta	:	My good fortune has arrived.
Na	:	It is.
Na dat time	:	That is the time.
Nada	:	Nothing
Na fight?	:	1. Rebuff to someone being unduly aggressive. 2. Is it by force?
Na go bi dat?	:	Are you going ?
Na im	:	It is.
Naif	:	Knife
Nait	:	Night
Na one	:	Exclusive or distinctive item. Eg That Bobo Opon na one.
Na kwensh	:	See Na die.
Na so	:	1. That is true. 2. That is how e.g. Na so e come dabaru everything.
Na so?	:	1. Is that how it is now? 2. Is that true?
Na so I see am o!	:	That's the way it is.
Na una sabi	:	That's your business not mine.
Na wa	:	It is wonderful. Also Na wah.
Na wetin?	:	1. What is it this time? 2. So what?
Na you bico	:	You the man please!
Na you o!	:	You are the man! Also Na you we dey look o!
Na you we dey look o	:	We look up to you.
Na yua eye bi dis?	:	Long time no see.
Naija	:	1. Pertaining to Nigeria 2. Nigerian citizen e.g. Naija no go change.
Nak	:	1. Tell 2. Hit e.g. Why you nak me for bodi laik dat now? 3. Eat 4. What someone is wearing e.g. See the shoe wey e nak.
Natin	:	Nothing.
Natin spoil	:	1. No sweat 2. Hey, no worries.
Native doctor	:	1. Juju practitioner 2. Herbalist.
NEPA	:	National Electric Power Authority. Also

		Never Expect Power Always.
Next tomorrow	:	Day after tomorrow.
NFA	:	National Football Association. Also No future ambition.
NFAite	:	Student lacking in ambition.
Ngwo ngwo	:	Soup made from goat intestines, heart, liver, vegetables, onions and pepper. Served as a starter.
Nigerian factor	:	Excuse used to explain away failures in Nigerian organisations or government
Nko?	:	1. So what?
No	:	1. Did not e.g I giam chop e No chop. 2. Will not.
No bi?	:	Is it not?
No be me and you	:	Just count me out of that
No bi person	:	Persona non-grata E.g Dat one no bi person.
No bi classmate	:	Not in the same category.
No bi small	:	A lot. E.g. E get money no bi small.
No bi today	:	It didn't start today. e.g No bi today that man begin tief.
No dey	:	1. Not at home. 2. Not available.
No dey stay one place	:	1. Can't stay still. 2. Adventurous.
No dey take eye see	:	Can't see without touching e.g Dat guy no dey take eye see woman.
No do no do	:	Before I could say Jack Robinson.
No face	:	No time.
No how no how	:	One way or the other. Also - No do no do.
No go	:	1. Will not.
No know	:	1. Not aware.
No know im sef	:	1. Ignorant or clueless person 2. One with exaggerated ideas about their true station in life.
No size in London	:	Very large size E.g. Im leg na no size in London.
No wan hear	:	Refusing instruction or advice.
Not to	:	It is not.
Notice me	:	One desperately carving attention.

Now	:	Placed at end of question for emphasis E.g Wetin dey do you now?
NTA	:	1. Nigerian Television Authority 2. Gossip.
Number six	:	Intelligence.
Nyanfu-nyanfu	:	Plenty. See Borku and Plenti plenti.
Nyanga	:	Showing off. Also Nyanga Tolotolo.
Nyarsh	:	Bottom. Also Backyard.
Obey the wind	:	Skinny, Very underweight individual.
Obioma	:	See Mobile tailor.
Obito	:	1. All night wake.
Objectiv	:	Multiple choice examination.
Obobo canda	:	Light skinned person.(Derogatory).
Obodo	:	Homestead.
Obokun	:	1. Cat fish 2. Mercedes Benz limousine
Obrokotor	:	Obese person.
October rush	:	Frantic chasing of female freshmen (Jambitoes) in Nigerian universities by senior male students.
Oda	:	Other.
Odeku	:	Large bottle of Guinness stout.
Odu	:	Shady business.
Odudoof	:	(Derisory) Overweight individual.
Ofofo	:	Yoruba word for Gossip.
Oga	:	Person in charge. Also Oga pata pata.
Ogbele o!	:	Goodness gracious! See Ye pa!
Ogboju	:	Bluff your way through. See Bold face.
Ogbologbo	:	Old hand
Ogbono	:	Soup made from ground Ogbono seeds, crayfish, beef, dried fish, okra, spinach and pepper.
Ogi	:	Pap made from corn. Also Akamu.
Ogogoro	:	See Apketeshi.
Ojare	:	Said at the end of sentences for emphasis. E.g Comot for road Ojare!
Oje marina	:	Big lie.
Ojoro	:	Cheating.
Ojuju	:	Masquerade.
Okada	:	1. Name of Nigerian Airline. 2. Motor cycle

		taxi. See By air.
Okirikpotor	:	1. Eczema. 2. Dermatitis.
Okpetu	:	1. Trouble 2.It has happened!
Okporoko	:	Stork fish.
Okrika wake up	:	Second hand clothes. Also Gorgio Amadi.
Ol'boy	:	Yo my man.
Ole	:	Theif. Also Teif.
Olodo	:	Dunce.
Olofofo	:	Gossip (Yoruba word). Also Tatafo and Amebo
Olopa	:	Police officer.
Omi ni polish	:	Patent leather shoes.
Omo	:	1. Child 2. My friend 3. Popular detergent powder.
Omo ale trousa	:	Literally means Prisoner's trousers i.e. Trousers that barely reach the ankles. See Jump up pee. Also called Michael Jaskin.
Omolanke	:	Labourer for hire who carries goods in a large custom made wooden wheelbarrow.
Omoge	:	Fine girl. Also Chinani, Chickito, Gboyen, Si si and Babi.
Omota	:	Ruffian or rude boy.
One day one day	:	One of these days. Used as a warning for those involved in dodgy acts e.g One day one day monkey go go market e no go come back meaning everyday foe the thief one day for the owner.
One kain	:	Odd E.g Dat guy dress one kain.
One thousand and four	:	Popular block of flats in Lagos Island.
Onioburu	:	Night soil man. Also Agbepo.
Opaks	:	Worthless.
Opari	:	It is finished.
Opeke	:	Good looking girl. See Omoge.
Open eye	:	1. Wise up. 2. Become sexually active.
Open mouth	:	1. Talk e.g Abeg no open mouth laik dat.2. Astonishment e.g Ol' boy, the way dem spray money nyanfu nyanfu for dat party,

		Omo na so I open mouth.
Open ya sense	:	Use your intelligence.
Operation	:	Armed robbery.
Operation sweep	:	(Defunct) Special police anti-crime task force.
Opkor	:	Juju.
Opon	:	Yoruba word for prominent forehead. Also Crash helmet.
Oppressor!	:	Owner of big car.
Orenj	:	Orange.
Osa straight	:	Molue. Literally means Straight into the lagoon. Called so because of accidents involving Molue Buses plunging into the lagoon in Lagos.
Otopiapia	:	Rat poison.
Over-graduate	:	Postgraduate student. (As opposed to undergraduate).
Overs	:	Overseas.
Over stone	:	Disallowed goal when stones are used for goal posts and the ball goes directly above the stone.
Ovie	:	King.
Oyinbo	:	1. Caucasian 2. English 3. Big English words.
Oyoyo	:	1. Good times 2. Jollification.. See Ariya
Paale	:	Old man.
Paddy	:	Good friend.
Pafuka	:	1. Give up the ghost 2. Collapse
Pain	:	Physical deformity e.g Una sabi dat guy now, di one wey leg dey pain.
Pali	:	See Paddy.
Pammi	:	Palm wine taped from tree top.
Pammy	:	See Pammi
Pan cake	:	Make-up.
Panda	:	Cheap gold plated jewellery.
Pangba	:	Astonishing e.g. Dat man Byah byah na Pangba.
Pangolo	:	Tin can.

Panla	:	Dried stork fish. Also Opkoroko.
Papa	:	1. Dad 2. Granddad 3. Old man.
Papa battalion	:	Man with many children.
Papa dash	:	Hand me downs from a man.
Papa dozen	:	See Papa battalion.
Papa-lolo	:	Dandy old man.
Parapo	:	Kinsman.
Parsha	:	Partiality. See Fren fren.
Pata	:	Underwear.
Pata pata	:	Completely.
Patch am	:	Managing.
Pay smol smol	:	Pay for goods in instalments.
Pepper	:	1.Trouble e.g. You go see pepper.
Pepper don reach	:	I am alright financially
Pepper eye	:	1. Jealousy 2. Sour grapes.
Perm	:	1. Commit to memory 2. Woo a girl.
Persin	:	Person.
Petty trader	:	Road side vendor of assorted cheap articles.
Phichemba	:	Physics, Chemistry and Biology.
Pickeh wey say im mama no go see, im sef no go sleep	:	Admonition to disobedient child - "You think you are giving me trouble but it's you who will suffer most."
Pipo	:	People.
Piss for bodi	:	1.Incontinence of urine 2. Paralysed by fear
Pkomo	:	See Ponmo.
Pkaje	:	Share of fraud money. See Cut.
Pkokiripko	:	Rackety.
Pkopo garri	:	Dried Tapioca usually eaten with salt and ground nuts.
Pompoo	:	Navel.
Plant	:	Electricity generating plant. Also Gen or Standby Gen.
Play	:	1. Trick e.g. No play mi wayo jo.
Plenti plenti	:	Abundant.
Pollute	:	Fart. Also Mess.

Pololo	: Prostitute. See Ashewo.
Ponmo	: Boiled animal hide. Also Pkomo, Show-boy and Rain coat.
Popular jingo	: Man about town.
Popular side	: 1. Cheap seats 2. Standing only tickets in stadium.
Populo	: 1. Cheap seats. 2. Cheap or very common article.
Port	: Port Harcourt. Town in Rivers state, Nigeria. Also called the Garden city.
Poto-poto	: Mud.
Poundi	: Pounded yam.
Pozza	: Poser. See Alan Pozza.
Pregnapoline	: Pregnant lady. See Get belle.
Presido	: President.
Press	: 1. Demonic oppression especially in bed at night 2. Ironing of clothes. 3. To be dominated during soccer game.
Price	: 1. Haggle over price with market trader. 2. Inquire as to the cost of items for sale.
Proper proper	: Very well.
Provisions	: Tinned beverages.
Puff puff	: Fried balls of flour.
Pull your ears	: Get ready to run off.
Pump	: Public or outdoor tap.
Pure water	: 1. Bottled water sold by street vendors in Nigeria 2. A very common commodity. e.g Dat car dey everywhere laik pure water
Push me push you	: See Apketeshi.
Put	: Appoint to position.
Put am for ground	: Floor with a punch.
Put eye	: Look at something with longing.
Put fire	: 1. Stir up strife 2. Depress the accelerator pedal. (speed up) 3. Incite/goad two quarrelling parties into a fight.
Put mi for trouble	: Get me into trouble.
Put leg for road	: Start going.
Quaya	: Choir.

Quayet	:	Quiet.
Quanta	:	1.Collide 2. Fight 3. Clash
Quarter pass four	:	Squint.
Quench	:	1. Switch off e.g. quench dat light. 2. Die e.g. Di man don quench. Also Yamutu.
Queer-queer	:	Useless. See Ye-ye.
Quick	:	Used to comment on 1. Punctuality e.g. Since im promotion e no dey quick return from work 2. Rarity e.g Rain no dey quick fall this time of year
Ra-re	:	Trendy guy.
Rain beat you	:	Drenched in the rain.
Rain coat	:	See Ponmo
Raise hand	:	Salute e.g. I raise hand for you o!
Rake	:	Empty boasting.
Ranka dede	:	Hausa greeting.
R.R.S	:	Rapid Response Squad. (An arm of the police Force).
Reach	:	1. Arrive e.g. Which day you reach? 2. Afford e.g. Na dat one my hand (pocket) reach.
Reach ground	:	Completely.
Reach mai place	:	Pay me a visit. e.g. you come town no even reach mai place.
Ready made	:	Off the peg (rack) and ready to wear.
Reign	:	In vogue e.g Na dat trousa dey reign now o.
Reign pass	:	Out of fashion.
Remain small	:	1. Nearly 2. Almost.
Remember me	:	Remind me.
Remember the day yua mama born you	:	Threat e.g. I go beat you sotey you go remember the day yua mama born you. Means the beating will cause you to relive your birth.
Remi	:	(Derived from Remnant). Left overs. Also Chop remain.
Return match	:	Returning faulty electrical goods to point

		of purchase especially at Alaba International market.
Rhyme	:	Go well together e.g Dat yua trousa no rhyme di shirt.
Richard Lander	:	One who uncannily times his visits to your house to coincide with meal times.
Rimuv	:	Remove.
Rockeez	:	Party.
Rofo rofo	:	Rough.
Room and parlour	:	One room apartment rented out to families with shared toilet facilities. The room is usually divided with a curtain into the sleeping area (room) and the sitting area (Parlour). Mats are placed under the bed to be fished out at night for the kids to sleep.
Rush	:	1. Struggling for a place on a bus e.g. Na when I dey rush for Molue na im pick pocket teif mai money. 2. Flow. e.g. The pump dey rush well well.
Sabi	:	Know.
Sabi book	:	See Know book.
Sacrifice	:	Bribe to Police at road junctions.
Sagalo	:	Overhead kick in Football game.
Saka	:	Know too much (sarcastic) e.g Na you saka.
Sake of say	:	The reason is.
Sake of what?	:	Why should that be?
Salenza	:	Exhaust pipe if vehicle. Derived from Silencer.
Salot	:	1. Salute 2. Greetings
Samba	:	1. Bottom. 2. A generous rear end. See Yarnsh.
Samma	:	Hit e.g I go samma you slap o! See Mammar.
Sam-sam	:	1. Never 2. Not in a million years. Also Lai-lai.
San sand	:	1. Sand 2. Dirt.
Santana	:	also Apku. Named after the car which

		normally comes in white and handles smoothly like Apku.
Sapele water	:	Native gin. See Apketeshi.
Saraa	:	Sacrifice. (Yoruba word.)
Satellite	:	1. Abbreviation for Satellite Town , Lagos. 2. Large head scarf worn by women dressed in traditional attire.
Sawa	:	Sour.
Say	:	Is it not that e.g Say na you be di Oga?
Say wetin	:	1.Why? 2. What?
Scata	:	Scatter. Also Scata-scata.
School Father	:	Male mentor to junior student in Nigerian boarding school.
School Mother	:	Female mentor to a junior student in Nigerian boarding school.
Scope	:	1. To look at an object or person longingly 2. Tell a lie
Sebi?	:	Isn't it?
Sekon	:	Second.
See Blood!	:	Look at trouble!
See im place see mai place	:	We are close neighbours.
See Oba	:	See trouble; threat. E.g. If mai hand touch you you go See Oba.
See Pepper	:	See- See trouble.
See trouble!	:	What a fine mess!
Sef	:	1. In particular e.g. You sef. 2. Placed at end of question when irritated or impatient e.g. Wetin sef?
Senior	:	1. Elder 2. Someone in a higher class in secondary school.
Serve Juju	:	Worship idols.
Set	:	Hi-fi system. See Gbedu and System.
Set blow	:	Adopt a fighting stance.
Shack	:	1. Drink alcohol. 2. Be intoxicated or mesmerised by anything e.g. The house wey e build juss dey shack am.
Shackeez	:	1. Act of drinking. 2. Alcoholic drinks. Also

		Shak.
Shaded up	:	Wearing dark sun glasses.
Shakabula	:	Dane gun.
Shakara	:	1. Showing off. 2. Boasting about the impossible. See Raking or Draw rain.
Shake bodi	:	1. Spend some money 2. Pay the bill.
Shaki	:	Sheep or cattle cooked intestine.
Shako	:	Yoruba word meaning Show off.
Shalanga	:	Pit latrine.
Sharrup!	:	Shut up.
Sharp mouth	:	1. Acid tongue 2. Gift of the garb.
Shenj	:	Change.
Shenlele-coolele	:	Chant usually sang by kids at each other before a fight in Warri.
Shey?	:	Yoruba word meaning- Is it not?
Shicoco	:	See Omoge.
Shift	:	Verb. Move out in convoy of cars.
Shimi	:	Slip worn under dress.
Shinani	:	See Omoge.
Shine	:	1. Look well 2. Look glamorous.
Shine eye	:	1. Keep your eyes open 2. Be on your guard
Shine shine	:	Glittering.
Shockazoba	:	Shock absorbers of vehicle.
Shoe maker	:	Shoe repairer.
Shomo	:	1.You know 2. You understand? Also You sabi say.
Shoo!	:	1. Wow!
Short knicker	:	Shorts.
Show	:	1.Make life difficult for you e.g I go show you o!
Show boy	:	See Ponmo. Also Pkomo and Rain coat.
Show face	:	1. Turn up. 2. Show up briefly at a function to avoid being accused of snubbing the host.
Sime sime	:	1. Weak 2. Too gentle e.g Ol' boy, why you dey make Sime sime.
Si si	:	Young trendy girl.

Sista : Sister.
Six to six : ref. Apku. Phrase coined up because some claim a meal of Apku can keep hunger away for 12 hours.
Skenchi : Greedy.
Slacki : Slow thinking person.
Slap : Walking e.g As man no get car na so so slap man dey slap go everywhere.
Slipas : Slippers.
Small chop : Pre meal appetisers such as Chin Chin, Peanuts, Puff Puff and Kuli Kuli.
Smallie : Small statured individual.
Small-small : 1. Gently . Also Sofri sofri. 2. Little by little.
Small time : 1. Next thing you know. 2. Before you know it.
Smell : Get close to e.g. No rake how you enta Concord when you never smell Muritala before.
Smol : Small.
Soak away : Septic tank.
Soak garri : 1.Meal of Garri mixed with water 2. Financial hardship e.g. As dem never pay us e bi laik na garri we go dey soak.
Soakeez : Act of drinking garri.
Soda : Wield together.
Soja : Soldier. Also Soja man.
Sokoto : Traditional trouser.
Sontin : Something.
Sontin dey do you : There is something wrong with you.
Sontin dey there : There's something special going on.
So so : 1. Something always being done e.g. Na so so drink e dey drink.
Sotey : For such a long time.
Soyoyo : Trendy.
Sound you : Slap you in the face.
Soup wey sweet na money kill am : Good things cost money.

Spark	:	Lose temper.
Spin	:	Woo a girl. Also Toast , Approach, Tune, Give raps and Baze.
Spoots	:	Designer or very nice clothes. See Sputs.
Spoil	:	Talk badly of someone behind their back. e.g I hear as you dey spoil me for dat party.
Stock Fish	:	Chemically dried fish
Stone ground	:	1. Fall heavily e.g See how e take bodi stone ground.
Stomok	:	Stomach.
Stranger	:	Visitor.
Stroke	:	Tease. See Yab.
Strong head	:	1. Stubborn 2. Persistent.
Stud	:	Rough tackle during football game e.g No stud me o! 2. Hamper one's progress.
Suegbe	:	1. Dunce 2.Slow person.
Suffer head	:	1. One prone to recurrent hardships.2. Poor man.
Suffer man	:	Poor man.
Suppose fit	:	Should be able to.
Suppose to	:	Should.
Suya	:	Barbecued Beef or chicken served with special Nigeria spices.
Taba	:	Tobacco.
Taim	:	Time.
Tanda	:	1. Stand 2. Loitering.
Taffia	:	Gossip.
Take	:	1.How did you do it? e.g. How you take build house on yua salary?
Take breeze	:	Sit out in the fresh air.
Take eye see	:	Look without touching e.g why you no fit take eye see Gulder i.e Can't you see a bottle of Gulder without wanting to drink it?
Take Garri from mai mouth	:	Interfere with my livelihood.
Take light	:	Power cut. See NEPA.

Take me shine	:	1. Show me up 2. Look good at my expense
Take style	:	1. In a round about sort of way e.g the tailor take style get the dress o! 2. Use of guile e.g the bobo wan take style thief mai money
Talk anoda thing	:	(Dismissive) .Say something better.
Talk true	:	Singing a different tune. e.g when you hear Koboko for yua nyansh you go talk true.
Tap leather	:	Play football.
Tap soccer	:	See Tap leather.
Tapping	:	Stealing.
Tapping electrons	:	Caressing a Lady.
Tatafo	:	Gossip.
Them say	:	I heard it on the grape vine.
Them send you	:	Were you sent to torment me?
Thermacool	:	1. Relax 2. Chill or Stay cool. See Coolee. 3. Brand name of refrigerator.
The thing bi say	:	The fact of the matter is.
The thing wey-happun for fowl-haus dey happun-for chicken haus	:	What's good enough for the goose is good enough for the gander.
Tinigboko	:	Extremely thin individual.
Tiro	:	Khol used as eye liner.
Tip	:	Dribble opponent during football game.
Titi	:	Young girl
Titrate	:	Urinate especially at road side or in a bush.
Toast	:	Woo a lady. Also Spin, Approach, Base and Tune.
Today na today	:	This problem must be fully resolved today
Tokunbo	:	(Yoruba word) 1. Second hand goods. 2. Child born overseas
Tolotolo	:	1.Turkey. 2. Show of e.g E dey make Nyanga Tolo tolo.
Tombo	:	Palm wine. See Palmmy. Also Tombo Liquor.
Tommorow	:	Procastination.

To nonsense	:	To excess E.g E Grab muscles to nonsense.
Too dey	:	1. Always doing something. E.g. You too dey snore.
Too get	:	1. Have in abundance.
Tori	:	1. Interesting or humorous story.
Tori get k-leg	:	The situation has become complicated.
Tori get many leg	:	See Tori get K-leg.
Toro	:	1. Old Nigeria 3 pence coin with circular hole in it's middle. 2. Problem e.g. Dat one na yua Toro.
Toronto	:	Fake goods.
Tortoise car	:	Volkswagen 'Bettle'. Also Volks.
Tory don wowo	:	The story or situation has turned ugly.
Totori	:	1. Tickle 2. Excite
Traficate	:	Indicate while driving. (using the turn signal in your vehicle)
Travul	:	Travel.
Trekeez	:	Act of walking. See Legedis Benz, Foot wagen and Footron.
Tri	:	Three.
Trousa	:	Trouser.Also Trousees
True true	:	Most definitely.
True to God	:	I swear.
Try	:	1. Did well. 2. Tried you best. 3. Sarcastic use when someone offends e.g. Ol' boy , you try as you come finish the last iced water for fridge.
Trying	:	Doing very well.
Tu	:	Two.
Tu tu	:	Two each.
Tuffia	:	God forbid!
Tuke tuke	:	Buses used for transport. See Danfo.
Tune	:	See Toast.
Tuwo Shinkafa	:	Hausa meal made from mashed boiled rice and served with soup.
Ukodo	:	Meal of yams, spices, fish and pepper soup boiled in the same pot.
U.I.	:	University of Ibadan

Una	:	You people.
Uselu	:	1. Area in Benin city where the Psychiatric hospital is located. 2. Mad man 3. Eccentric. See Aro.
Vamoosh	:	1. Make hasty retreat.
Veks	:	Vex.
Venue	:	Location of party.
Vess	:	1. Vex. 2. Provoke to anger.
Vex-comot	:	Storm off in anger.
Viagragra	:	1.Viagra.2. Aphrodisiac.
Vibrate	:	1. Exert one's self. 2. Show off one's grasps of a subject.
Village persin	:	Someone who hails fron one's tribe or village
Wad	:	Rich e.g Dat business man wad well-well.
Wadded	:	Rich e.g Di guy dey wadded no bi small.
Wado	:	Urhobo greeting e.g Internet surfers Wado.
Wahala	:	Trouble.
Waffi	:	Warri. Town in Delta State, Nigeria.
Wak	:	Eat.
Waka	:	1. Walk.2. Frequent visits to a Juju practitioner e.g. Dat man sabi waka o!
Waka about	:	1. One who is always on the road.
Waka-jugbe	:	One constantly loitering about.
Waka waka	:	See Waka about.
Waka pass	:	To act as extra in Nigerian movie. i.e. - to have a walk on role.
Walahi	:	I swear. Also Walai.
Wan	:	One.
Wan wan	:	One each.
Watch night	:	1. Night vigil 2. Security guard. See Mayguard
Wata	:	Water.
Wata and garri-make eba	:	Rude reply to a question beginning with 'What'.
Wata pass garri	:	Things have reached breaking point.
Waya	:	1. Wonderful 2. Tough like steel wire. 3.

Pangs of hunger e.g. See how hungry waya man.

We two : The two of us.

Weak for bodi : In a state of shock e.g Dat news make us weak for bodi.

Wear : 1. Board a bus e.g I go wear bus reach Tinubu.

What's doing you? : What is wrong with you? Also Wetin dey do you?

What's your own? : What's your problem? also - Wetin be yua own now? And Na wetin?

Which day? : When? E.g Which day you begin go gym?

Which one : 1. Hello e.g Ol' boy which ones now. 2. What is e.g Which one be dis?

Which one you dey? : 1. What's wrong with you? 2. Whose side are you on anyway?

Whinch : Witch.

Whinchi : 1. Bedevil.

Who born? : Derisive. Used when someone claims to be able to do the unattainable. 1. You can not do it e.g. Who born monkey?

Who born monkey? : See Who born.

Who know man : 1. Nepotism. 2. Being well connected especially in government.

Who no know-go know : Threat meaning - Whoever is claiming not to know will know without a shadow of doubt. Also Who no sabi go sabi.

Woman Lappa : Man easily controlled by his woman.

Won : One. see also - Wan.

Wor wor : Ugly.

Wuru-wuru : Underhanded methods. See Mago mago.

Xerox : 1. Plagiarism. 2. Examination malpractice of copying someone's work. Derived from Rank Xerox. Also - Dub.

Yakata : 1. Heavily e.g. I juss fall Yakata.

Yallow : Light skinned person especially when using skin lightening creams. Also Yallow babi.

Yam : Large calf muscles.
Yama-yama : Nonsense!.
Yamiri : Cannibal.
Yamutu : 1. Die 2. Break down.
Yanga : 1. Pride. 2. Flamboyance. Also Nyanga.
Yawn : Loneliness. See Gba Winter.
Yellow fever : 1. Traffic warden with bright orange khaki shirts. 2. Lady who bleaches skin lighter. (derogatory).
You go know yourself : Threat e.g I go so beat you eh, you go know yourself. Also- You go see Shege and You go see pepper.
You go see : (Threat) You will see. Also You go see blood.
You hear? : Do you understand?
You meet me well o : Type of greeting used when a visitor who stumbles on you at meal time.
You no get work? : Don't you have something better to do?
You never chop? : 1. Haven't you eaten? 2. Why are you acting so weak? e.g which one you dey waka laik say you never chop. Also - Abi you never chop?
You sabi now : You know how it is.
You're on o! : You are the man!
Your hand reach : 1. Afford e.g Na dat one my hand reach meaning That's what I can afford.
Your money don come : You have hit the jackpot.
Yua : Your.
Zero one zero : (University slang) No breakfast , have lunch and no dinner due to financial hardships.
Zero zero one : Eat only dinner.
Zombie : Derogatory name for Soldiers originally used by Fela Anikulapko-Kuti.